Interpersonal Processes in Groups and Organizations

Interpersonal Processes in Groups and Organizations

Sara B. Kiesler

National Research Council
National Academy of Science

AHM Publishing Corporation
Arlington Heights, Illinois 60004

ISBN: 0-88295-451-2

Library of Congress Card Number: 77-86018

*Credit note: The extended quotation beginning
on p. 179 is from MAN AND WORK IN SOCIETY, ed.
by Eugene Louis Cass and Frederick G. Zimmer,
© 1975 by Western Electric Company, Inc.
Reprinted by permission of Van Nostrand
Reinhold Company, a division of Litton Educational Publishing, Inc.*

778

Contents

ACKNOWLEDGMENTS

I wish to recognize and thank the following persons for their encouragement and help: Barbara Paschke, Donn Parson, Patti Plamann, Benita Anderson, Maureen Trobec, and my husband, Charles Kiesler.

Foreword

The growing awareness of the importance of organizations in our lives has created interest in understanding them. We are interested in individual and interpersonal behavior in organizations. We are aware that organizations influence us and that through our participation we can change organizations. We realize that organizations have subgroups, structures, and task and administrative processes. We understand that organizations are affected by technology, other organizations, and by general social and economic conditions. We also perceive that organizations can be used by their members in order to achieve personal goals.

Given the wide range of problems and issues, there are many theoretical approaches, schools of thought, and very different methods for studying organizational phenomena. This diversity has resulted in a growing, vigorous,

and exciting field of study. It has also given
rise to a wide variety of academic courses and
research interests.

The books in this series are more than a
collection of separate surveys. They have been
integrated to provide a clear picture of the
scope of organizational behavior, to insure
consistency in approach, and to portray coherently the relationships existing across sub-
problem areas. Each book cross references the
others, and together they provide an up-to-date
working library for any person seeking to
understand the field of organizational behavior.

To achieve these goals of integration and
completeness, six outstanding scholars and
teachers with experience teaching in business
schools were assembled to write the first six
books in this project. Two are social psychologists, three are specialists in organizational
behavior, and one is a sociologist. The wide
range of topics was first drawn up and then
divided into six groups. Each of the authors
then worked with the series editor to draw up
a detailed outline of his or her portion of the
whole book. Care was taken to insure that each
author understood how he or she related to the
whole series, that each author had a theme
for each chapter, and that these themes were
consistent within individual books and across
the series as a whole. When the independent
writing of each book was completed, the author
and the series editor went over each manuscript
painstakingly to create a solid part that was
consistent with the whole series. One of the
features of this series is that each book examines its topics in terms of behavioral processes. Behavior is seen in terms of complex
interrelated sequences of contingent events.

Each book is written so that it can stand
alone and so that it connects across the others
in the series. Thus, any single book or any
combination of books can be used in the classroom. In addition to the coherence of an integrated series, the integration itself helped
to reduce the length of each book and hence

reduce the direct costs to the student. The author of each book had the primary responsibility of writing on his or her assigned topics. But when a topic from another book was needed, the author could count on its being adequately covered. Thus, each author could stick to specific topics and refer to the other books for more detailed explanations for other topics. Together these books provide adequate coverage of the main topics, a compendium of ideas about organizational behavior, and a source of new ideas and critical references.

The books in the series were written primarily for beginning M.B.A. students at a respectable college or university. Some of these schools require two semesters or three quarters of classes in organizational behavior. For these, we recommend that all six books be used. Some require a semester of classes. For these we recommend any three of the books. Those requiring one or two quarters should use two or four of these books.

Kenneth D. Mackenzie
Lawrence, 1977

A Social Psychological Approach to Interpersonal Behavior

I have searched in vain during the last year for any
unusual organizational structures, procedures, or
programs which prevent corruption . . . . I can find
no magical solutions for bringing about an anti-cor-
ruption climate.—Joseph D. McNamara, Chief of the
Kansas City, Mo., Police Department (1974)

Chief McNamara's words point out what anyone
knows who has ever closely observed an organization or group. No bureaucratic arrangement
of people, jobs, or rules can solve a group's
problems. No technical innovation or reorgani-
zation plan can by itself improve an organization. No path heads straight to institutional
success.

The reason is that groups and organizations are comprised of human beings whose relationships are complex—more complex than the
finest machines humans have ever created. Human

relationships are affected by individual conceptions of reality, expectations and aspirations, needs and commitments. Perceptions and motives affect the impact of bureaucratic and technical facets of the environment on relationships. Moreover, relationships affect other relationships. People do not act alone, though they often think of themselves as independent. Theirs is a human, a social, environment, as well as a physical one. Groups learn values and derive beliefs from each other and cause changes in each other's behavior. These phenomena are complex, dynamic, interpersonal processes.

The purpose of this book is to bring to your attention what we now know about interpersonal processes. The theoretical approach taken (that is, the assumptions, hypotheses, and concepts) is that of social psychology, a discipline in the social sciences that studies human behavior in its social context. This discipline stands among (and has strong ties to) the study of individual psychology, the sociological study of groups and social institutions, and the study of organizational behavior.

WHY INTERPERSONAL PROCESSES ARE IMPORTANT: THE CASE OF POLICE CORRUPTION

The quotation heading this chapter was taken from a paper presented at the 1974 American Psychological Association meetings in New Orleans. In this paper, Chief (and Dr.) McNamara traced the history of police corruption and various attempts to correct it. He noted that, almost from the time police forces were organized (only about 130 years ago), corruption was a problem. In the eastern cities, politicians interfered with police work; in the old West, sheriffs were commonly bought. Corruption functioned not only to line individual pockets, but to smooth the way for the

new industrialist entrepreneurs and provide
social mobility for immigrant groups.

Since political machines were actively involved in the encouragement of organized,
pervasive corruption, reform effects naturally
centered upon the independence and profession-
alism of the police. Reformers believed that
structural changes in the organization would
be sufficient to achieve police integrity. So
did classical organizational theorists. Max
Weber (1947), the German scholar, described the
efficient ideal organization as having these
characteristics: (1) clear division of labor,
(2) definite responsibility for job performance, (3) specialists, (4) a hierarchical
structure, (5) formal rules, (6) unbiased treatment of workers and clients, (7) recruitment
of managers on the basis of ability, and (8)
job protection.

Reforms introducing civil service, tenured
jobs, and political independence made most
police organizations superficially fit the Weber
model. Still, corruption continued. So another
bureaucratic solution was proposed: the internal affairs unit that would identify and control corrupt practices. Yet even an internal
watchdog was no panacea, and to this day attention still focuses on police corruption.

A lack of understanding about human social
behavior and how humans organize themselves was
one reason why bureaucratic innovations, such as
the internal affairs unit, were often imple-
mented in a manner and form that were ineffective in minimizing police corruption. Hit
or miss attempts to change the work environment,
without any empirically defensible theory about
why individuals behave as they do, had hit or
miss effects. For example, internal affairs
units were usually not established in a way
that would destroy a climate of opinion tolerant
of corruption, or its social rewards, and, in
fact, often had the opposite effect. The
presence of a watchdog committee implied that
all police officers had to be watched. As a

result, honest officers were encouraged to
have closer ties with the dishonest ones; the
reporting of dishonesty was left exclusively
to those who had that "role"; and resentment
toward the internal affairs unit—other police
officers—was increased. At the same time,
officers assigned to the internal affairs unit
were freer to collect graft than before.

There have been some successes in reducing
police corruption. For example, in Kansas
City, Clarence Kelley (who at one time was
head of the FBI) increased pride in integrity
by rewarding and publicizing it, maximized
peer group pressure against corruption, and
promoted police cohesiveness. Periodic trans-
fers from sensitive positions to minimize temp-
tation were made a matter of policy, rather
than an arbitrary punishment for a few. These
administrative actions were largely consistent
with what social psychologists and other social
scientists have learned about interpersonal
processes. The actions took advantage of positive interpersonal forces and reflected the
fact that corruption is not simply a selfish,
unethical act, but is one component of interpersonal behavior within the context of an
organization.

Applying Knowledge of Interpersonal Processes

Many people believe today that the successes
and problems of most groups and organizations
have a significant social and interpersonal
cast to them. Successes and problems are not
simply technical or economic in nature. Few
people realize, however, that knowledge of
social and interpersonal processes is rarely
applied in a simple, direct manner as one
might apply knowledge of how a lock works.
Having just argued that interpersonal processes
are important, it must be said, too, that
knowing about them does not guarantee improve-
ments in practice.

It is not easy, even in the most enlightened organization, to arrange procedures, make decisions, or devise policies that positively and effectively influence behavior, especially in a relatively free society that is dramatically changing and in a world whose nations have an ever greater economic, political, and social impact upon one another. Even were our understanding not so limited, there are barriers to the use of knowledge. Hard data from the laboratory or the survey researcher's files are not dumped in neatly arranged packages on the desk of an administrator. Nor do they tell the administrator what to do.

The knowledge we do gain about interpersonal processes or anything else from social science must be attached to values and attitudes; and goals and decisions must coincide with the constraints of practical necessity, political feasibility, and actual resources. People who have decisions to make and actions to take sometimes either scorn the apparently abstruse results of research or too readily adopt some of its fads. Instead, consider that social science is useful, but not in the same way one uses a machine. It should be approached as one uses a good, well supported idea.

Good ideas pay off because they reveal problems and conditions which narrow human choice. In the last fifty years, understanding of how people are affected by public attitudes and norms, social policies and institutions, and family and work environments has grown quite a bit. Here, for example, are a few things we did not know fifty years ago:

* Institutional neglect of the need for emotional contact—even when physical needs are well met—cause workers to languish and children to die.

* Emotional stress, including the stress of a "better" job, causes physical disease.

* Abuse or discrimination, sometimes directed at people "for their own good," teaches them to abuse and discriminate in turn, and damages their self-esteem.

* Programs for the disadvantaged sometimes widen the gap between them and the majority because the majority gain more from the program than the disadvantaged.

* Employee attitudes usually affect productivity more significantly than do the physical amenities of a work place.

* When people make decisions, their attitudes are likely to change.

* When each individual in a group makes a "rational" choice, the effect can be that the group as a whole behaves irrationally.

* The best decisions in many organizations are not those that are based on a rational ordering of preferences.

* Many unpleasant kinds of behavior, such as aggression, arrogance, or shyness, are caused or exacerbated by the labels that people attach to other people who are different.

* A group, team, or organization can fail because it is too highly motivated.

Most of these ideas are old hat now, but they did, in their time, lead to the better identification of problems and to more informed decisions. Sometimes, they pointed toward more sensible ways of doing things.

In recent testimony to the United States Congress (1976, pp. 3, 6), Herbert A. Simon described a use of social science that is most applicable to this book:

> The function of social science, like all science, is to explain the phenomena, not to advocate actions to change them. . . . What it does is to give us new insight into the mechanisms that govern the

phenomena, and that have to be taken into account
in any effort either to preserve or change them.
. . . .

The typical output of basic research is publication
in the open literature, where it is available to
anyone who can and will read it. But applied research
may also reach its end use through this route. The
general diffusion of knowledge through publication
is especially important when the final application
requires a large number of people, and particularly
people who are not professionals but laymen, to take
action or to change their habits. Many American
people take daily vitamin supplements with their food.
(I don't wish to argue that they take the right
amounts!) They have certainly not read the original
research reports on which estimates of human vitamin
requirements are based. Those estimates have trickled
down from their research sources through many steps
of successive popularization, finally finding a place,
for example, in standard cookbooks. General dissemination of information through a multitude of channels
is what I call the "public diffusion model."
   This kind of diffusion and popularization accounts
for a very large part of the use of knowledge developed by the social and behavioral sciences. One
reason is that much of such knowledge is important to
us as citizens and participants in the political
process.

Simon's explanation of the utilization process fits well with the findings of University
of Michigan researchers Nathan Caplan, Andrea
Morrison, and Russell Stambaugh (1975, p. 18):

   Although a respondent may have given as an instance
   of his use of knowledge that he was influenced by an
   idea which he attributed to the social sciences—such
   as the belief that people's attitudes tend to follow
   their behavior rather than their behavior being
   governed by their attitudes—he cannot name a study
   or demonstrate the validity of that assertion.

The researchers interviewing these policy-
makers were able to identify 575 instances in
which the officials had used specific ideas from

social science to create or inform themselves
about public policy. Sometimes the ideas were
based upon their reading of professional jour-
nals or of staff papers based upon hard data,
but more often (as we have seen) the ideas
were in the form of general knowledge learned
from texts, popular books, magazines, government reports, and newspapers. Nevertheless,
the use of their knowledge was diverse and
impactful:

* A decision to establish large-scale programs
  to deal with alcoholism was based on social
  science data indicating that alcoholism is
  more serious (e.g., in causing reduced productivity and family disruption) than the use
  of drugs like marijuana and heroin.

* The feasibility of the volunteer army was
  evaluated by means of social science data.

* The planners of federally subsidized building
  programs used social research to design
  architectural arrangements that reduced
  vandalism.

* Auto safety requirements were developed by
  using information from research on public
  acceptance of seat belts and other safety
  measures.

* National health insurance proposals were
  designed that took account of the large
  behavioral component of disease and cure
  discovered by researchers.

In all, 13 percent of the policy issues
mentioned were national in scope, 50 percent
affected significant population segments, and
37 percent affected administrative decisions
to reorganize or change policy within an
agency. Application of social science research
may not have been as wise, as direct, as fast,
or as informed as we might wish, but it was,
in fact, made.

ASSUMPTIONS ABOUT PEOPLE

Using a social science depends on understanding the assumptions on which the science is based. According to social psychologists, people have physiological, emotional, and cognitive needs. People ordinarily act to satisfy these needs in what they themselves consider to be a reasonable manner. They may take into account how others have behaved in the past, what others might want now, possible consequences, and social standards.

Whether a person is intrinsically rational or irrational, selfish or altruistic, aggressive or pacific, good or bad—such questions are moot. A label such as "stubborn" does not help us to understand why a person offers resistance to a new idea. Instead, one must discover the conditions that the person feels and sees and hears.

The purpose of most research in social psychology is to discover these conditions and in doing so, to establish the reasons for variations in behavior. These reasons are described in terms of concepts like "self-esteem," "achievement motivation," and "equity." Concepts help us to see patterns and grasp the essentials of social behavior. Concepts, however, are open to alternative interpretations because we attach different values to them. This is a major reason why knowledge from research helps us to explain phenomena but does not tell us what is right or wrong. Concepts also reflect what is assumed to be important. The concept "childhood," for example, is said to be a rather recent cultural invention—an invention that reflects a modern concern with the special characteristics and development of children (Aries, 1962). (You can see children viewed merely as little adults in medieval paintings.) Below are described some things that social psychologists think are important.

VIEWS OF REALITY

One characteristic of people that most social

psychologists stress is that their actions and
reactions to social stimuli are modified by
their views of reality. That is, they act in
response to how they think and feel about their
environment, not to its objective qualities.
Individuals' interpretations of reality are
more important in influencing their behavior
than reality itself. Suppose we illustrate
by examining the finding (e.g., in Strodtbeck
and Hook, 1961) that the person most likely to
be elected chairman of a group or foreman
of a jury is the one who sits at the end of a
rectangular table. The head seat is real. We
can all agree on its physical location. If
physical location were the reason for winning
elections, we should be able to create
leaders by simply placing individuals in
strategically located seats. But we cannot.
The reason is that it is not so much a person's
physical location, but interpretations of the
meaning and cause of a person's location that
affect group members.

The point was demonstrated quite clearly by
Charlan Nemeth and Joel Wachtler (1974) have
argued that the occupation of a head seat is
not the same thing, psychologically, as the
choosing and taking of a head seat. While
a head position might symbolize authority or
provide relatively greater access to other
group members, the taking of the head seat is
probably far more important. This act, not
mere occupation of the seat, is what fosters
the perception that a person has confidence
and authority. Further, it is this perception
that aids the occupant of a head seat in
leadership and influence attempts.

Nemeth and Wachtler made their point through
an experimental study. They showed that people
who had been randomly assigned to the head of
a table had little influence on others, but
people who had apparently chosen that position
had great influence. According to private
attitude measures, the influence of those
who had chosen a head seat was created by the

perceptions of them as confident and consistent
persons. The results did not show that physical location is of no importance, but rather
that psychological views of reality alter
its effects. Where one chooses to be or is
assigned by others can indeed say a great deal.

   You may recall squabbles among delegates at
the peace talks during the Vietnam War that
centered on the size and shape of the table.
Deciding who would sit where was an important
barrier to beginning the discussion on peace.
Why? Not because table shape affects the flow
of communication, but rather because where one
is allowed to sit (at the end of a rectangular
vs. a square table, for example) is assumed to
reflect differences in power. In fact, the
struggle about this procedural problem was
used to test the power and will of the parties
and to set the stage for how to solve other
issues.

THE IMMEDIATE SITUATION

   Most social psychologists interested in group
and organizational behavior think that people's
immediate social surroundings are very important. To illustrate, a few years ago an
English manufacturing company whose main offices were based in London decided to move to
a newer building. While there were numerous
amenities there were fewer offices with
windows than in the old building. Therefore,
plans had to be worked out concerning who would
have to give up an office with a window. Meanwhile, an American who had been hired by the
company to take over a position in middle management arrived in London. Not knowing of the
company's desire to apportion offices according
to a plan, and too shy to bother people by
asking, the American simply looked around the
new building, chose a desirable office with a
window, and had his crates delivered there.

   What happened next? (1) As soon as the other
employees saw the American's boxes in the new

office, they ignored the impending "plan" and put their personal materials in the most desirable offices still available. (2) Since they had promised to come forth with a rational procedure, the members of top management decided to announce a plan for office space. But offices had already been taken. Therefore, management agreed to a plan which accepted the fait accompli—"first come, first served." (3) The shy American who so stirred things up was viewed as a comer and rose quickly in the hierarchy.

Thus, an accidental circumstance created by someone who did not know the company and was fearful of bothering others had impact on the company's procedures and "planning," and on the development of his career. To put this another way, views of reality and, in turn, behavior—or reality itself—were influenced by situational constraints.

What happens in any situation is affected, of course, by the particular individuals who experience it. Unfortunately, research on groups has been a bit too neglectful of differences among people, and only recently has much attention been paid to the interaction of personal traits and the situational environment (e.g., Mischel, 1968). For example, does personal immaturity wipe out all the benefits that usually accrue to people when they are given more responsibility at work? Such interactions are incompletely understood and are beyond the scope of this book. Their existence is mentioned here so you will understand that most of the discussions of people in this book do not presume everybody is the same. No generalization holds for everyone. When we speak of the effect of situations on interpersonal processes, we make a probabilistic statement about what is generally true. No book can point out all the exceptions to such a statement, though they surely exist.

MOTIVES

People who study group and organizational behavior emphasize motivation. Motives are the
fuel for behavior. Wanting to succeed, for example, makes you work hard. Motives also direct behavior. Because of your desires, drives, purposes, and aspirations, you prefer to do some
things more than others. You obviously cannot
satisfy all your preferences. For example, it is
usually not possible to express all your anger
at someone and also keep all their affection.
The relative strength of motives can determine
which of many actions you take.

If we are to understand how situations affect people, we must understand how situations
affect their motives. One way situations affect motives is by offering different incentives. Incentives such as economy, security and
services affect the motives people have for
various actions and resources, i.e., affect
their preferences.

Management wants to implement a new procedure
in a factory, say. Their incentive is reduced
cost of the process. The production supervisor announces that a new set of machines will
be installed. But the employees view the new
machines as a threat to their preferences for
security and job autonomy, and their incentive
to change is not very high. Now we see a situation alter the array of incentives: The union
enters the case and insists that the innova-
tive machines be a bargaining issue in contract
talks. With this step, the issue enlarges beyond efficiency and security, to matters of
commitment and facesaving. The employees, to
the extent of their identification with the
union, have yet another incentive to resist
change. The managers, on the other hand, have
more incentive to implement change. In short,
the situation affects motives which in turn
affect behavior.

VALUES

Society has been described in terms of three major characteristics: (1) the economy and the system of occupations; (2) the polity and forms of political participation, and (3) the culture —the meanings and symbols attached to life (see Bell, 1973). Culture is especially important to interpersonal processes. If you introduce any two people who have experienced the same culture into a new situation, the chances are pretty high that their behavior will be more alike than will the behavior of any two randomly selected people (Pepitone, 1976) and that they will get along better than randomly selected people. The reason is that they share beliefs and values which derive from a common culture. Such values and beliefs (in "freedom," for example) are not necessarily precise guides to action because they can be variously interpreted, but they do serve to point toward consensus on social standards and goals or to support actions otherwise desired.

Social psychologists can illustrate the importance of values by turning the tables on themselves and examining their own history. For example, back in the 1930s, during the Great Depression, most people in this country believed in growth, in the panacea of material progress, and in the value of conquering nature. Industrial ingenuity and productivity, it was believed, would solve the nation's problems. Watchwords in all sorts of organizations (schools, factories, and farms) were efficiency and growth; to attain these ends, managements brought in efficiency experts who experimented with changes in illumination, studied fatigue, and did time and motion studies. Some of these experts discovered that employee attitudes and relationships were often more important than plant conditions—that the real barrier to increased productivity lay in reducing worker resistance to change and poor morale (see Mayo, 1933; Haire, 1954; Allport, 1968). Today we might wonder where this all-

consuming interest in worker productivity has
gone. Actually it has not disappeared, but
other beliefs and interests have tempered it,
such as a concern with the scarcity of our
natural resources, with the quality of life,
and with the bargaining position of unions.

Most of what constitutes the field of social
psychology today has been studied by Americans
in response to American problems. In doing so,
American social psychologists have sometimes
been unaware of how their choice of problems
and concepts reflects the values of their
culture. Recently, European social psychologists (Israel and Tajfel, 1972; Apfelbaum,
1974) have pointed out that many issues Americans have studied are phrased in terms of the
needs of a quasi-capitalistic, democratic
society. The central theme of research on
group and organizational behavior has been
productivity, particularly the productivity of
workers rather than leaders. For example, prior
to their famous study of resistance to change,
Coch and French, two social psychologists,
were asked by the owner of a pajama factory
how to overcome the reluctance of employees to
comply with new, more efficient work rules.
Coch and French (1948) tried to show that allowing workers to participate in the formulation and planning of innovation decreased
their resistance to it.

Here are a French psychologist's observations:

> The general perspective remains that of management,
> since the stages of the process of change are de-
> fined as "resistance," i.e., as obstacles to the
> effective implementation of what *must* come. The issue
> of *who* wishes the changes to be introduced and *whose*
> interests they would serve is not even touched upon;
> nor is anything said about the possibility that re-
> sistance might be legitimate, that its roots may be
> in the objective situation. (Moscovici, 1972, p. 28)

Researchers are trained to be self-conscious
about their biases, to build safeguards against
bias into their research designs and to take

care in drawing conclusions. Nevertheless, they and the people who provide financial support for their work, are influenced by values, especially in their choice of problems to study. In this book I have tried to represent the points of view of both employers and employees, the powerful and powerless, the advantaged and disadvantaged. To the extent that I have succeeded, however, I can claim no moral superiority. The values of the 1970s, as compared to the values of the 1940s, are far more supportive of recognizing various group interests.

SUMMARY

Interpersonal processes are psychological phenomena that influence human interaction in groups and organizations. In this introductory chapter it is argued (using corruption as an example) that interpersonal processes affect all facets of experience in groups and organizations, such as bureaucratic strategies for solving organizational problems. Knowing about interpersonal processes is useful for attaining a greater understanding of how groups and organizations behave and might behave, even if one cannot change that behavior.

To begin, four psychological principles comprise the fundamentals of interpersonal processes. These are (1) that people respond and act on their views of reality, not its objective qualities; (2) that people are influenced by the immediate (social) situation they perceive themselves to be in; (3) that people act on motives that they bring to situations as well as motives altered or created by situations; (4) that interpersonal actions are guided by values and beliefs which derive from the culture in which people live.

2

The Human Environment

In most sports, group training can be very advantageous. The group will offer a competitive situation.
. . . Most important, training with a group should
motivate and inspire each competitor to try harder.
—Al Raine, Head Coach, Canadian National Ski Team
   (1974)

In the minds of many people, the formula for
success consists, on the one hand, of one person imbued with tremendous energy and motivation and, on the other, of a noisy audience or
team. The successful person has had a lifelong
ambition; the people around the person are a
source of stimulation and challenge. In ath-
letics, the phrases used to describe what is
needed are "drive" and "psyching up." There is
an element of reality in this notion, but it
is much too simple and sometimes very wrong
because it fails to account for the psychological complexity of people. In many social
situations neither high motivation nor the

presence of others leads to increased success.
A better way to understand how people succeed
—and how they attain other goals, including
interpersonal ones—is to discard such simplistic notions and to study how the human environment, the world of people, shapes the views of
reality, the situations, the motives and
values of individuals.

In 1897 psychologist N. Triplett had his
students wind fishing reels either alone or in
the presence of other students. The students
who worked in the presence of others wound the
reels more quickly than those who worked
alone. This was one of the first attempts to
study systematically how the human environment
influences an individual. Does the presence of
a group always lead to better performance? Do
others increase the motivation to succeed? Is
increasing the motivation to succeed always
productive? These questions were asked by researchers, efficiency experts, industrial and
military planners, and athletic coaches. The
answers turned out to be not quite so simple
as the quotation heading this chapter implies.
People in groups have a much richer impact on
each other than many think. People affect not
just the competitive urge, but also desires for
friendship and solidarity and the search for
meaning in everyday life. They affect, as
well, views of reality—what is perceived to
be true and what is expected will be true.
They affect beliefs and values and the emotions
attached to them, and they affect pedestrian,
everyday habits. Sometimes these psychological
effects are beneficial to performance on
tasks; sometimes they have just the opposite
influence.

It is easier to grasp the impact of people
on people if we begin with the simple situation of one person working in the presence of
another person. We shall therefore start with
the several ways that the mere presence of
another can affect one person. Then we will
move to the effects of interpersonal interactions, and it will become clearer how complex

arrangements of the human environment into
groups and organizations affect the individual.

THE PRESENCE OF OTHERS

Social psychological theory was undeveloped
until about the 1940s, so researchers interested in the effect of the mere presence of
other people on an individual's performance began by trial and error. They put together
various combinations of audiences, workers,
and tasks to see how individual performance
was affected. As is sometimes the case with
this scientific strategy, a large number of
studies produced varying results which could
not be explained parsimoniously. Many researchers found that work was improved by the
presence of others (they called this phenomenon
"social facilitation"); but others found that
work was negatively affected. Since investigators had used all sorts of tasks—from wind-
ing fishing reels to mathematics—and had
varied the social context in several different
ways—from having people work on the same task
in different rooms to having people work on
different tasks in the same room—it was impossible to sort out why social facilitation was
obtained at one time, poorer performance at
another. But by the mid-1960s psychological
theory was more sophisticated. Experiments
with animals had led to a fairly good understanding of some situations which help learning. It was now possible to look back at studies of social facilitation with some reasonable,
testable hypotheses in mind.

In 1965, Robert Zajonc published an article
in *Science* which reviewed the social facilitation research literature. He pointed out that
stress, anxiety, or stimulation increases physiological arousal and he noted that arousal
increases the speed of behavior (cf. Weiss and
Miller, 1971). (Simply put, if a lion chases
you, you run faster.) Zajonc argued that other
human beings are arousing, so in their presence

the speed of a person's task performance should increase. An increase in speed, however, does not always improve performance on tasks. Errors may increase as well. Anyone who has taken a timed exam while being watched has felt this phenomenon in action. The presence of others, though it may be "motivating," can be a source of mistakes, too. Therefore, performance will be improved only if the task is simple to perform (e.g., running) or is well learned. On a task that requires finely-tuned skills or is complex or not well learned (so that errors predominate), increased speed from the presence of others would merely reduce accuracy.

In 1966, Zajonc and Sales showed research volunteers (subjects) a number of "foreign" words. They practiced pronouncing some words over and over, other words very little. Then the subjects were asked to look at some patterns projected at high speeds on a screen. Although the patterns were actually meaningless, the subjects were led to believe that the words they had been shown earlier were being projected. The subjects more often reported seeing the words they had practiced than the words they had not practiced, and, further, they saw the words they had practiced more often when an audience was present. Zajonc and Sales concluded that since "well learned" responses were increased in the presence of others, their hypothesis was supported.

Nicholas Cottrell (1968) has argued that the mere presence of others is not only arousing when others are evaluating a person. True or not, knowing one is being evaluated clearly increases the importance of success. The arousing effect of the presence of others may occur most of all because people are trying harder or are trying to look good. In accord with this hypothesis, Cottrell et al. (1968) demonstrated that the mere presence of a blindfolded student did not significantly affect the performance of experimental subjects, whereas a student who was there to observe the subjects did influence their task performance. In the observer's presence, the subjects performed better on well learned tasks, more poorly on unlearned ones.

Since it is the meaning of others' presence and not their physical proximity that is the most significant factor in arousing others, it is reasonable to assume that other people can affect performance even when they are not physically present. Merely knowing that others are working on the same task or that others will evaluate one's work may be as effective in activating behavior and changing performance as their actual presence. For example, Dashiell showed back in 1935 that individual speeds on simple tasks were enhanced when subjects knew that others in the same building were working on the same tasks.

To review, thus far we have seen that the presence of other people can cause you to do things faster and that the question of whether doing things faster helps or hurts overall performance depends on the task. If working fast doesn't create mistakes, you are better off; if working fast causes you to lose accuracy, you are worse off. Two hypotheses attempt to explain why the presence of other people can make you work more quickly. The first one is simple: the physical presence of others is arousing. The second is more complicated: the perception that others are observing or competing with us causes us to worry more about our probable success or how we will be evaluated. Both of these hypotheses have merit. We know, for example, that animals —though they probably don't worry about success—do become aroused in the presence of other animals. There may be some parallel instinctive activating mechanism in humans which causes arousal in the presence of others. But Cottrell's studies suggest that the meaning we attribute to the presence of others is far more important.

There are many examples in the research literature of how other people affect us

differently because of differences in the
meaning their behavior has for us. The last
ten years has seen phenomenal growth in theory
about attributions of meanings—the explanations we attach to others' behavior and our
own. If you think about why you feel shy when
speaking before a group, the importance of
attributions of meanings will be apparent. The
meaning you attribute to those coughs at the
back of the room affects you, not the noise
itself.

ATTRIBUTIONS AND EMOTIONS

A demonstration of how other people alter our
attributions was conducted by a group of researchers at Columbia University. Stanley
Schacter (1964) and his colleagues were interested in how people experience emotion. Our
bodies, they argued, do not distinguish among
emotions very well. Whether we are very happy
or very angry, the physiological responses
seem to be similar—increased heart rate, per-
spiration, shaking. Therefore, emotion must
involve some combination of physiological
arousal and thinking. Perhaps we feel a particular emotion like sadness because of the way
we explain and give meaning to the arousal we
experience. If so, then people around us could
influence our emotions by giving us ideas of
how to interpret our arousal.

The first study of emotion to test this
idea was performed by Schachter and Jerome
Singer (1962). Under the guise of an investigation of a new vitamin, some subjects were in-
jected with epinephrine, which causes physiological arousal; others, with a placebo (an
inert substance). Some subjects receiving
epinephrine were correctly informed that the
drug caused physical symptoms such as increased heartbeat and palmar sweating, but
others were either misinformed that it caused
nausea and dizziness or not warned of any
symptom.

The two latter groups of subjects would have

had no ready explanation for their agitated
physical state. To provide one, Schachter and
Singer manipulated the social context. Half the
subjects were paired with a confederate who
acted nearly euphoric; he threw paper airplanes
about the room and aimed paper balls at the
wastebasket. The remaining subjects were
paired with a confederate who acted angry; he
pretended to resent the experiment and stomped
from the room when a questionnaire made inappropriate queries. The conditions and
results of the experiment are illustrated in
Table 2.1.

The subjects' own feelings were dramatically
affected by a combination of receiving epinephrine and observing the confederate's behavior. The subjects receiving a placebo did
not report feeling particularly aroused or
emotional regardless of the confederate's behavior, but the subjects receiving epinephrine
reported experiencing relatively strong feelings. Of the latter, those who had been correctly informed that epinephrine would cause
arousal symptoms felt that arousal, physically, but they felt less emotional than those in
any other epinephrine group. Those who had
been misinformed or not informed about epinephrine's physiological effects reported feeling emotional. The emotions they felt were
"happiness" if the confederate had acted happy
or "anger" if the confederate had acted angry.
Schachter and Singer concluded that (1) un-
explained arousal and (2) "cues" from the behavior of others and the context of their
behavior—that is, the situation—caused these
subjects to attribute particular emotions to
themselves (see Figure 2.1).

A few other studies have provided somewhat
more support for the prediction that both physiological arousal and the social environment
cause emotional attributions. For example,
people ordinarily feel anxious if put in a
darkened room, but when they are in an encounter group with others, they feel warmth
and sexual attraction for each other (Gergen,

TABLE 2.1   Emotions as a Function of Arousal and the Situation (Adapted from Schacter and Singer, 1962)

| | Situation | |
| | Euphoric Confederate | |
Arousal	Subjects' Self-report[a]	Subjects' Behavior[b]
Low: Placebo	1.61	16.00
High: Epinephrine Informed	.98	12.72
High: Epinephrine No Information	1.78	18.28
High: Epinephrine Misinformed	1.90	22.56
	Angry Confederate	
Low: Placebo	1.63	.79
High: Epinephrine Informed	1.91	-.18
High: Epinephrine No Information	1.39	2.28
High: Epinephrine Misinformed	Condition not run	

[a]For both Eurphoria and Anger conditions, the higher the score, the happier and less angry the subjects felt.

[b]For the Euphoria condition, the higher the score, the more happy subjects acted. For the Anger condition (different scale used), the higher the score, the more angry subjects acted.

Gergen, and Barton, 1973). Many people feel sick if they first use marijuana alone, but attribute the same experience to a high when they learn from others what marijuana is supposed to do (Becker, 1953). Further, arousal actually caused by anticipated shock is attributed by men to be a feeling of attraction

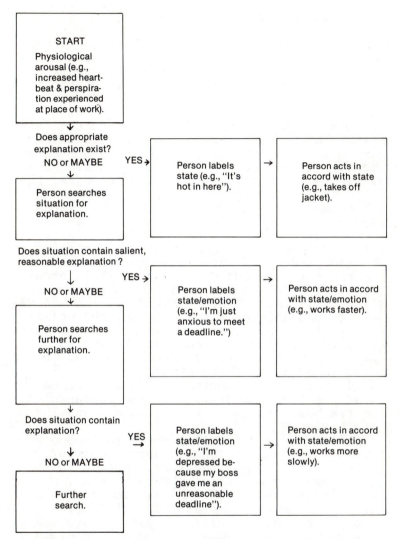

FIGURE 2.1 Schachter's Theory of Emotion: A Schematic Example.

if a pretty woman is around, but dislike if a plain woman is present (Brehm et al., 1970).

ATTRIBUTION THEORY

Attribution theory is actually not a formal theory but rather an approach to understanding all the ways that people try to make sense of situations by explaining the causes of their behavior and the behavior of others (cf. Heider, 1958; Jones et al., 1972; Harvey et al., 1976). Basic to the approach are the twin assumptions that (1) we all systematically organize information about ourselves and others and (2) that we compare sets of possible causes of events in an attempt to see which offer the most reasonable explanations.

Suppose a student fails a test. The teacher examines the available information, such as whether or not the student has failed in the past, whether few or many other students failed the same test, and whether or not the student has regularly attended classes. This information tells the teacher something about the consistency of failure by the student, the uniqueness of the student's failure, and the possibility of extenuating circumstances. With these clues to the possible cause of the student's failure, the teacher will decide whether it occurred because of the student's lack of ability or lack of motivation or perhaps because the test was difficult. The explanation the teacher decides on is called a "causal attribution."

People make attributions about their own behavior as well as about others' behavior. Suppose, for example, that the teacher in the last example always feels "funny" (e.g., his heart beats faster) when he has to talk to a group of parents. According to attribution theory, the teacher will explain his arousal in a way that seems most reasonable to him. His explanation may be obvious (e.g., he expects to be criticized). Yet if he has no ready explanation for feeling "funny" (if, for instance, he knows the parents and is sure they like and agree with him), he may look further for an explanation of his physical state. If teacher-parent meetings always occur near dinner time, he might explain his feelings as "hunger." If he has a troublesome student or two, he might feel "guilty." He thus may attach an emotional label to his feelings that helps him explain the events around him. Obviously such attributions as we make concerning our own behavior may have consequences that are as important as those we use in explaining other people's behavior.

An interesting facet of attributions is that the actors and the observers in a situation often come to opposite conclusions about why things occur. If I am a failing student (the actor) and you are my teacher (the observer), it is quite possible that I will think I failed because of something you did (e.g., made up a hard exam), whereas you will think I failed because there was something wrong with me (e.g., lack of ability).

Actors and observers see behavior from opposite perspectives. When I am acting, I cannot focus on my own behavior very well. The situation and other actors are what I see best, and what I see best influences the alternatives I consider. I am therefore more likely to consider other people's motivations or personalities or the constraints of the situation than I am to consider myself as a cause of events. Yet from the perspective of others in the situation, it is my behavior that stands out most and that is likely to be examined as a possible cause of events.

The actor-observer difference is particularly important when people are participating in an interdependent but somewhat conflictful relationship with each other, as in families or work groups. Here the "observer" is not simply a disinterested spectator, but someone who has something to gain and lose by the actor's behavior—particularly self-esteem and other personal rewards. The "actor," in turn, is also an interested spectator of the observer's actions. There will be an understandable

tendency towards self-protection and towards
reinforcing self-interested views of the relationship—not necessarily because anyone is
selfish, but because the stakes are relatively high. It is even possible that the more
a person gives to another and to a relationship, the greater the tendency to differ with
the other in explaining the causes of behavior towards the other. Figure 2.2 illustrates some data from a study of young couples
to show some of the behaviors that they explain
differently. It does not take too much imagination to think of instances in which the same
sort of phenomena could apply to business,
political, or other kinds of relationships
where people work closely together and where
conflicts of interest arise.

Suppose you are in charge of a work group.
From your perspective, the strengths and
foibles of regular group members will stand
out. You may feel a bit separate from them.
You may blame their personalities, abilities,
or motives if anything goes wrong. Meanwhile,
your behavior stands out from their perspective more than their own does, especially
since you have power. This lack of a mutual
perspective can lead to major conflict and
breakdowns of productivity because both you
and the group members are failing to see how
your own behavior affects decision making and
communication. Given some area of disagreement,
for example, you could be wondering why they
don't see the point while they are resenting
your pushiness.

Though differences of attribution separate
people during difficult times, those same
differences do not always bring people together
when times are better. For instance, if a group
is successful, the leader may not attribute
the good outcome to the work of the group
members and the members may not attribute the
good outcome to the quality of their leader.
What happens sometimes is that people
attribute good events to themselves; they
take credit for successes they can claim.

Type of Behavior	Example: Behavior of Actor	Actor's Explanation of Behavior	Partner's Explanation of Actor's Behavior
Avoiding or exacting behavior	Man quits competition in sports.	Circumstances: *"It's too time-consuming, I'm too busy."*	Actor's characteristics: *"He's too lazy. No competitive spirit anymore."*
Inept or socially rejecting behavior	Woman is extremely pessimistic about world.	Actor's beliefs: *"I'm being realistic and merely conveying the facts."*	Actor's characteristics: *"She's close-minded in that she only sees what is wrong."*
Activity disliked by partner	Man gets drunk.	Activity is desirable: *"It's a release and I enjoy it."*	Actor's characteristics: *"He's addicted and has no self-control."*
Emotional or aggressive behavior	Woman yells and swears in arguments.	Partner is responsible: *"I'm so mad because he can't see how wrong he is and can't understand me."*	Actor's characteristics: *"She can't stand to be quiet and, above all, lose an argument."*
Irresponsible or annoying behavior	Man fails to do something.	Actor's characteristics: *"I'm forgetful."*	Actor's characteristics: *"He's inconsiderate."*

FIGURE 2.2 Some Examples of Prominent Actor-Observer Differences: Attributional Conflict in Young Couples (Adapted from Orvis, Kelley, and Butler, 1976)

Because attributions are self interested, actors and observers in successful groups, unsuccessful groups, troublesome situations, and
happier situations explain what is happening
differently but usually in a manner that reinforces their own self-esteem.

ATTRIBUTIONS AND SELF-CONFIDENCE

Are you *really* a good leader? Several researchers interested in attributions (e.g., Weiner,
1970), have pointed out that to be successful
we need to attribute good characteristics
to ourselves. The leader will gain confidence
(and behavior that reflects confidence) by
attributing good things that happen to such
abilities as considerateness and creativity.
To have confidence, faults should not be ignored, but should rather be viewed as changeable (e.g., needing to try a bit harder). Unfortunately, many people attribute negative,
hard to change characteristics to themselves,
such as lack of intelligence, or shyness,
merely because other people treat them as if
that were true. Probably, too many good words
have been written about taking the other fellow's perspective. Thinking about what other
people think of our mistakes (given the actor-
observer difference) can be misleading.

Attributions can interfere with one's self-
confidence, as when one thinks, "They must be
just waiting for me to make a mistake." As long
ago as 1924, Floyd Allport wrote that the
presence of others was inhibiting; subjects who
were to "free associate" any word with a word
given by the experimenter used more impersonal
words in the presence of others than they did
alone.

One might think inhibitions would be stronger
if one were with strangers or a hostile audience, but sometimes just the opposite is true.
Researchers Brown and Garland (1971) asked
subjects to sing a song in the presence
of their friends or in the presence of some

strangers. They found that the subject's songs
were shorter in the presence of friends than
with strangers. This study is only one of several that show how supposedly supportive others
can inhibit us. In sports, it has been demonstrated that teams which are very cohesive and
friendly can perform very poorly. Teammates may
not want to take risks that could make them
look bad in front of their friends, or may
fail to play aggressively because their friends
would view them as selfish.

SOME ATTRIBUTIONAL TRAPS

Attributions often explain not just the
causes of present behavior, but also behavior
in the foreseeable future. Good students often
worry about their next test because they have
attributed their past good grades, in part,
to good luck and think bad luck must come
sometime soon (the gambler's fallacy).

Using the expectations of others to predict
the future can get one into this attributional
trap. If others are prejudiced about a group
we belong to, for example, they may expect us
to fail. This expectation can reduce our
motivation to perform well (cf. Kiesler, 1975);
it leads us to believe that the odds in the
situation are against success.

Ordinarily people want to perform well, but
what if others will like them less if they do?
In that case they may attribute lack of motivation to themselves and not try so hard. Research
on the performance of women and minorities
(particularly on tasks associated with white
masculinity) shows that these persons, even if
they know they are competent, may try less hard
in the presence of others (e.g., Morgan and
Mausner, 1973).

People may be motivated to perform less than
their best if success is socially inappropriate,
if they will be punished for success, or in
deference to others. Administrators sometimes
contribute less in a group when they want to

give others the chance to succeed, but more
commonly it is the lower status individuals who
fail to participate.

Another attributional trap is labeling
feelings as fear or anxiety when these labels
are inappropriate. People who have serious
emotional problems do this, but all of us
experience inappropriate anxiety at one time
or another. In this case the presence of others
may be relaxing (Kiesler, 1966; Amoroso and
Walters, 1969). Studies of anxiety have shown
that many people (particularly first born or
only children) will seek out others when they
are anxious, and that the presence of others
in the same boat can indeed reduce anxiety
(Schachter, 1959; Wrightsman, 1960)—providing
one doesn't blame them for how one feels! Attributional analysis suggests that relaxation
in the presence of others occurs when their
action or demeanor suggests that the situation,
while unpleasant, is not really dangerous or
important. In a performance situation, of
course, this attribution could be either helpful or detrimental to success, depending on the
requirements of the task for high or low
arousal.

Social Comparison

We have seen that the behavior of others affects how we define our emotions, our attitudes about ourselves, our perceived abilities,
and, in general, how we make sense of the
world. One aspect of this process involves
comparing ourselves with others. For example,
seeing yourself as a good student depends partly on how studious you think you are in comparison with other students. This use of the
behavior of others for information about oneself is called "social comparison." There
are three rules of perception that explain why
we need to employ social comparisons (cf.
Hastorf, Schneider, and Polefka, 1970). First,
there is the rule of limitation. It is only

possible to evaluate the qualities of any
entity—that is, to know how good or bad something is—by comparing it with other entities.
This means that self-evaluations are learned
in part by comparing ourselves with others.
(This is not the only source of self-evaluations, however. For example, we also compare
our present behavior with our past behavior.)
Knowing how we are different and what makes
us individual comes from social comparison.
For example, our skin defines us as human. But having skin does not contribute to
our unique self-definition—everyone else has
skin, too. But if we consistently have the
clearest, rosiest, finest skin, then we feel
attractive. Our self-definition is therefore
dependent upon our observations of others'
similarities and differences.

The rule of limitation also affects how we
compare ourselves with others. We can know
about ourselves only to the extent that our
qualities can be measured. In comparing qualities of physical objects, we have yardsticks,
weights, and other objective tests. But for
qualities of people we usually have fewer such
tests. There are no physical measures of beliefs, motives, opinions, skills, and goals,
so our comparisons are fairly rough and usually limited to classification and relative
judgments. They depend more upon what others
say and do, and how they look, than upon what
they physically are.

Next is the rule of organization. We organize
our perceptions so that information about ourselves and others fits into categories. We
learn through people's behavior what the categories are and how to fit our behavior into
them. For example, one category is "friendliness." As we grow up, we learn that being
polite to strangers, telling another a secret,
smiling at a party, and shaking hands all fit
into this category, and to the extent that we
do these things as much or more than others we
have evidence of our own friendliness.

The rule of organization goes hand in hand

with the rule of meaning. That is, categories of information are coherently organized and weighed so that they make sense. We do not ordinarily think of a person as both friendly and hostile. These traits seem inconsistent.

We group categories and traits meaningfully. Friendliness often goes with cooperativeness, and the two may seem to be the reason why a person is a good worker. Such a chain of perceived characteristics is an implicit theory of personality which ties perceptions together so that some things about a person explain why other things about him are true. Obviously, some kinds of information contribute more to such attributions than others. Friendliness, for example, is usually more important in our culture than forgetfulness. When a person loses his glasses, we infer much less about him than if he smiles a great deal.

Although people from the same culture will generally use the same categories when evaluating others and themselves, there are also individual differences. Some people, for example, give the category "intelligence" unusually great importance. They have an implicit theory of personality that makes intelligence a strong determinant of how a person is evaluated. For these people, intelligence is seen as the reason for other good qualities, such as being a good worker.

If you think about what categories of information are most important to you when you evaluate people, you may learn something about yourself. What you pay attention to reflects your own implicit theory of personality and has a strong effect on how you evaluate yourself. For instance, do you often notice how much drive for success others have or don't have? Or have you repeatedly remarked on other people's appearances? If so, you are probably using those categories to evaluate yourself.

THE GROUP

One of the important ways in which individuals

categorize and organize information about
people is to attach them to groups. Different
characteristics can be attributed to different
groups although there will often be overlap.
By organizing the world of people into groups,
the task of processing and organizing information becomes much easier. In some instances,

Sometimes by identifying people as members of
a particular group, we then "know" them since
we perceive them as having the qualities we
attribute to the group. This group stereotype may be so clear to us that we never have
to meet any members of the group to feel we
can predict their behavior or describe their
personalities.

A group stereotype does not necessarily have
to be learned from personal experience or from
others' accounts although it often is. Our
language is sufficient to provide some attributions. The name of a group, for example, may
cause one to assume that people in a group have
a particular trait. Imagine what you might think
of a person who belongs to an organization
called "Freedom Fighters." Now try the same
thing about someone who belongs to "Inheritors
of the Earth" or "Smokers Unite." Naturally,
you don't really know what the person is like,
but if you are asked for a best guess, symbolic
associations will guide your imagination.

The organization of the world into groups
strongly influences the process of social
comparison. Individuals are especially likely
to compare themselves to other people in their
own group (cf. Neath-Gelvin, 1975). The mere
fact of belonging to a group implies that
we have something in common with the other
members of the group, and that something will
often be inferred to go far beyond the simple
fact of joint membership. Joint membership,
by the perceptual rules of organization and
meaning, implies similarity along other
dimensions. "Birds of a feather flock together"
is a valid description of what we infer from
group membership.

But it is not just a law of perception that induces individuals to compare themselves to others in their group. Doing so is useful. Consider, for example, a situation in which two people score extremely high on a test measuring law aptitude. If one of them is a member of your own group (a graduate student in a business school, say) and the other is not (a first-year law student), the performance of the former is much more likely to be used in assessing your own aptitude to practice law. Comparing yourself to someone in your own group gives you more useful information about yourself (e.g., what your chances of success are if you apply to law school). Mark Zanna and his colleagues (1975) have shown experimentally that social comparisons with members of an individual's own peer groups are much preferred to those with members of other groups.

IMPACT OF THE GROUP: MEMBERSHIP AND REFERENCE GROUPS

Research on social comparisons is one part of the evidence for the very powerful and direct impact of people in our own group on our feelings, attitudes, and behavior. For example, Morse and Gergen (1970) demonstrated that favorable comparisons with similar others tend to raise the level of self-esteem, whereas comparisons with dissimilar others do not. But which of the many groups in which we hold membership will have the greatest effect?

In name, all of us belong to hundreds of groups: the human group, the male or female group, a political group, a neighborhood, a social class, an occupational group. Clearly, some of these groups are more important to us than others. If we share membership with a group of strangers on an airplane, they may have a momentary impact on our feelings, but it probably will not last beyond the trip. In contrast, people with whom we have an ongoing relationship, or at least care about, have a much more impactful and lasting

effect. Indeed, we do not even have actually
to belong to a group for its members to have
an important effect on our behavior. All that
is really required is that we have some psychological involvement with them. For example, if
we aspire to membership in a country club, we
may compare ourselves to the members of the
club.

"Reference group" is the term used for any
set of individuals with whom we have some psychological involvement; actual membership is
not required. "Membership group" is the term
for any set of individuals with whom we are
classified according to some objective criterion of similarity; psychological involvement
is not required. It is largely the reference
group that has psychological impact. Kurt Lewin
(1948, p. 134) made the point early: "Similarity between persons merely permits their
classification, their subsumption under the
same abstract concept, whereas belonging to
the same social group means concrete, dynamic
interrelationships among persons. A husband,
a wife, and a baby are less similar to each
other, in spite of their being a strong natural group, than the baby is to other babies."

The distinction between a reference and a
membership group is of more than academic interest. For instance, demographers and political scientists have discovered that one's
social class, whether defined by educational
level, financial status, or profession, is not
necessarily the class with which one identifies
(e.g., Centers, 1949). The class one identifies
with can be a better predictor of one's con-
sumption, fertility, or voting (e.g., Douvan,
1956). The sex researchers (e.g., Kinsey,
Pomeroy, and Martin, 1948) found that sexual
behavior conformed to that of the social class
people felt a part of, or aspired to, even
when by objective criteria they were not members of it. Personality theorists discoverd
that traits such as authoritarianism (which
had formerly been thought to develop early in
life) changed in accord with the adult reference

group (e.g., Siegel and Siegel, 1957). The designers and users of IQ ability tests found that the reference group influenced people's (supposedly innate) intelligence score by affecting their motivation to do well on the test, their patience with the examination procedure, their interest in the questions, and even their willingness to accept a high score as valuable (see especially the discussion of black culture and tests in Jones et al., 1972). In these areas of behavior, and others, the reference group has tremendous influence.

FRIENDS, ALLIES, AND ENEMIES

It does not take much for a person to feel psychological involvement with others. A group's name, sharing a common crisis, or just being told one is classified in a group ("social labeling") may cause one to adopt it as a reference group. For example, Henri Tajfel (1970) brought some young boys into his laboratory to work on some tasks, after which monetary rewards were to be distributed. Some of the boys were told they were in "Group X" and some were not assigned to a group. He found that boys assigned to Group X unfairly distributed too much money to other members of Group X and too little to those not in the group, whereas unassigned boys distributed the money equitably. Yet the boys in Group X had never seen the others in their group, had never interacted with them, and knew nothing whatever about them.

Why did the Group X boys give their members more money? Mere assignment to Group X may have suggested some common interest or deserving characteristic. People not in the group would by contrast seem less similar, less deserving. Perhaps assignment to Group X suggested to the members that the experimenter wanted Group X treated in a special way. Tajfel's experiment does not answer the question, but it is quite

possible the boys of Group X assumed their
group was superior.

Most individuals learn that they are basically good, that their own beliefs are correct,
and that their own feelings are based on reality. People in their own groups are perceived to have similar worthiness, beliefs,
and feelings. Since attributions and judgments
are relative, people in other groups appear to
be less worthy, less similar.

The assumption of own group superiority
is a psychological basis for prejudice against
groups to which one does not belong. It is
a bias that reinforces the feeling that members
of the reference group are friends, groups
supportive of the reference groups are allies,
and other groups are quaint, or strange, if
not enemies. (Does former President Nixon's
enemies list come to mind?) It is a bias
that makes us cultural absolutists instead
of cultural relativists. And it is a bias
that has continuing effects, positive as well
as negative. As favoritism toward one's
own group develops, the assumption of
commonality of interest and similarity with
the people in it increases, too. For instance, husbands and wives assume their
opinions are more similar than is really
the case.

Several interpersonal phenomena affect the
perceived difference between "we" and "they."
For instance the actor-observer difference of
perspective can produce a tendency to see the
behavior of other groups as caused by negative
personality traits, abilities, or motives, but
to see our own group's behavior as a (reasonable) reaction to people or situations (Storms,
1973). If they quit their jobs, they are lazy;
if we quit, it is a response to unpleasant
working conditions or a better offer. If they
make war, they are an aggressive people; if we
take up arms, we are only defending what is
ours. This is one source of what is called
"ethnocentrism," or an exaggerated view of

the importance or superiority of one's own group.

THE GROUP IMAGE

The reference group defines a set of individuals who feel some psychological involvement with one another, and as we have seen, membership in such a group creates an image of the group as a set of people like oneself. The result in some cases is not a feeling of special importance or superiority but just the opposite. If you belong by reason of luck or choice to a group which is maligned by others or which fails, the group's negative image tends to fall on all its members, you included. The unfortunate irony is that you and the others in your group may be seen as more similar to each other (in a negative sense) than you really are, while at once your individual behavior is attributed to your own traits and dispositions. In other words you are given a label, such as lazy, because of your membership in the group, but any evidence of laziness is viewed as your own doing!

Social labeling is a term used by sociologists (cf. Tannenbaum, 1938; Becker, 1963; Schur, 1971) to denote the way people label nonconformist or minority groups and attach a group image of deviance to them. All heroin and cocaine users are addicts; the elderly are frail; people who don't mow their lawns are eccentric. Those so labeled often tend to act in accordance with others' expectations— to become as they are labeled and to feel closer to people similarly labeled even though they may have little in common with the group except the label (Storms and McCaul, 1975). Many sociologists believe that much deviance in our society is caused by social labeling and not the other way around.

FUNCTIONS OF GROUPS

So far we have described relatively passive interpersonal processes, involving little or no interaction with group members. But individuals do join groups, defend groups, socialize with group members, work with them, and try to influence them. Why do individuals interact in groups? Why do they sometimes accept severe personal hardships to stay in groups? One reason is that individuals have strong needs to interact; another is that groups create the need to interact, and to interact in particular ways. Each process has important effects on the individual as well as on the individual's group.

THE INFORMATIONAL FUNCTION

Stereotypes provide some information about ourselves and other people. Passive observations provide more. But even more information is gained by interacting with members of a group. By observing how others act toward us, we obtain information about how correct our own behavior is. Acting in ways that will provoke a reaction from others also gives us information. Or we may ask others for their opinion, and others may give us advice. Interaction provides us with information that we can use to assess ourselves, predict outcomes, and decide how to act in the future. Interaction in groups can help us interpret our personal goals and give them significance.

THE INTERPERSONAL FUNCTION

Another function that groups serve is to make it possible for us to satisfy interpersonal needs. Consider, for example, Abraham Maslow's (1954) hierarchical list of human needs. First are the physiological needs such as for food and water. Next are the needs for safety and

security. Then, if these are satisfied, come
the need for love and the need for esteem (including the need for status or respect from
others and the need for achievement and success). Finally, there is the need for self-actualization. All are satisfied through membership in groups.

Physiological needs, of course, demand that
one belongs to a family or its substitute when
one is young, and to a work group when one is
older (although it is possible to write books
alone in the wilderness). Safety in our society
demands group affiliation: a country, a town,
a family that can pool resources for protection
and defense. The need for love and esteem requires belonging to at least one group since
neither can be satisfied alone. Honorary
societies, for example, may have nothing to
give members except prestige, but people
covet their membership, even in equalitarian
societies. Another related need is the need
for power, which obviously is satisfied by belonging to a group that one can influence. Even
the self-actualization need, which Maslow
characterized as being uniquely personal, probably cannot be satisfied without a group that
in some way rewards this fulfillment and provides a standard for measuring its success.

THE MATERIAL FUNCTION

Groups do not just satisfy basic physiological and psychological needs, but also provide
material and practical aid for maintaining
one's standard of living and working. Belonging to a group or organization may provide
facilities that an individual cannot afford or
obtain alone, as belonging to a country club
provides the swimming pool, tennis court, and
the golf course an individual could not afford. Belonging to a travel group may provide
cheaper air fares. The pooling of resources
also may enable one to reach personal goals
that would be difficult to reach otherwise.

Groups and organizations can exert political pressure that have more effect than when the effort is not so coordinated. Problem solving groups can put their heads together and correct each other's errors to solve problems.

The importance of their material function to many groups becomes clear when one observes what happens to groups which were formed to achieve some material gain and then either fail dismally or succeed completely. Leaders are replaced (Hamblin, 1958); new goals, perhaps interpersonal ones, are created (Pepitone and Kleiner, 1957); factions erupt over alternate activities (Leighton, 1945).

THE GROUP AS MOTIVATOR

So far, the group has been characterized as helping to serve the needs and goals that individuals bring with them to the group. But groups create needs and goals, too. In fact, many groups wield considerable power simply by being able to create new motives, intensify old ones, or cause people to reinterpret their previous desires. There are two major ways that this can happen. First, the activity and interaction of group members can create or intensify individual motives. Second, group activity and interaction can cause group goals to be developed and interpreted.

INDIVIDUAL MOTIVES

In the simpler case, the group interaction causes feelings to be experienced that are attributed to the group and create motives oriented toward the group. If the group activity is arousing and is labeled in accord with cues provided by group members, the individual's attribution of emotion will have been caused by the group process (Kiesler and Coffman, 1975). For example, what would be the effect of joining a group of people for lunch and perceiving that they, not the temperature of

the restaurant or the quality of the food,
have made one feel good? If one joined the
group out of curiosity but then attributed
warm feelings to the others, one would be
more motivated to return or to try to gain
their approval. In this manner, a group can
create new motives that weren't there when the
person joined it.

Direct communication from others during group
interaction can also create new motives. For
example, imagine that someone points out that
you are particularly competent in solving certain problems. You may never have noticed this
before, but now, having been rewarded, your
efforts in this direction will be increased.
Or suppose that group members nod their heads
in agreement whenever you speak. You will then
be much more likely to speak up in the group.
You may become the group leader. A group can
create motives by rewarding and punishing such
behavior during group interaction.

One interesting manner in which groups change
individual motives occurs as conflict among
individuals arises within a group. Intragroup
conflict can become so engrossing that its
importance for the individuals involved is distorted. They spend a good deal of time thinking
about the conflict, discussing it with others,
and trying to resolve it.

GROUP GOALS: RATIONALES AND OBJECTIVES

The second way that groups create motives
is by developing and reinterpreting group
goals, which then guide the behavior and
attitudes of individual members. One group goal
found in nearly all groups is group maintenance; group members decide it is important to
keep people attracted to the group and maintain
group membership. To do this, the group has to
find some justification for being, if one has
not been obvious. Therefore, group members will
tend to interpret their actions as having a
group-oriented purpose.

One can observe, for example, what happens in

the beginning stages of an encounter or T-group
(directed training group for learning about
oneself and groups through experience [Bennis
and Shepard, 1965]). The members sit there
waiting for the group leader or "facilitator"
to tell them what to do. But he or she does
nothing. People in this situation will usually
begin to talk, making suggestions about what
ought to be done. Often there is an argument
about why they are there. To learn? To learn
what? Some members suggest that the group is
learning how groups operate. Others believe
that the group is teaching them about themselves ("personal growth"). Others urge that
the group provide practical advice that the
members can use in their jobs. Out of discussion, conflict, and interpersonal bargaining
arise group goals.

Since group behavior often seems oriented to
discovering some reasonable goals, rather than
being directed by them, one might be more
accurate to call its discoveries "group rationales" rather than "group goals." A goal implies
that the group is working toward something
that first existed as an end; rationales are
purposes the group develops and elaborates
to give meaning and value to its activities.

Most groups have two kinds of goals: (1) subordinate or long-range goals, such as making
a profit or having a happy marriage, and (2)
specific objectives, such as selling more cars
in February, 1981, than were sold in February,
1980, or finding a movie both husband and wife
will enjoy. Superordinate goals are usually
poorly operationalized, that is not clearly associated with immediate objectives, and they
often fail to direct group decisions. They are,
however, useful as group rationales.

Goals such as personal growth, education, or
social change sound good and are capable of
justifying various actions. For example, a
school board goal might be quality education,
but its immediate objective, cost cutting.
These seem contradictory, but actually
the stated goal of quality education

can be cited as a reason for cost cutting and
can improve the acceptability of the immediate
objective by virtue of its mere existence as a
superordinate goal.

Sometimes, group rationales have an advantage
over true goals because they give a group flexibility. Were a school board's actions pre-
determined by a single-minded, clearly articulated goal related to quality education, it
might soon find itself at loggerheads with
local councils, the mayor, or the state legislature. A school board must find ways to satisfy teachers, legislators, reporters, princi-
pals, parents, superintendents and taxpayers.
It must have unspoken objectives, such as inducing teacher groups to agree with parent
groups or quieting some extremists who see
schools as a source of particular irritation.
Rationales aid the group in providing some
reasonable response to outside demands and in
making some satisfactory decisions because they
help to bring different interests together and
to inspire individuals to act as the group desires.

All groups create, recreate and elaborate
goals as the group members interact with each
other. This task is not simple, whether we
speak of superordinate goals or immediate objectives. To agree on goals, group members must
bargain; they must deal with concrete events
that impinge on the group; and they must consider the resources of the group.

INTERPERSONAL BARGAINING. Interpersonal bargaining over goals in groups is often a matter
of resolving a conflict between two or more
subgroups or coalitions that have different
ideas about what the group is for and how it
should function. This conflict is not necessarily admitted by group members. For example,
weak subgroups often have a hidden agenda
through which a struggle for influence is attempted. Bennis and Shepard illustrate this
phenomenon in a T-group:

Two opposed subgroups emerge, together incorporating most of the group members. Characteristically, the subgroups are in disagreement about the groups' need for leadership or "structure." One subgroup attempts to elect a chairman, nominate working committees, establish agenda, or otherwise "structure" the meetings; the other subgroup opposes all such efforts.

In many groups, particularly large, heterogeneous organizations, subgroups are divided by status and professional credentials. At stake for each subgroup is the utilization of its particular competencies and the protection or growth of its hierarchal position and profession. In large organizations employing engineers and scientists, conflict may exist between the two subgroups about project objectives (Evan, 1965). The conflict stems both from their wanting to use their own skills and from loyalty to their professions, as contrasted with their loyalty to the organization.

Robert Merton and others (e.g., Thompson, 1961) suggest that subgroups divided by specialization may be so attached to their own methods that the methods become goals. For example, people outside a budget office frequently accuse budget officers of believing the organization exists for the purpose of operating budget procedures.

A person dealing with a large group is shortsighted if he or she assumes that the apparent goals of one subgroup, even the so-called decision makers, have a monopoly on the rationales or objectives of the entire group or organization. Lower status subgroups often have considerable informal power and can block not only the implementation of policies set by their higher status leaders (Mechanic, 1962) but the policies themselves. For example, Scheff (1961) reported a case in which failure to reform a mental hospital was mostly the result of opposition by hospital attendants. The attendants, upon whom the physicians were dependent for the day-to-day operation of the hospital, would neither accept the need for reform nor the need for a reformist ideology.

The bargaining through which subgroups come to agree on goals for the entire group is incompletely understood, but in the end, agreement usually obtains on highly ambiguous aims, which individuals can interpret from their own perspective. Management policy in a large organization may view the ambiguous goal of organizational success as one in which after-tax profits are increased (the objective here is to increase profits), whereas individual executives and workers may perceive the same goal to mean financial reward to themselves (the objective here is to increase salaries). The bargaining process continues until some semblance of stability is achieved (Cyert and March, 1963), and even then it is likely to start all over again when a concrete conflict of interest arises.

In large organizations, operating policies and measurable objectives reflect continuing tradeoffs and previous commitments. Objectives will be somewhat inconsistent with each other and with superordinate organizational rationales (cf. Simon, 1976). Tradeoffs such as "We'll fill the empty staff positions in your unit if you will support our other budget allocations" do not quite fit with the organization's goal of rationally allocating resources. Such tradeoffs, however, are necessary and lend a modicum of stability to organizations. Moreover, tradeoffs are useful for setting precedents when there exist poor guides to action. In fact, it is usually tradeoffs and the commitments they produce that create goals, not the reverse.

GROUP EXPERIENCES. The experiences of the group are a second influence on the development of group goals. Goals which relate to different levels of achievement, such as increasing sales, reducing crime, or stabilizing costs are

affected by whether the groups has been suc-
ceeding or failing in the recent past (Zander
and Medow, 1963; Stedry and Kay, 1966). Success and failure create a search for "better"
objectives, which, in turn, affect what the
group is supposed to be aiming toward in the
long run.

Alvin Zander has done the most research on
group experiences and goals. He has found that
groups most often raise their objectives after
success (but not so high that success is jeop-
ardized) and less often lower them after
failure. This may be because the challenge of
setting higher objectives is more pleasant than
the necessity of lowering them (Zander, 1968)
and because groups are less likely to believe
they have failed than succeeded (e.g., Medow
and Zander, 1965). Zander notes that a study of
United Fund campaigns in 149 cities over four
years showed that failing campaigns in one
year were rarely followed by lowered objectives
in the next, but successful objectives were
nearly always followed by higher objectives
(Zander and Newcomb, 1967).

Zander has also found that external social
pressures influence both the specific objectives and the rationales of groups, especially
if sanctions are threatened (Zander, Medow, and
Dustin, 1964). In the federal government and
nonprofit organizations, such as educational institutions, the influence of outside pressures
is especially strong because so many people
have a potential interest or actual stake in
their activities and there is no easy way to distinguish reasonable from unreasonable objectives.

An organization that is uncertain about its
objectives and stature will be open to pressures from the public, industry, Congress, or
other groups to adopt various new objectives or rationales, and it may actually do
so to acquire legitimacy or, some argue, to
reduce uncertainty. The recent movement toward
basic skills in the schools is an example of a
changing rationale due to external pressure.

Schools moved toward practical competence and away from personal development as a rationale for their activities.

GROUP RESOURCES. A group's resources are usually related to its choices of rationale and objectives. Daniel Batson is a researcher who argues that, while the superordinate goals of many service organizations sound totally unselfish, their actual, operational objectives and methods more often reflect the interests and resources of their own personnel rather than the needs of their clients.

In one study, Batson (1975) employed twenty professional counselors from a seminary and twenty nonprofessionals to run a simulated referral agency. Each heard a series of cassette recordings in which clients discussed their problems and blamed them on their environments. Batson found that, even though all clients requested help in dealing with their environment, professional counselors, more often than lay persons, referred clients to agencies that change individuals (e.g., mental hospitals) rather than to agencies that change individuals' environments (e.g., employment agencies). Batson obtained similar results when he compared other professional groups, Social Security claims representatives and clinical psychology graduate students, with lay persons. Why? Batson says that the professionals perceived their major resource to be a competence in helping individuals change and adapt to society rather than in protecting individuals from society or changing society. Their advice was thus consistent with their own resources. Their goals were to accomplish what they had been trained to do.

EFFECTIVENESS OF GROUP GOALS

Group goals influence individuals in the group because they help keep the group together, steer its activities, protect it, and

influence the development or procedures, roles
and rules. Some group goals are sufficiently
inspiring that they motivate tremendous individual effort. But some group rationales are
more useful to individuals than others.

Group Activity

When a group's rationale or superordinate
goal is accepted by the members of the group,
it will have more power to influence their
activities. Greater acceptance leads to better
group maintenance and coordination of effort
(Horowitz, 1954). Unfortunately, clear rationales, which are also more likely to influence behavior than vague ones (Raven and
Rietsma, 1957), are less likely to be found
acceptable by group members. Thus, it is often
difficult for a group to have both acceptable
and clear rationales.

James March and Herbert Simon (1958) propose
that groups solve this dilemma by agreeing
upon operational objectives that are minor in
comparison to the superordinate goal. For example, they say, a business firm may understand to some degree how its specific actions
affect its share of the market, but may understand less clearly how its actions affect
long-range profits. Therefore, the subgoal of
maintaining a particular share of the market
may become the effective criterion of the
action. The police might operationalize their
rationale of protecting law and order by
creating the objective of maximizing the number
of arrests and convictions. A professional society may exist to advance the profession it
represents, but have an operational objective
of obtaining high attendance at meetings (Cartwright and Zander, 1968).

While the development of operational objectives increases the power of the group over its
members, it may not actually enhance the level
or quality of their performance from others'
perspectives. Capturing the market, if profits

are not increased, may not satisfy stock-
holders; compiling a good record of arrests,
but not reducing the incidence of crime, will
be unsatisfactory to the public; winning popular acclaim for a research paper, but not
publishing it in a scientific journal, will not
impress some scientific audiences.

INDIVIDUAL BEHAVIOR

Even when a group's performance is objectively mediocre, having agreed upon a rationale and
a set of objectives makes people feel psychologically useful and dependent upon one another
and causes them to assign roles to each other
and to agree upon rules for interaction. A
classic study of the effect of common objectives on group interaction was conducted in
1949 by Morton Deutsch, who divided psychology
classes into groups, some of which he induced
to have a cooperative, common objective (by
offering rewards to the group as a whole for
success) and some of which he discouraged from
agreeing upon objectives (by offering rewards
to individuals for success). Everyone worked
on the same kinds of problems, which included
the solving of puzzles and human relations
problems. Deutsch found that the "cooperative"
(common objective) groups coordinated their
efforts more, gave more diverse contributions,
subdivided their work, were more attentive to
each other, communicated more clearly to each
other, were more orderly, felt more obligated
to others in the group, were more friendly,
and in some respects performed better. They
did not work more quickly, or produce significantly more, or get significantly higher
grades, but they did do somewhat higher quality
work on the problems. The cooperative experience, then, facilitated interpersonal interaction, even though performance levels were
not really so different from those in the
"competitive" groups.

Group members with a common objective in the
Deutsch study were not just better organized

but more friendly to each other. Remember that friendship can be a two-edged sword. Feelings of friendliness and involvement cause group members to be concerned about each other's behavior and attitudes. Members who contribute to objectives will be evaluated highly, but those who do not or who violate the consensus will be punished. Through social comparison, the self-evaluation of members will be affected by such evaluations. Members who are well regarded in the group will come to think well of themselves, and their own levels of aspiration will approximate group standards. On the other hand, members who are not well evaluated will come to think less well of themselves.

Common objectives and rationales elicit a pecking order that is not simply external but is also a systematic variation in the way group members privately feel about their own worth and esteem. Those at the bottom of a highly cohesive group may not be as well off as they would be in a less cohesive group. In conclusion, group goals certainly have an important effect on individuals, but they are sometimes not as effective as individuals think they are.

SUMMARY

Groups and organizations consist of people who affect one another. The influence they exert is not simple, for even one person cheering another's performance can have the opposite, undesired, effect. The effect of others on an individual's performance depends on (1) the nature of the task, especially whether it is simple and well learned or complex and not well learned, and (2) the individual's interpretation of cues or information from the others' presence. In general, people's feelings about themselves are influenced by the information other people communicate and by the social context of

that information. Some kinds of information make
people feel nervous, so they hurry and make
mistakes on tasks; others can cause people to
interpret a state of physiological arousal as
anger or happiness. A current theory of emotion
states that emotions consist of both physiological arousal and the information people have
about the arousal for explaining it.

Attribution theory is an extended theoretical
approach for understanding how people explain
events. People organize information about themselves and others and then select the most
reasonable explanation for their own and
others' behavior. People usually explain behavior in a manner that is self complimentary,
but sometimes they do not, particularly when
others label them and treat them as though
they were responsible for their own hardships.

A major source of information for individuals is other, similar individuals. Social
comparison is the process whereby people compare themselves to similar people in order to
evaluate themselves. Usually people look to
their own groups for similar people with whom
to compare themselves, especially groups with
which they are psychologically involved. Groups
to which people feel psychological attachments,
or reference groups, also have functions other
than informational ones. They satisfy interpersonal needs, such as the need for affection,
and material desires, such as wanting access
to a swimming pool.

In serving the motives of individuals, groups
influence individuals. People find that their
groups are not mere collections of individuals,
but that the group as a whole makes demands
through its objectives and rationales. For
example, suppose the group must agree on a
good reason for its perpetuation and therefore
discovers a new group "goal" (a rationale).
The effects this event has on group members include creating the need to justify individual
objectives in light of the apparent group goal,
and forcing people to bargain over them. Whether

group goals are a good thing for either the
individual or the group depends on one's perspective and one's opinion about their genesis.
Many goals are an outcome of commitments which
arise from interpersonal bargaining, outside
events that happen to occur, and existing resources of the group.

A NOTE ON THE ORGANIZATION AS A GROUP

Ordinarily when one refers to a business,
agency, or other institutional group, it is
called an "organization," whereas an informal
collection of individuals with psychological
ties to one another is called a "group." An
important question to ask is whether the difference in terms has serious implications for
the functioning of members. Most social psychologists will argue that basic interpersonal
processes affecting behavior in organizations
as compared to groups are precisely the same,
but that the social environment is different
enough in organizations to justify separate
study.

One obvious difference between an organization and a group is that an organization is
actually composed of several groups and the
effect of intergroup interaction is significant. So is the potential conflict between
rationales for a group within the organization
and rationales for the organization as a whole,
and for within-group versus between-group
images, motives, and resources,

Another difference is that organizations are
characterized by levels of power and by differentiation of functions and tasks across
groups within the organization. Different tasks
lead to many different rationales, rules, and
procedures. These levels and divisions and
differences are not arbitrary. Of great interest, therefore, is the process by which
people organize themselves (cf. Mackenzie,
1978; Weick, 1969).

Third, organizations are often more formal, more permanent, and more authoritative than small groups. There are rules, titles, and special rewards that the members recognize as legitimate; there are traditions and myths (that may or may not be functional). Informal rules within small groups and even rules for behavior between strangers may operate with the same underlying causes, but the legitimacy and public nature of organizational rules make them potentially much stronger. Moreover, since many organizations are accountable to other organizations and to the public, decisions and actions may take on extra importance, as if one is playing for keeps.

The organization is indeed a complicated group of groups. Yet one can approach an initial understanding of organizations by studying the single group and the interpersonal communications, attitudes, and behaviors that occur in and among groups. In the next chapter we begin that task.

3

Interpersonal Communication

An ailment called "lack of communication" has taken
the place of original sin as an explanation of the
ills of the world, while "better communication" is
trotted out on every occasion as a universal panacea.
It is guaranteed to appear at least once, and usually
several times in any TV panel discussion. Usually it
is offered with the mock modest air of one who is
making a substantial contribution which is bound to
be well received, while the correct response is
solemn nods all around, strongly reminiscent of the
amens in church. Indeed, ritualization of the whole
sequence is far advanced. — Charlotte Kursh (1971)

When people are together, there is never an
absence of communication. Even being ignored
transmits meaning—more, in fact, than a
"Hello" which, being a common politeness, says
little about the speaker (cf. Geller et al.,
1974). This chapter is designed to describe
the communication process, including nonverbal
aspects of it. We shall be looking critically

at what is commonly assumed to be good and bad
communication and see whether those diagnoses
accurately reflect the experiences of the interacting parties. In the course of the discussion, you will observe the complexity of
the communication process and perhaps understand why research on its causes and effects
is yet relatively undeveloped.

VALUES AND COMMUNICATION

A quotation from an essay by Charlotte Kursh
was chosen to begin this chapter because it
illustrates a major problem in the study of
interpersonal communication—that is, a tendency by scholars, as well as the public, to
make value statements about communication that
have no empirical support. For example, as
Kursh argues, "lack of communication" is a
common diagnosis for unsatisfactory interpersonal interactions. If that does not seem to
fit the bill, then one might blame poor or bad
communication. School boards that cannot gain
support for sex education, or community
councils whose plans for water fluoridation are
denounced as an attempt to poison people, may
blame themselves for not communicating "effectively" or may derogate their opponents for
"clouding the issue" or "misleading the public." The opponents may object to the projects
on the grounds that officials did not accurately or honestly inform the public. Value statements such as these may have no basis in fact
and may distort the objective study of communication.

Such statements are, however, interesting behaviors in their own right. They are a form
of metacommunication, or communication about
communication. Looked at in this light, they
appear to be a code for a failure to achieve
desired and equitable outcomes. To say, "We
(You) did not communicate effectively," is to
say, "We (You) did not win the argument,"
"They refuse to budge on the issue," or "They

hate us." The metacommunicator, by placing blame on the communication process, may ignore the real, tougher source of difficulty—that is, a conflict of interest.

Meanwhile, the lamented communication process may actually be functioning rather well, considering everyone's different objectives. It may be, for example, that the appearance of not listening to the spokesman of another group satisfies one's need to appear loyal to one's own group (which may be more interested in group solidarity than in resolving conflict with the other group). It is important, then, to think critically about value-laden conclusions about interpersonal communication. This does not mean, however, that one should never express them. Sometimes, blaming some aspect of the communication process for interpersonal difficulties will effectively delay a standoff or an escalation of conflict. Moreover, a comment on the communication process is often well suited to an exchange of good intentions and regard for others even when its ostensible purpose seems only to be a delivery of factual information.

THE COMMUNICATION PROCESS

The requirement that speakers and listeners both know a language is just the first step in communication. For between speaker and listener occurs a complex process involving the speaker's inferences, perceptions, expectations, and intentions; the formulation of messages, and the messages themselves; and the understanding of messages as influenced by the listener's perceptions, inferences, expectations, and intentions. A simple exchange of information is affected by all of these and, in fact, becomes somewhat more than an information exchange.

Figure 3.1 (cf. Johnson, 1969) shows a diagram of a single question and answer. An office manager asks a truck loader at a company

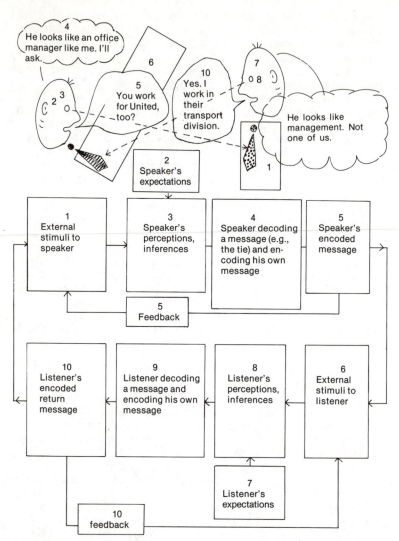

FIGURE 3.1 Diagram of a Simple Exchange of Information

party for employees and relatives, "You work for United, too?" The speaker is not simply asking about the other's employment, but is responding to particular assumptions created

by their presence in a common situation, is
trying to place the other in or out of his own
reference group, and perhaps is wondering if
their relationship might be encouraged. His
message is formulated or "encoded" in a way
calculated to get the information he wants
without offending the other or seeming to be
too egocentric (he does not ask, "Are you an
office manager like me?"). The listener, however, understands more than the words he hears;
he infers some labeling intent—perhaps because
he is uncomfortable in the setting (and in his
tie) and expects peculiar social games in a
company mixed-status gathering. He decodes the
message as including the additional question
of whether he is a white-collar type like the
questioner, and his response, "Yes, I work in
their transport division," is a defense
against publicly admitting to lower status as
well as an attempt to supply the requested
information. The office manager probably understands this quite well.

Thus, the communication process involves an
exchange of symbols according to a code that
both parties have learned, with variations due
to different interpretations of, or experience
with, the code and different attitudes, perceptions, and motives. Doubtless, both men
implicitly understand that the question is
loaded and the answer, vague. But in the social
environment in which their exchange takes
place, the code is an appropriate means for
exchanging information while maintaining face
for both parties and avoiding embarrassing
commitments.

INFORMATION EXCHANGE: FROM FACT TO FICTION

The study of the effects of language on human
behavior is called communication pragmatics.
Understanding these effects depends not simply
upon a grasp of interpersonal processes but
also on an examination of the nature of language itself.

Take a simple question asked by a new acquaintance: "What do you do?" You will probably answer with a description of your occupational status: "I drive a truck" or "I am a graduate student." You have learned that "do" in this context means "work"; the word "do" is a symbol that refers to a particular concept, or referent, "work." But in different contexts the same symbol has other referents. In the phrase, "What can I do for you," the reference is to helping someone, not to occupation. This difference between the symbol and its referent is important because the meaning of language depends upon learning the association of a symbol to various referents or other symbols (which have referents).

What is communicated are symbols, not referents (cf. Katz, 1947). This would not be much of a problem for interpersonal communication if referents were simply physical objects; one could avoid misunderstanding by pointing to them. But referents are also events, relationships and values, which cannot be pointed to. Speakers may use symbols differently than listeners, who may misunderstand what the speakers meant. For example, an employee describes a friend who never takes pencils from the office as "naïve." The listener, who thinks not taking pencils is simple honesty, believes the employee is referring to the social behavior of the friend. There is, then, the potential for conflict between the private meaning that a person wants to communicate and the meanings the person actually communicates. This is particularly true when people come from different groups or cultures. Shared meaning is much more likely when there are shared experiences and learning about referents and their symbols, so that language is used in the same way by speaker and listener.

An exchange of factual information, therefore, is both more and less than that. It is less because not facts (referents) but symbols are exchanged and in the process some facts are altered, left out, or drowned by "noise" (extraneous stimuli). It is more because it is not machines but humans who communicate, and they exchange self-presentations, attitudes, and values, as well as factual information, usually according to culturally acceptable norms.

Some observers of the communication process have suggested ways in which the exchange of information can be made clearer. Here are four pointers for the educated layman from popular books or texts on communication:

1. Do not assume that a word or phrase always has the same meaning (from Lee, 1970). American negotiators, after World War II, used "democracy" to mean voting for candidates and protection of minority opinion, whereas Russian negotiators used "democracy" to mean racial equality and Communist dominance. Naturally, the use of two kinds of democracies led to friction when specific policies regarding Eastern Europe were to be negotiated.

2. "Learn to distinguish between factual and inferential statements" (Tubbs and Moss, 1974, p. 130). Although a statement of fact can be made only after observation of some object or event, many people assume the factuality of their inferences. The problem is of particular concern in groups. When inferences are passed off as fact, the discussion tends to subordinate the search for objective information to a contest to show whose statements are most factual.

3. Avoid simplistic dichotomies and analogies (from Katz, 1947). The English language has many pairs of opposites: black and white, success and failure, honest and dishonest. People use one of these when the truth is somewhere in between (e.g., sometimes honest, sometimes dishonest). Dichotomization affects not just information, which is likely to be oversimplified or misleading, but also attitudes and actions. According to Katz, American dichotomous views of German guilt after World War II (i.e., all Germans as bad; all Allies as good) initially led to a dichotomous view of

punishment (all Germans punished; all Allies rewarded). American troops were forbidden to speak with any Germans, which was relatively severe punishment for German children, mild punishment for Nazi leaders.

4. Set clear objectives for the goals of communication. This piece of advice is exemplified by the following (Anderson, 1971, p. 111): "The discussion process functions at its best [when] . . . the purpose [is] . . . *exactly defined* and *accepted*."

A major problem in exchanging information in groups and organizations, where motives, goals, and values can vary enormously, is that people may not agree on the purpose of communication. Some participants may view the exchange not to solve a problem or share information, but as a chance for people to convince others about an issue or to exert power (in fact, these are likely to be motives, more or less, in any communication situation). Thus, in addition to the apparent reasons for the communication exchange, there may be hidden agendas (goals of interaction that are not expressed openly).

Hidden agendas often lead people to misunderstand the motives behind their words. One way to deal with this is for participants to agree upon the objectives of the discussion. For example, they may agree to set aside discussions of long-term group goals in order to exchange information about a particular issue. This technique is designed to avoid drifts to irrelevant topics and force attention onto important issues, even when potentially full of conflict.

THE REWARDS OF POOR COMMUNICATION

In spite of all earnest advice to the contrary, people, including the communication experts themselves, continue to communicate "poorly"—to confuse symbol and referent or uncertain and certain referents, to use dichotomies and unclear analogies, to fail to

formulate objectives. In the most serious of
conferences, as well as in chance and brief
encounters, we see unclear, imprecise communication, fuzziness, double talk, lying, and
misuse of words. It can be argued, however,
that such behavior is neither good nor bad, but
well serves the motives of people to present
themselves favorably, maintain their relationships, behave in socially appropriate ways,
maintain or increase their power, maintain
self consistency, avoid or carry out commitments, and feel free and flexible in social
interaction.

Consider, for example, the executive's assistant who is instructed to make sure that
office employees take just a ten-minute coffee
break in the morning. The message he sends
looks like this: "Please remember to limit your
coffee breaks." Now certainly the message seems
imprecise; the word "limit" is used as if it
had a single meaning, but it does not, and so it
violates the first item of advice listed above.
The boss in likely to perceive the message as
bad communication. Nevertheless, if we consider the interpersonal situation, there is
good reason for the message; it may have been
chosen for its very imprecision. The assistant,
caught between a need to satisfy the boss and
the motive to be liked by those he or she
supervises, encodes a message that complies
with the boss's demand, yet avoids confrontation and the explicit use of power.

Unclear communication is sometimes called
"double talk." Double talk is a message that
is presented as if it had one meaning, but
it actually has more. It is a message that is
so ambiguous that the listener can read into
it almost anything. The Central Intelligence
Agency, according to Victor Marchetti and
John Marks (1975) has used double talk in order
to cover up behavior that is unacceptable
(except to the initiate). Thus, the word
"disinformation" is used, not "lying"; and
"assistance" is given to various groups, not
gifts of military equipment.

Double talk qualifies as bad communication,
but its vagueness is precisely what makes it
valuable, at least to speakers of it or their
organizations. Without a simple, clear referent, their forecasts will always be right,
their intentions honorable, and their actions,
desirable. For example, a CIA head who asks a
group of officials for permission to "disin-
form" the public of another country is committed to no particular prediction or act.

The use of jargon creates uncertainty in
one's audience at the same time that it leaves
the impression that a group knows how to
handle severe problems. Marchetti and Marks
(p. 310) quote a statement by columnist Stewart
Alsop explaining why the Kennedy administration
approved the disastrous Bay of Pigs invasion of
Cuba: "The answer lies somewhere in the mys-
tique of the secret-service professional *vis-a-
vis* the amateur. Somehow in such a confrontation, the amateur tends to put a childish
faith in the confident assertions of the professional."

Double talk, then, can be a powerful form of
communication in spite of its lack of meaning-
fulness. The CIA, of course, is not the only
organization that uses double talk effectively.
The military use of "pacification," the union
use of "job actions," the Nixon White House use
of "not operational," and, of course, my own
"we" instead of "I"—all are double talk.

Failing to cummunicate clearly may be psychologically protective. Take, for example, a
college-educated supervisor who, in upgrading
his department, insists upon systematic record
keeping, but is blocked by a foreign-born warehouse distributor whose lack of English has
caused him for years to keep records in his
head. The foreman accuses the distributor of
stubbornness; the distributor accuses the foreman of elitism. The foreman does not know
that the other man can't read English, but the
distributor, of course, does not want to admit
that he cannot keep written records. Their
problem seems one of unclear communication, for

their inferences about each other are inaccurate and they are not telling each other how the situation really affects them. But actually there is communication going on in this exchange, and exposing the facts will not alter the problem, which, in this case, is a real conflict between one person's interests and the other's resources. The supervisor cannot improve his department without written records, and the illiterate distributor cannot keep them. The function of vague communication in this case is to postpone the real problem but also to protect a relationship from dissolution. With a delay, other experiences might lead the men to respect each other and to resolve their differences happily.

Unclear communication also has the function of serving dominance and control motives. It is valuable to the party with less power, for it enables one to benefit from manipulation of information. Thus, one can avoid punishment by giving vague explanations for mistakes and can use the white lie to avoid offending or to flatter the more powerful. Distortion of information is not in keeping with the aim of being truthful, but it may actually reduce some negative effects of power inequalities.

Those who have high power also use distortion. Their purpose is to maintain or increase their control and influence. From the powerful, the effect of information distortion is likely to be strong indeed. This is because power is dependent upon the control of resources, one of the most important of which is information. The powerful have at hand relatively more information they can choose to distribute, withhold, or distort. Moreover, in doing so they can give the impression of having more power (including information) than is actually the case.

It has been said that power in groups and organizations accrues to those parties who can best control the distribution of information, because information controls uncertainty (Crozier, 1964; Thompson, 1967). Power via

uncertainty control in a state university was
studied intensively by Gerald Salancik and
Jeffrey Pfeffer (1974). State universities are
at the mercy of outsiders for their funds, and
the source of funding is probably the major
source of uncertainty. One may hypothesize that
units which contribute to reducing the uncer-
tainties of funding by attracting federal contracts and grants gain the most power and command the most favorable internal fund allocations. Salancik and Pfeffer discovered this to
be the case, in spite of the fact that chair-
persons and deans did not want it to be so.

Another benefit of poor communication can be
improving persuasiveness. For example, since
budget decisions are based not so much on the
criterion of meeting organizational goals but
rather on who deserves benefits (Wildavsky,
1961), departments are usually careful to communicate what they think they deserve to administrators when they present their case. The
Salancik and Pfeffer study indirectly supports
this hypothesis; subunit heads who were asked
to rank their preferred bases for budget allocations showed a definite bias toward criteria
that would favor their own department. Indeed,
those who participate in budget allocation decisions are undoubtedly often faced with arguments from powerful units that they deserve
greater funding to maintain their success,
while less powerful units argue that they deserve funding support to become more successful.

The military is an organization where one
can observe poor communication that, in fact,
is much more persuasive than would be clear,
truthful communication. One can see this oc-
curring in recruitment of troops as well as in
presentations to Congress when budget allocations are made: "Senator Stuart Symington has
pointed out that scare stories about Soviet
military strength appear at congressional
budget time in springtime Washington as regularly as the cherry blossoms" (Marchetti and
Marks, 1975, p. 296). Congressmen may know that

the military overestimates its needs, but they cannot vote (publicly) against "maximizing strength" or reducing "enemy threat."

Politicians are another group famous for persuasive but unclear communication. Consider a Congressman's use of "hard-working Americans" in a speech. The politician may use a false comparison which implies that other nationalities are lazy, yet also demonstrate his loyalty. He certainly has a better chance of being elected than if he shades his description: "Americans are sometimes hard working." (In fact, his use of exaggeration is not really false, for just about everyone understands what he intends: "We Americans are good fellows." An unspoken code makes the assertion politically true, if not literally so.)

Studies of conflict show that groups are sometimes more effective in moving toward agreement when they do not communicate clearly. Groups with unequal power structures are especially likely to reduce the cooperative exchange of information (Okun and DiVesta, 1975), but it is to their advantage to distort or withhold information. Given real conflicts of interest and differences in attitudes, values, and motivation, it is unlikely that one can legislate, by communicating, a common ground. The participants usually must compromise on some ill-defined objective (possibly avoiding the real issue) and then go on bargaining, complete with hidden agendas and "consensus by misunderstanding" (Kursh, 1971).

COMMUNICATION IN THE SERVICE OF INTERPERSONAL CONCERNS

It should be apparent by now that interpersonal communication, even when there is specific information to be exchanged, will be affected by psychological motives and goals. Social psychological researchers have neglected the causes and correlates of communication in favor of examining the effects of communication.

The limited amount of research on how communication varies means that one must speculate, considering what is already known about interpersonal processes. Here, I assume that people have different reasons for communicating and that the way they communicate is affected by their interpretations of the responses they expect to receive.

ASSESSING OTHERS

One reason to communicate is to find out where one stands. The studies reviewed in Chapter 2, showing that people have a need, particularly when uncertain, to evaluate their opinions, plans, or characteristics, suggest that messages will sometimes be used not to communicate information but instead to provoke a reaction. Included among these types of communication are boasting and showing off (meant to provoke reassuring admiration), floating of ideas (meant to elicit information regarding their acceptability), and staring (meant to induce another to make the first move).

Individuals and groups sometimes make seemingly accidental statements in order to assess how others feel about them or their ideas. A governmental agency may leak some information about a proposed policy in order to assess how favorable the public response will be; the policy can be abandoned if the response is unfavorable. In personal encounters, one can arrange for messages to be overheard or passed through a third party. A person can discover what others think, also, by speaking just to see how much attention the speaker received, by flattering or insulting another to see if the evaluation is reciprocated ("fishing"), or by "throwing out ideas" in order to observe reactions to the speaker, not the ideas. All of these communication strategies for assessing others' reactions are especially likely to be employed when people do not know each other well; men and women who often lead small groups come to expect a great deal of it during

initial encounters among people and first
meetings of groups

PERSUASION

The purpose of much communication is to influence or change others, and many studies have
examined the effectiveness of different kinds
of communication. Few researchers have studied
which communication strategies are used in
different influence situations. We do know,
however, that influence attempts are affected
by the speaker's need to avoid offending the
audience, which might derogate the speaker, and
to minimize reactance (an audience's attempt
to freely choose opinions). Also, a speaker
needs to avoid using up power in the influence
attempt. A delicate balance must be maintained
between using enough persuasive force to produce change but not so much that the influence
attempt backfires.

There are several studies of persuasive communication that show how people try to maintain
this balance. Manis, Cornell, and Moore (1974)
asked subjects to pass on information to an
audience and found that they biased their messages in a manner that would be acceptable to
the audience. Hazen and Kiesler (1975) showed
that speakers in planning a persuasive message
were more likely to avoid stating conclusions
or asking for specific action, the greater the
gap between the audience's initial attitude and
the position advocated by the speaker.

Abraham Tesser, Sidney Rosen, and others
have performed a series of experiments showing
that communicators are reluctant to communicate
bad news: This they called the "MUM effect"
(Rosen and Tesser, 1970; Tesser, Rosen, and
Conlee, 1972).

Johnson, Conlee, and Tesser (1974) recently reported a study that concerned the
communication of news to a student that she
would have to participate in a study using
severe shock. The higher the subject's

self-reported fear of a negative evaluation
from the student, the more likely the subject
was to withhold the bad news. Studies suggest
that communicators consider the possibility of
rejection when encoding messages and distort
messages so as to please recipients. In addition, messages are more likely to be distorted
when communicator and audience are dissimilar—
in attitude, power, or experience.

Distorting a message so that it pleases an
audience or making it seem less controversial
may, of course, have the effect of producing
no change in the audience at all, because the
audience is not aware of a need for change.
Whether this is a bad or good state of affairs
depends upon whether change is really desired
(perhaps, as in politics, it is simply exposure
that the speaker wants) and, if desired,
whether it would benefit both or just one of
the parties.

Irving Janis, Howard Levanthal, and other
researchers have shown that maladaptive responses to stressful medical procedures, such
as operations, can be reduced by providing
accurate information and specific instructions
(e.g., Janis, 1958; Johnson and Levanthal, 1974;
Vernon and Bigelow, 1974). In this case, unclear messages make the audience more anxious.
In contrast, the politician who makes clear
a stand regardless of the audience's initial
attitudes is taking a risk.

One difference between situations in which
clear communications have positive or negative
effects lies in the perceived intent of the
communicator. When an audience perceives that
the message is meant to benefit them and is sincere, a clear, direct approach is effective.
Even direct threats may be useful if the intent seems benevolent. Mogy and Pruitt (1974),
for example, showed that when a threatener's
costs were perceived to be high ("This will
hurt me more than you"), the credibility of a
threat was high, and so was compliance. Whether
communicators regularly encode messages with
these considerations in mind is not now known.

We do know that, whatever their strategy, communicators do consider the audience reaction.

Communicators think of their own costs, too. They avoid wasting time on people already committed to a position and they focus their communications on those who are perceived to be malleable, such as people who have already shown outward compliance (Sampson and Brandon, 1964). This tactic has the advantage of saving power (since unsuccessful influence attempts reduce one's credibility) and giving the appearance of discretion.

POWER

Communication is used to gain and maintain power. We have already seen how language (e.g., double talk) is used to serve dominance objectives, whether they be driven by a need for power as an end in itself or by an interest in solving important problems or in helping a group. It has been noted, too, that communicators take into account their audience's position and that they are more likely to distort information when their audience is dissimilar. This suggests that dissimilarities of power alter communication.

People with high power are potentially able to be either more exploitive or more trusting than others; they have more freedom to communicate because they are relatively secure. The conditions under which they take the more or less benevolent course is unknown.

Dutch psychologist Mark Mulder (1960) claims that the exercise of power per se can be so reinforcing that communications from the powerful are likely to become insensitive to the needs of others. Edwin Hollander (1958) proposes that the powerful, in gaining leadership by carefully conforming to the wishes of a group, build up "idiosyncrasy credit," which allows them to violate social niceties more than others do. On the other hand, Solomon (1960) found that in a game situation higher power persons engaged in more "trusting" (coop-

erative) behavior. At this point, all we can
state is that the powerful use a wider range of
communication than the less powerful—they are
more free to be benevolent or distrustful.

More research is available on communication
to the powerful. Several studies have shown
that both low power and high power people communicate more often to those with high power
(e.g., Hurwitz, Zander, and Hymovitch, 1968;
Kelley, 1951). People with low power approach
those with higher power with deference and
flattery. Zander, Cohen and Stotland (1957),
in a study of relations among psychiatrists,
psychologists, and social workers, showed
that the latter groups, who felt less powerful,
sought out contacts with the more powerful
(psychiatrists), sought advice from them, and
praised them, whereas the reverse was less
frequent.

It was suggested earlier that those with low
power may distort information in order to
protect themselves (a tactic commonly observed
in formal organizations, where higher officials
are kept unaware of problems at lower levels).
Perhaps people praise and listen to the powerful to protect themselves. The studies that
have been performed seem to indicate that
the less powerful communicate in ways that will
induce the more powerful to use their power
benevolently. We know little, however, about
how or when they communicate to change the
power relationship itself.

Little of the research on communication
focuses upon the communication between the very
powerful and the relatively powerless (e.g.,
General Motors vs. the individual owner of a
Chevrolet), particularly when they are in conflict. Most conflict models assume that each
party has something to bargain with. Only a
few have asked how the less powerful "fight
City Hall" or use communication for revolutionary aims. One of these few is John Bowers
(1974), who has constructed a model of influence strategies between large institutions and
their individual clients. His is a social

Bowers' model emphasizes the costs of gaining power and maintaining it. Institutions, he proposes, employ their least costly response, usually avoidance, to complaints (petitions) from their powerless clients. Institutions relinquish power (e.g., make restitution for damage, flexibly define rules, let clients determine policy) only when the client can make the preferred institutional response too costly.

Illustrative is an exchange Bowers observed between a passenger about to board an airline—although he had not gotten his ticket properly processed—and a stewardess who insisted he return to the gate. The passenger petitioned for his seat anyway since the crowds made it likely he would lose his place if he went back to the terminal. The stewardess inspected the ticket again and told the passenger he had to return (avoidance being her least costly response). The man persisted; he demanded that his ticket be honored. Her response was the next least costly. She insisted ("procedural counterpersuasion") he must return since she had no power to permit boarding (the common separation of policy making and policy implementation makes this a workable response in many institutions). But the man stayed, raising his voice in objection ("nonviolent resistance"), and there arose a publicly tense situation. Finally, the stewardess called her supervisor, and within minutes an official arrived to seat the passenger ("adjustment"). In this situation, then, the institution gave in to the client only when avoidance and persuasion were made too costly. A simplified matrix, showing each party's various alternatives ordered by increasing cost, is depicted in Figure 3.2.

In Bowers' view the powerless increase their power by making the malevolent actions by the powerful too costly and thereby reducing the alternatives. More research will be needed to find whether this process holds for political changes of power as well as for other power

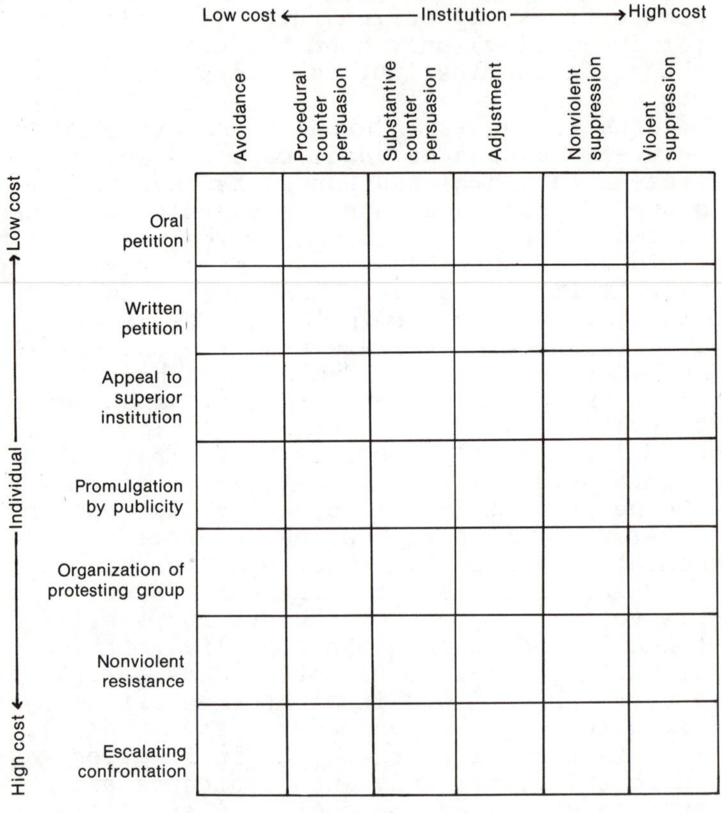

Note: Adapted from Bowers, 1974

FIGURE 3.2 Matrix Describing Alternative Transactions between a Disgruntled Individual and an Institution to which He Complains

alternatives in private institutions. To speculate on one implication of Bowers' model, if

an institution makes limited adjustments, a revolutionary change in power is unlikely. At this point, the individual (or group) will be motivated to maintain the gains already won and avoid more costly confrontations.

SELF (AND OTHER) PRESENTATION

People communicate to be liked and respected. The ability to artfully present oneself without appearing to be self-aggrandizing, and to act as if convinced that one is behaving commendably helps satisfy these motives. How people manage this in so many different situations has been of interest to a number of researchers. The person who stimulated much of this research is Erving Goffman, the sociologist, whose books include *The Presentation of Self in Everyday Life* (1959), *Stigma* (1963), and *Behavior in Public Places* (1966). Goffman (1959) argues that much of our everyday communication is analogous to a theatrical production. As actors, our appropriate roles are communicated as well as our public opinions and personalities. To Goffman, the object of a performance is partly to sustain a particular definition of the situation. In the eyes of others, an actor's performance represents his or her claim as to what reality is. By enacting an appropriate script, the actor can be viewed favorably, gain influence, save face, and ensure comfortable interaction. Acting in a role does not imply the person is not a unique individual, rather conformity to a role may actually protect a person's privacy and freedom to be different. If the person can choose a role, so much the better, for the role may be nicely fitted to his or her own particular situation and interests.

Goffman's approach has greatly influenced current research on self-presentation. The effects on self-presentation of the "stage" (situation), the "plot" (definition of situation by players or audience), and the "role" (social role) are being studied.

The work of E. E. Jones and his colleagues (e.g., Jones, 1964) on ingratiation tactics is interesting. Suppose we assume a motive to present the self favorably on a certain occasion, such as an interview between a young man, a private, and his captain. Jones formulates several possible ingratiation tactics that either might employ: flattery, agreement with the other, getting the other to talk about himself, doing him a favor, or showing off one's own best qualities. But the difference in the two roles will partially determine whether these ingratiating techniques are useful, ineffective or even backfire. The more powerful captain, for example, will seem weak if he agrees too much with the private. But the private has to be careful too, for the more he agrees, the more he seems to be agreeing simply because he is the more dependent (Jones and Wortman, 1973). Each person's role has associated with it a script appropriate to the situation—a particular style of self-presentation that goes with the role—and he cannot deviate too much in presenting himself.

In experimentally examining self-presentation tactics, researchers have asked subjects to try to make a good impression on another person; other subjects have been asked to present themselves accurately. The studies indicate that people trying to look good describe themselves favorably, exaggerate their strengths (Gergen, 1965), and try to match the self-presentation style of the other—boast if he boasts, reveal secrets if he does (Gergen and Wishnor, 1965; Schneider and Eustis, 1972). Also, those who are instructed to ingratiate themselves are nonverbally more positive (they smile and nod their heads up and down) and talk more (Rosenfeld, 1966).

But roles alter tactics. For example, upperclassmen in a Naval ROTC program, when ingratiating themselves, only agreed with lower status freshmen about issues unrelated to school or the Navy, presumably so their superior expertise would remain unquestioned. In contrast, the freshmen agreed with the upperclassmen on academic and naval subjects, but not on miscellaneous topics (Jones, Gergen, and Jones, 1963).

These studies may be criticized on the grounds that instructing subjects to ingratiate themselves revealed strategies that people do not ordinarily employ. But in a number of other studies, there were no instructions to ingratiate; the situation has been manipulated so that subjects had something to gain if they made themselves attractive. Many of these studies have demonstrated not only that people do use ingratiation tactics appropriate to their role but that they are sensitive to whether others play their role (e.g., Jones, et al., 1965).

There are some who say that the self-presentation behaviors common in today's society are antithetical to the development of intimacy and trust among individuals. In his popular book, *The Transparent Self* (1964), Sidney Jourard asserted that ingratiation tactics, rigid conformity to politeness norms, and safe, superficial relations are too common, especially among men, at the cost of mental health and the establishment of close relationships. Studies of self-disclosure and openness show that, while people who are already intimate are relatively open with each other, acquaintances avoid personal disclosure unless they are isolated (Altman and Haythorn, 1965; Taylor, Wheeler, and Altman, 1973). There is some evidence that people dislike intimate self-disclosure in others (Kaplan et al., 1974); and, in a developing relationship, disclose themselves only gradually (Altman and Taylor, 1973).

Why are people apparently so cautious about disclosing themselves? You may think of many reasons: to avoid embarrassment or to avoid seeming to be ignorant; to remain independent; to maintain an impression of being normal. To disclose anger is to risk needless anger in return; to disclose fright is to risk the appearance of weakness; to disclose love is to risk being considered a pushover. In short, self-disclosure of one's "true" self will be avoided unless the risks of doing so are low or trust is already established. In any case it will be approached slowly.

There is also an unwillingness of people to jeopardize existing relationships by being very revealing. Often, the more intimacy they desire, the more afraid of being open they become. Openness should not be encouraged unthinkingly, however. For example, people do not like to hear bad things about themselves, no matter how honestly spoken. The closeness that results from sharing positive feelings is matched by estrangement when negative feelings are aired openly.

One should consider the effect of the immediate situation, too. Most people learn early when to be open and when to be circumspect. Children are reminded to be on their best behavior when guests arrive; parents become anxious when their children act out their feelings in public. Children learn that in some situations it is appropriate to tell white lies, to pretend affection, and to hide displeasure.

In most situations there exist norms, or shared expectations, about the degree of disclosure that is appropriate. Zick Rubin's (1975) study in an airport lounge is illustrative. College students approached people waiting at the airport and asked them to participate in a class project on handwriting analysis. The students showed the subjects a sample of handwriting, either copying it from a card or writing it spontaneously. The message varied from being low in openness (e.g., "Right now I'm collecting handwriting samples") to medium openness (e.g., "I've made several good friends, but I still feel lonely a lot of the time") to high openness (e.g., "I think that I'm pretty well adjusted, but I occasionally have some questions about my sexual adequacy"). Rubin found that the degree to which subjects reciprocated any disclosure in their own handwriting sample was a function of how much the students had revealed. When the students had copied the message, the subjects reciprocated with more disclosure the more the student had disclosed. In contrast, when the students spontaneously wrote a highly revealing message, subjects did not reciprocate. This resulted because the students' intimate revelations, when they were spontaneous and not a regular part of the class project, were simply inappropriate.

In situations when disclosure is appropriate to one's role, openness is of benefit. Thus, in therapy, openness is to the advantage of the client (assuming the therapist is competent). The confidentiality of the relationship lowers the risks of abandoning one's usual roles (wife, husband, employee, boss). Carl Rogers' (1967) advocation of openness makes sense in this setting, but imagine the concern of a client's family, friends, and co-workers if the client exerted the same degree of disclosure (which probably includes revealing negative feelings and disloyalties) in daily life.

TEAMWORK

Communication with, in, and among groups requires, on occasion, that the group act as a team in presenting itself to others—there is an audience to consider (and this goes, too, for coalitions, committees, or other subgroups within the group). To protect the team against ideological attack or embarrassment and to ensure that united action is possible, teamwork in self-presentation is required. The team must appear to be in agreement, and not just publicly, for a united stand will be more believable if it appears that group members arrived at their opinions independently. Teamwork requires cooperation, and so the team members communicate to learn what the public line is to be, consult one another secretly

about the position they will take publicly,
wait for the official word before taking a
stand, and restrict intra-team disagreements
until out of public view (Becker, 1963). Communication in groups then, is affected by the
requirements of the group's presentation to
outsiders.

The decision making process also affects
group communication. Teamwork is required to
make group decisions, whether the decision is
how to solve a problem, where to go for dinner,
whose house to meet at, what the agenda for
discussion should be, or what to do about
Sally, who always arrives late for the party.
Because the individual concerns of members
must be considered, group decision making involves seeking and listening to information,
opinions, and feelings; expressing the same;
and agreeing on some decision rule, such as
unanimous voting for arriving at a verdict or
a consensus.

Leaving the question of decision rules,
which obviously require teamwork, for later
(see Chapter 9), consider the teamwork involved in discussion prior to a decision.
Members must coordinate their efforts (so
that, for example, all do not speak at once),
should consider as much relevant information as
possible, should take into account emotional
issues, and should behave in accordance with
social norms. Naturally, two or more of these
considerations may conflict. For example, even
when all have an equal amount of information
and, presumably, the same right to express an
opinion (e.g., in juries), the norm that high
status persons are accorded more deference
dictates that some members speak more often
than others.

Cultural and group norms develop to organize
the discussion process, and this imposition
of structure influences group communication.
For example, the group leader (e.g., the chairperson) is expected to guide the group and,
as we have mentioned earlier, also has more
power to control discussions.

Groups are marked by leaders' talking more
(e.g., Simon, 1967), regulating more (e.g.,
Strodtbeck, James, and Hawkins, 1957), asking
more questions, giving more orientation, and
providing more negative reactions to deviant
opinions (e.g., Strodtbeck and Mann, 1956).
Other frequent speakers in the group seem to
be those who have a task or work role in the
group rather than a socio-emotional role—a
distinction suggested by Bales (1970). In say,
a twelve-person jury, we might find a central
work group containing five to seven high
participators who conduct most of the work of
the jury (e.g., convincing the minority to
change).

Who else in the group turns out to be a high
participator? The group's opinion of the individual and the nature of the decision to be
made are apparently as important as individual
tendencies to dominate, seek information, or
affiliate. People who are consistently rein-
forced by others (via head nodding, for example) will become high participators, and
people who appear to be withdrawn or silent
types will become talkative if others reward
their talking or give them more opportunity
(e.g., by leaving the room) to assert themselves (Mulder, 1974). Speakers are also those
who feel they need information, and information
has a high value for uncertain individuals for
whom the decision is important (Lanzetta,
1967; Lanzetta and Driscoll, 1968; Crawford,
1974).

It is ironic that those in a group who actually have the least amount of information,
i.e., those with low power, are least likely to
seek it. This phenomenon is explained by their
lack of knowledge about the existence or source
of information and their lesser involvement in
power struggles and group decisions. The least
powerful are more concerned with the drama of
decision making and with the impact of decisions.
It has been suggested that the limited degree
to which people rebel might be explained in
part by this spectator-like orientation to the

decision making process (Edelman, 1964). On
the other hand, the tendency for those in
power to seek information leaves them open to
be influenced by that information. Control goes
two ways if those with less power insist on
being heard.

COMMUNICATION AS CAUSE AND EFFECT

One of the difficulties of studying interpersonal communication is that each message
is both a response to messages and a cause of
new messages. As each person speaks up, others
talk back, new people participate, and the
social situation changes. In a classic study,
Jacobs and Campbell (1961) gradually replaced
members of a group with new members. The researchers found that new members' judgments regarding the movement of an "autokinetic" light
were influenced by a group norm, but also that
the relatively fresh judgments of the new members influenced the group. Although on each
trial judgments of the light were relatively
uniform, by the time the original group had
been completely replaced, the original group
norm had completely disappeared. What happened
was a circular process whereby new members
were both influenced by communications from
old members and affected old members.

The transactionalists (who mainly rely upon
observation and description of the communication process rather than on experimental techniques) believe that to study the effect of
isolated communication variables precludes our
understanding of the process as a whole. Examine, for instance, the diagram in Figure 3.3,
which describes the transactional view of one
interaction from the perspective of each
participant. The man and woman are assumed to
be communicating with each other, not at each
other, and each person's overt message, covert
perceptions, and perception of the perceptions
of the other are assumed to be part of the communication process. This view is far different

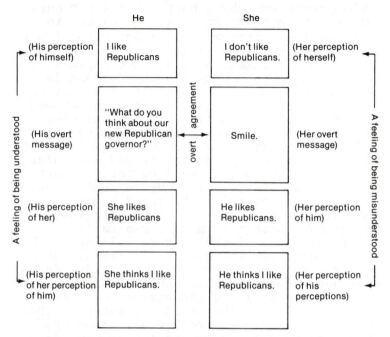

FIGURE 3.3 Feelings and Perceptions in a Single Trans-
action

from the traditional sender/receiver conception
of communication and is much more difficult
(though not impossible) to examine experimentally. It is only recently that social
psychologists and communication researchers
have experimentally tested a few hypotheses
derived from transactional ideas. We must for
the present consider the transactional approach
to communication as an heuristic device, not a
testable theory.

THE SELF-FULFILLING PROPHECY

Transactionalists have embraced the self-
fulfilling prophecy hypothesis, first proposed
by sociologist Robert Merton (1948, 1957). The
self-fulfilling prophecy, as you may know, is

a phenomenon whereby expectations about oneself or another person cause one to act in
a manner that confirms the expectation. A person who expects to be liked acts in a friendly
manner and is liked; a person who expects to
be hated acts in a defensive manner and is
hated. One person can also fulfill his prophecy
(expectation) for another. A boss who expects
a lazy subordinate will oversupervise him,
which will have the effect of reducing the subordinate's initiative. A boss who expects initiative will be looking for it and rewarding
it, causing the subordinate to feel and act as
if he has initiative. The boss's communication,
then, has the circular effect of causing the
subordinate to affirm the boss's original expectation, whether or not it was false.

Most evidence of the self-fulfilling prophecy
is indirect. Robert Rosenthal's (1971) work in
classrooms is best known. In one study (Rosenthal and Jacobson, 1968), the researchers
selected a school and administered IQ tests to
all the children. They told the teachers that
the tests measured "intellectual blooming."
They also randomly selected twenty percent of
the children and told the teachers that these
children had scored particularly well on the
test and could be expected to make remarkable
progress during the school year. Eight months
later, this group of children, who had been no
different from the others except in the eyes of
the teachers, showed a higher average gain than
their classmates.

The recent development of techniques to
measure nonverbal communication by Albert
Mehrabian (1968), Howard Rosenfeld (1967), and
Robert Kleck (1968), among others, has made
possible the unobtrusive identification of
communication behaviors that transmit expectations to others. A two-part study by Carl Word,
Mark Zanna, and Joel Cooper (1974) provides
direct evidence for the self-fulfilling
prophecy. Two experiments were performed in
the context of a job interview. In the first,
naïve, white undergraduates interviewed black

and white confederates who posed as job applicants. Although the black applicants behaved
in the same manner as white applicants, they
received shorter, more halting interviews and
less "immediacy," a word that means closeness
(such as close physical distance, leaning
toward another, and eye contact).

In the second experiment, Word, Zanna, and
Cooper demonstrated that communicated expectations are both understood and reciprocated.
Naíve, white applicants were interviewed by
white interviewers, confederates who had been
trained to approximate the kinds of behavior
received by black and white applicants in the
first experiment. The results indicated that
subjects treated like the black applicants
in the first experiment performed less ade-
equately and were more nervous in the
interview situation than subjects treated like
the whites. The subjects treated like blacks
also reciprocated by moving farther away from
the interviewer and rating him as less adequate
and friendly. This pair of experiments supports
the transactional view of communication circu-
larity. The results also have obvious implications for such social problems as minority un-
employment and school failures.

SPIRALS

Escalation and de-escalation of attitudes
occur during communication as well as fulfillment of expectations. Take, for example, the
following interaction between a man and a
woman which spirals the relationship to a
greater degree of intimacy:

He: "You look nice today."

She: "You look well, too. I like your shirt."

He: "Maybe we could have dinner together
      sometime."

She: "I'd love that."

He: "Want to go tonight?"

She: "Sure, that would be just great. I haven't been going out much lately."

He: "Well, then, why don't we go someplace special? I've been lonely, too, so we deserve it."

What has happened during this conversation is that the man's feelings have been intensified by the woman's reactions, and hers, by his reactions. As a result, the relationship has become more intimate.

Communication spirals also expand disagreements into full-fledged argument:

He: "Would you mind wearing a dress?"

She: "You don't like my slacks?"

He: "I didn't say that. I said you should wear a dress."

She: "Don't tell me what to wear."

Communication spirals occur because our behavior may be rewarding or punishing. Reward intensifies good feelings; punishment, bad feelings. Reward encourages affection and confidence; punishment encourages avoidance, hostility, anger, and retaliation.

The people in communication spirals are (usually) unaware of the spiraling effects of their own behavior. They are each focused upon the other's behavior and feel their own to be an appropriate response rather than a cause.

Researchers interested in attribution theory, such as Michael Storms, 1973; E. E. Jones and Richard Nisbett (e.g., Storms, 1973; Jones and Nisbett, 1972) argue that each person has a unique visual orientation toward others (people cannot observe themselves communicating). As a result, responsibility for events appears to fall on the other person. Storms (1973) has provided strong evidence that one can alter attributions of causality by changing visual orientation through use of videotape. Subjects who had conversed with a new acquaintance were later shown a videotape of either themselves or the other person in that discussion. Those who saw themselves attributed more causality for their own behavior to themselves than did those who saw the other person.

Katz (1947, p. 20) has illustrated the effect of different orientations in one business setting, especially as they are magnified by the different experiences of each party:

> Granted that industrial disputes have as their bedrock real and immediate differences in economic interest, it is still true that these differences are augmented by the inability of each party to under·· stand the opposing point of view. The employer, owner, or superintendent, through his executive function of making daily decisions and issuing orders and instructions, acquires a psychology of management. He can understand, though he may dislike, a union demand for more wages. But when the union requests, or even suggests, changes in the conditions of work or changes in personnel policy, he grows emotional and objects to being told by subordinates and outsiders how to run his own plant. For their part, the workers have little understanding of the competitive position of the employer. Since the employer enjoys a new way of life luxurious in comparison with their own, they find his plea of inability to pay a higher wage laughable.

Transactionalists such as Benjamin Whorf (1956) and Paul Watzlawick, Janet Beavin, and Don Jackson (1967) have described communication spirals in a different way with, nevertheless, the same general conclusion. They propose that participants in an interaction always perceive what is called "punctuation" in the sequence of events. Punctuation organizes events into a pattern of cause and effect, or start and finish. Accordingly, disagreement about how to

punctuate the sequence of events is at the
root of countless relationship struggles. The
marital problem described by Watzlawick,
Beavin, and Jackson (p. 56) is a good illustration:

> Suppose a couple have a marital problem to which he
> contributes passive withdrawal while her 50 per cent
> is nagging criticism. In explaining their frustra-
> tions, the husband will state that withdrawal is his
> only *defense against* her nagging, while she will
> label this explanation a gross and willful distortion
> of what "really" happens in their marriage; namely,
> that she is critical of him *because of* his passivity.
> . . . their fights consist of a monotonous exchange
> of the messages "I withdraw because you nag" and "I
> nag because you withdraw."

Disagreement about punctuation is what the
attribution theorists would predict for nearly
any communication between two people, since
each actor would explain behavior in different
ways. Naturally, the disagreement on punctuation could have either deleterious or beneficial effects on the relationship. If the
behavior of each is punishing, the relationship
spirals to a less friendly level; if the behavior of each is rewarding, the relationship
spirals to a more friendly level.

Conflict between two people is clearly exacerbated by differences in punctuation, and
it is obvious that conflict between two groups
or two nations spirals in analogous fashion.
Take, for example, Joad's (1939, p. 69) description of an arms race:

> [Nations regard the armaments of other nations as a
> menace to peace, and are] accordingly stimulated to
> increase their armaments to overtop the armaments by
> which they conceive themselves to be threatened. . . .
> These increased arms being in their turn regarded as
> a menace by nation A whose allegedly defensive arma-
> ments have provoked them, are used by nation A as a
> pretext for accumulating yet greater armaments where-
> with to defend itself against the menace. Yet these
> greater armaments are in turn interpreted by

neighboring nations as constituting a menace to themselves and so on.

Where does the spiral stop? All spirals, even
positive ones, have limits. Wilmot (1975, pp.
127-128) provides the following example. An individual with a high self-concept promotes
positive response from others, which in turn
enhances his self-concept. "But if the self-
concept continues to be encouraged, he will
eventually reach the stage at which he considers himself superior to others. At that
point, negative responses from others will go
to work on him to lower his self-concept."
In like manner, a poor relationship must stop
spiraling, or else each person thinks so little
of the other that the relationship is dis-
solved.

Most relationships that are maintained fluc-
tuate between progressive and regressive
spirals. They have ups and downs. Consequently,
individuals in relationships are forever feeling worse and worse, then feeling better and
better, and so on. As time goes on, the fluc-
tuation stabilizes somewhat. In long term
relationships, people learn to anticipate the
consequences of their messages and thus can
moderate their effects.

PARADOX

At least two messages are communicated in
most human relationships. One message pertains
to the information, opinions or feelings the
speaker desires to transmit. The other message
pertains to the relationship itself. Paradoxes
occur when the messages contradict each other,
placing the audience in a "double bind."
Double binds occur every day:

Supervisor to an employee: "Just pretend I'm
not here and go
on with your
work."

Employee to a supervisor: "Tell me exactly what to do so I can do my work independently."

Sign on a roadway: "Do not read road signs"

A co-worker: "I won't give you advice, but I think you should do that the other way."

These paradoxes can be funny, but they can also exacerbate interpersonal problems. This happens when the double bind frustrates the listener's idea of fair play by making his or her most potentially rewarding behavioral alternatives costly as well:

Company policy: "Employees must join the Union . . . Employees who participate in Union strikes or 'slow downs' will be dismissed." (The company is communicating on two levels. It is supporting union membership, but disciplines the employee for acting as a member.)

Prisoner's dilemma: "We won't be able to put you away long if neither you nor your partner confess. On the other hand, if you trust him but he turns state evidence, you'll go to jail for a long time while he gets off."

Catch 22: "You must obey Rule 1, but if you do you will violate it because it is subsumed under Rule A which requires the opposite action."

The individual caught in these double binds

cannot act directly, but must search for hidden
meanings, vacillate, or freeze. Such a person
is a victim, whose confusion, frustration, or
hostility adds a costly dimension to ordinary
relationships in groups and organizations. Remember, however, that paradoxes are equally
effective in freezing aggressive, anxious or
hostile spirals: When hostility is met with
neutrality, and anxiety with calm, then,
paradoxically, less is more.

SUMMARY

When people communicate, they usually accomplish, or mean to accomplish, more than the
simple transmittal of information. People communicate for many reasons, such as to assess
where they stand with others, to persuade
others, to consolidate or gain positions of
power, to defend themselves against the powerful, to make a favorable impression on others,
to improve or protect close relationships, and
to provide an image of unity in their groups
before outsiders. Because various aims and
interests are served by interpersonal communication, it is usually incorrect or overly
simplistic to blame most interpersonal or
group problems on a lack of communication or
poor communication.

Communication involves (1) the encoding of
perceptions and inferences about reality into
symbols, or language, (2) the transmitting of
messages via symbols, and (3) the decoding by
an audience or listener of the symbols. This
process results in a set of perceptions and
inferences about the speaker and the relationship as well as the content of the intended
message. Thus the effects of the communication
process include changes in views of the communicator (such as the realization that a
complainer will not back down) and changes in
the relationship itself (such as the escalation
of good or bad feelings). Communication can
thus exacerbate or alleviate problems in groups

and organizations. Given escalating aggression,
for example, a communicator can counter
pleasantly (paradoxically) and stop the spiral.

Norms and Roles

Most individuals in this total membership group [students at Bennington College] went through rather marked changes in attitudes toward public issues. . . . In most cases the total membership group served as the reference group for the changing attitudes. . . . The general trend . . . is from freshman conservatism to senior nonconservatism. —Theodore Newcomb (1952)

"Do you remember when he first came, Charles? It was fascinating. He lay very low at first, drinking us in: the games, the vocabulary, the manners. Then, one day it was as if he had been given the power of speech, and he spoke in our language. It was amazing, like plastic surgery." —John LeCarre (1970)

In our society, when husband and wife appear before new friends for an evening of sociability, the wife may demonstrate more respectful subordination to the will and opinion of her husband than she may bother to show when alone with him or when with old friends. . . . When each member of the marriage team plays its

special role, the conjugal unit, as a unit, can sustain the impression that new audiences expect of it.
—Erving Goffman (1959)

The quotations heading this chapter illustrate a very special power that groups have
over individuals, a power to influence the way
group members think and how they behave through
group norms. Group norms are shared expectations and guidelines for belief and behavior,
such as the collective attitude that spouses
should be respectful toward each other in public or that all in the group will favor liberal
candidates for President. Norms like these act
somewhat as a nonhuman member of the group who
supervises social interaction, insuring that
individuals behave as though they belong to
the group, care about it, and do not disrupt
its functioning. Group members pay attention
to this "supervisor" and show allegiance to it
in exchange for the rewards of belonging to
the group.
Norms develop as people in a group come to
agree that certain beliefs are true and certain behaviors, appropriate. Of course, not
all thought and behavior in a group is guided
by norms. While norms do provide boundaries
for much of social interaction, there are situations in which norms are not well developed
or could not be enforced, as in the realm of
private charity, food preferences and some
encounters between strangers. In addition,
many normative beliefs and behaviors have wide
latitudes within which people can vary, are
not considered important enough to enforce, or
contradict other normative behaviors and hence
are ignored.
Norms can guide nearly any type of belief or
behavior, but some areas of life are more
likely to be governed by norms than others.
Every human group, for example, has developed
norms for appropriate sexual behavior between
adolescents and for acceptable types of physical aggression between two males. Thus, in our
own middle class today, there is a norm among

teenagers which encourages sexual experimentation but not marriage and there is a norm for
boys which permits the use of fists in a fight
but not fingernails.

Groups have norms of self presentation (e.g.,
how much people smile and how closely they stand
together); they have norms for dress (e.g.,
jeans, dark suits); they have norms for addressing people of different status (as in "Sir,"
"Madam," and "Hey, kid!"). All groups have
norms directing which persons are to receive
which resources and rewards—these include
norms of reciprocity. They have norms, some
of them explicit rules, to manage conflict,
bargaining, and disagreements. They have norms
distributing different tasks, group functions,
and positions in the group hierarchy, and
opinions on culturally relevant topics such
as religion, government, health, work, money
and possessions. These include what economists
call "tastes," which determine in most areas
of life the things that people want to possess.
Finally, there will be norms about norms, that
is, shared expectations about what norms are
to be strictly enforced and what norms can be
safely ignored. These norms, especially,
adjudicate conflicting expectations, such as
exist between profit making and generosity.

Norms pervade our lives and have great
importance in groups and organizations. Nonetheless, their influence is often overlooked.
People usually are poor judges of each other's
conformity to norms. They overestimate the
uniqueness of each individual, underestimate
the force of the situation, and fail to see the
person's similarity to others as created by the
situation. They cannot perceive the uniformity
that norms bring about. Yet look in on any
randomly selected scene in the everyday life
of a home, factory, or office, and you will
find that most of the interpersonal behavior
that takes place, as well as most of the beliefs, are normative in character. Behavior
and belief in groups is, on the whole, shaped
and guided—supervised—by norms.

WHY NORMS EMERGE IN GROUPS

Norms emerge in groups because people and
their groups need norms and find that they
are useful. Norms help individuals (on the
average) attain their fair share of satisfaction and increase the regularity and predictability of social behavior. Because norms guide
how people interact, they prevent runaway selfishness and conflict, stabilize relationships,
and moderate the use of power. They provide
structure, strength and substance. To illustrate the usefulness of norms, it is helpful to
begin with two people who lack a norm but need
one. Examine Figure 4.1, which illustrates a
conflict between an employer and his employee.
Their disagreement is over the use of free
time. The employee often finishes his regular
assignment early. He would like to take a
coffee break during those periods, whereas the
employer would rather that he spent the time
inspecting his work for errors. If each were
to try to have his way (e.g., the employer
might interrupt the coffee break to insist on
an inspection), neither party would be satisfied (mutual dissatisfaction in the Figure is
represented by the integers 1,1). If just one
were to have his preference, the other would
always lose (4,1 or 1,4).

Suppose that during each free period the
employer threatened the employee with the loss
of his job or supervised him more closely.
In response, the employee might argue with
the employer or ask the union for help. But
doing so would involve moment-to-moment exercises
of personal power. Imagine how time-consuming
and stressful it would be if all similar conflicts of interest were resolved this way. To
avoid conflict or discussion each time a free
period occurs, and unpredictability of outcomes
for both, some rule covering the situation—a
norm—has to be established. The rule might
be that two coffee breaks per day may be taken,
while other free periods are devoted to

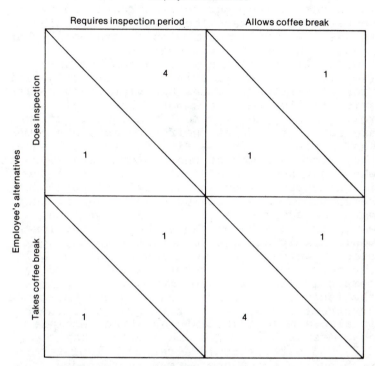

Note: Integers in the upper right-hand corner of each cell equal the net outcomes of the employer. Integers in the lower left corners equal the net outcomes of the employee. A comparison between the two integers in each cell indicates who gains most from that particular choice of alternative behaviors. The matrix is an over-simplification of reality, since it assumes only two alternatives for each person, fixed strategies, known outcomes, and a single simultaneous set of behaviors.

FIGURE 4.1 Allocation of an Employee's Free Time: Illustration of a Situation Requiring a Norm

inspection. Or it might be that all completed work is to be inspected, and afterwards the

employee's time is his own. Or an implicit
norm may arise without any discussion or planning: Inspections are done when the employer
is in the office, but coffee breaks are taken
whenever he is away. The solution, as Thibaut
and Kelley (1961) put it, is a "tradeoff" that
henceforth resolves the conflict.

When all parties in a situation can agree
(implicitly or explicitly) to a rule or definition of a situation, the behavior in that situation is likely to be smooth. The people involved will generally feel that their outcomes
are fair, given that their interests are somewhat different. The matrix of Figure 4.2 shows
the joint outcomes of the employer and employee
when they agree to a regular tradeoff. Although
if one person gives in (4,1 or 1,4) total outcomes will momentarily be higher than if they
agree to compromise (2,2), their agreement
would probably be unstable, because the loser
would likely agitate for greater gains, seek
other rewards (e.g., work less hard), or quit
the relationship. Therefore, a rule based on
compromise is likely to improve outcomes over
the long run, as long as each person knows what
to expect and sticks to the agreement. There
is also a more profitable solution. Because
outcomes of 4,1 or 1,4 are greater than
2,2, the parties could agree on a long-term
exchange in which one person is rewarded, then
the other (a 4,1; 1,4; 4,1; 1,4 sequence). Such
an agreement, however, would require a high
degree of mutual trust.

People in groups work out tradeoffs, as in
the previous example, all the time. Where
these tradeoffs concern similar issues, group
members eventually adopt expectations in common
as a guide, and a social contract is created.
This contract is usually an implicit agreement
which obligates each person to comply with the
shared expectations of the group. It thus becomes a norm that supervises behavior or belief and is enforced through social pressure.

Since any contractual agreement limits freedom, individuals lose, at the least, a measure

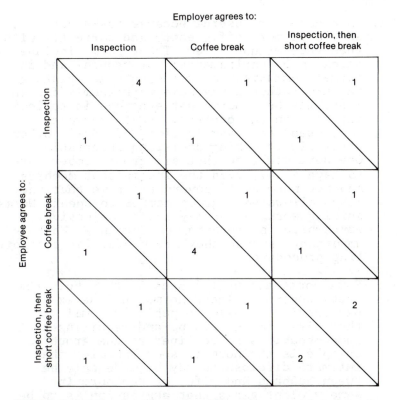

FIGURE 4.2 Illustration of a Situation in which Mutual
Outcomes May be Improved by a Tradeoff

of their flexibility by accepting norms. Even
the tyrant who hypocritically uses ritual, as in
the kangaroo court, loses the ability to implement punishments rapidly. His unfortunate subjects, who have little power to begin, gain
time and hope from the ritual but may lose the
initiative to rebel. Most norms, though dissimilar, are analogous. They restrict what people in
the group can do. Yet norms survive remarkably
well the inevitable resentments some people feel
about them and the periodic tests they are given.
The reason is that norms serve multiple interests

and needs.

1. Some norms are useful because tasks can be completed more efficiently and correctly with them than without them. These norms include sticking to parliamentary procedures and informal communication rules such as speaking in turn. Other norms make work seem efficient. There may be a norm that everyone is to look busy or, on the contrary, that everyone is to pretend the task is finished. Still other norms aid in making decisions acceptable. One norm might be that all group members are to have a say, even the incompetent members. Another norm could govern the time that the group allows each group member to speak. Norms guiding work may or may not be objectively worthwhile in improving performance. What is important is that they are useful for controlling procedure.

2. Some norms are useful because they hold the group together. These norms include expecting individuals to publicly commit themselves to the group, and requiring that some behaviors be confined to ghe group. An example is the norm in some families that intimate disclosures may be made only between husband and wife, or the norm in some violent gangs that aggression is to be displayed only towards members of other gangs. Other norms leave each person dependent on the group for material satisfactions, for example, a norm that causes farmers to buy and sell all produce at the community cooperative. These norms may, in effect, prevent members from leaving the group.

3. Norms satisfy personal needs for security, love, status, esteem, and power. Norms which supervise etiquette, for instance, protect each person from unpredictable

hostility, from loss of social position, and
from loss of face. Say an executive inquires
after the well-being of his assistant's
children, "Hi, Joe. How are the kids?" Joe
answers, "Just fine, thank you, Mr. Brown."
This exchange (whereby the employer, but
not the employee, is permitted to inquire
after the other's children) enables the two
people to exchange affection without jeopar-
dizing the status hierarchy. The norm not
only satisfies the need to be noticed, but
helps maintain a common definition of the
situation (e.g., undemanding and not threatening to a task difference). It helps everyone to get through interaction without
unpredictability, uncertainty, or embarrassment (cf. Goffman, 1959).

4. Some norms serve an informational use
   (Kelley, 1952). In the United States we
   have norms for evaluating what good government is, norms for judging success, norms
   for recognition of beauty, and even norms
   for reasonable sizes of one's family. These
   norms give "correct" information about
   reality in the face of ambiguity, they confirm one's opinions, and they help an individual to evaluate others and himself or herself.
   In fact, norms can be so useful in this
   respect that they can overwhelm what might
   be a more rational search for information.
   Groups that are uncertain or are under
   stress to make consequential decisions
   sometimes fear the consequences of a wide
   search for information. They adopt instead
   a strategy of reliance on what they are told
   or what is generally believed to be true.
   In the history of the United States we can
   find many examples of this overreliance on
   conventional wisdom in groups, such as occurred prior to the Spanish American War
   and the Bay of Pigs fiasco.

5. Related to the use of norms for information is their use for justification of actions (cf. Darley and Latané, 1970). Many norms are useful because they serve to explain and rationalize what people are doing or want to do. For instance, the norm "Be charitable" justifies gifts and bequests (whether or not they happen to be tax deductible). The norm allows people to maintain an altruistic self-image even when their actions are self-interested.

THE CONTENT OF NORMS

Norms can be roughly divided according to whether they supervise private beliefs and feelings, interpersonal communications, or overt actions. The three sections below illustrate the implications of norms that fall into each of these categories.

NORMS CONCERNING WHAT IS REAL OR TRUE: PRIVATE BELIEFS

In 1936, Muzifer Sherif (who was later known for his work on intergroup conflict and the development of social attitudes) asked groups of subjects to judge the apparent movement of a tiny light in an otherwise completely dark room. Earlier perception studies had already shown that a stationary light in a dark room appears to move because of the movement of the eyes, but individuals who are alone vary greatly in their perceptions of the distance that this light travels.

Sherif found that, as subjects in the presence of others continued to speak in turn, estimates of the light's movement converged. That is, with such a highly ambiguous stimulus, group members used others' judgments to help them make their own. Others defined the array of possible estimates, and the gradual accommodation of group members to each other eventually resulted in the abandonment of minority estimates. A closely arranged cluster of

judgments became more and more popular. Sherif
concluded that the growing uniformity of judgment, the judgmental norm, was caused by the
frame of reference that people in the group
provided for each other.

Sherif's experiments illustrate how people
rely on each other to frame judgments about
ambiguous physical phenomena, but it applies
equally to the formation of social judgments—
political preferences, opinions about social
policy, stereotypes, and feelings about other
people. As people in a reference group enter-
tain each others' opinions, a consensus about
the correct view develops, and those who join
the group are expected to believe the same.
The influence of the norm on belief, however,
will be strongest when the individual is initially uncertain about an opinion or when the
object of the evaluation is ambiguous, as in
Sherif's studies. If the individual is already
sure of a judgment (as when one can measure an
object, like measuring a table with a yard-
stick), group norms will affect private opinion
much less than if the individual is not sure
(cf. Festinger, 1954).

The use of norms to reduce uncertainty about
reality probably does not involve an active
search in which individuals choose membership
in a group in order to help them form opinions
and beliefs. Instead they usually join groups
that they imagine have similar opinions to
theirs (or they already belong to such groups).
Then other group members provide a frame of
reference for those opinions that happen to
be uncertain. Take voting, for example, which
is known to be heavily influenced by group
norms. According to a study described by Kaplan
(1968) of voters in Elmira County, New York,
80 percent of the Protestants and 36 percent
of the Catholics voted Republican. But also,
both groups voted as their friends did. The
minority of Catholics whose close friends were
all Republicans voted 61 percent Republican.
The Protestants whose close friends were all
Democrats voted just 21 percent Republican.

Thus, reference groups provided a framework
for voting. Most people voted as their reli-
gious group and their friends did. If the two
groups differed, however, they were most likely
to vote as their close friends voted, probably
because that was the group which provided the
greatest amount of uncertainty reducing information.

NORMS CONCERNING WHAT ONE SHOULD SAY: INTERPERSONAL COMMUNICATION

Even when a group member does not privately
agree with group actions or attitudes, he or she
may communicate agreement publicly because of
the obligation implied by norms to go along
with the group. For example, people who hate
singing aloud will usually do so in church
when it is appropriate. Groups expect people
to verbally fulfill a social contract, even if
private opinions or feelings diverge.

Observe what happens when a new member joins
a group. The person attends to what others are
saying, and in making an effort to win liking
and respect, gives off signals of the intention
to conform. The newcomer may not realize that
no one in the group is actually a true be-
liever; perhaps all are sticking to a party
line and go along with it to protect the
group's image.

Newcomers sometimes overdo compliance with
visible mannerisms and rituals, and inappropri-
ately claim true belief. They might not notice
the subtle ways in which other group members
deviate and, further, might feel too marginally accepted to try. To old timers such a
person's behavior will appear pretentious
even though it is sincere. Yet eventually, the
newcomer can learn what the real boundaries of
group norms are by watching others and by
paying attention to likes and dislikes, especially those that arise when no one else is
looking. Doing so frees the person to think
more independently while verbal behavior seems
compliant.

Solomon Asch (1956), in a series of classic studies, demonstrated the impact of norms governing what one should say on strangers put in a group. He showed lines of varying length to the subjects, and asked them to choose which one matched the length of a target line. This task would have been easy except for the fact that the subjects heard other members of the group giving incorrect answers. Asch had arranged the procedure so that the subjects had to announce their judgments after they had heard others speak; these other people were actually confederates who had been instructed beforehand to give certain answers, some of which were incorrect. Asch reported that a substantial minority of the subjects gave the same answers as the confederates (even when they knew very well that the other people in the room were wrong). This phenomenon of overt compliance with a group "norm" was most likely to occur whenever the other people in the group expressed unanimous agreement, i.e., more certainty.

Unlike the subjects in Sherif's experiments (1936) Asch's subjects outwardly conformed even when they were aware that the judgments of the confederates were incorrect (Figure 4.3). The norm affected what they said, not what they privately believed. This distinction between overt behavior and private attitude is important. Norms may govern both, but whether people have satisfied the norm ordinarily can only be inferred from their overt behavior. They cannot be faulted by others for disobeying the norm unless it is done overtly, for private beliefs can be hidden. Therefore, norms that have no information, justification, or emotional value to the individual may affect only outward behavior, and that behavior will change when he or she is away from surveillance. In contrast, norms that provide cues and frames of reference for the interpretation and explanation of ambiguous situations—as in the Sherif experiments—will need no surveillance or enforcement from others, because the norm is useful by itself.

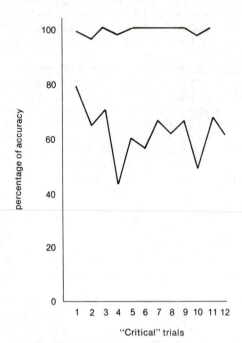

"Critical" trials

Note: Upper curve shows the accuracy of subjects who compared the length of lines without social pressure. Lower curve shows the accuracy of subjects who compared the length of lines with social pressure (i.e., six-eight confederates calling out incorrect judgments first). (Adapted from Asch, 1956)

FIGURE 4.3 Judgmental Accuracy under Social Pressure to Be Incorrect

NORMS CONCERNING WHAT ONE SHOULD DO: ACTION

There is a saying "You can lead a horse to water, but you can't make him drink." The proverb reminds one of a thorny problem in

groups: in many situations people can be induced to change their opinions, but not their
actions. They may nod their heads in agreement
with a group or offer supportive opinions and
advice, but when it comes time to act, they
give excuses and disappear.

One reason may be that action is more difficult than words. It often entails greater personal cost and risk; moreover, action requires
a favorable opinion toward action itself. Meanwhile, the group may be placated by words
alone. Verbal agreement gives the appearance of
good intent, so the group may accept the lack
of action as accidental or excusable.

Nevertheless, many norms require action. In
some street gangs, members must "slice" a member of another gang to show their commitment.
In committees, each member may be expected to
do his share of the work. Police recruits must
make a certain number of arrests. Professors
must publish. There are also norms, requiring
limited action, as in assembly-line cliques
which induce their members to limit their
output.

Group members get action by watching each
other and by implicitly setting behavioral criteria. Sometimes these apply in step-by-step
fashion. People are drawn to work for the
group or otherwise act in a manner that is easy
for them at first. Then they are gradually committed to a larger degree of action. The members of a violent gang, for example, may first
require new recruits to take a loyalty oath,
then to orally approve violence, and then to
acquire weapons, all of which gradually prepare
them for the more drastic action of hurting
others.

Jacob Varela (1971), a business consultant
familiar with social psychology, suggests ways
in which you can use surveillance plus the
small-step technique to induce people to take
action. He provides the following case of a
majority acting on a minority, which in broad
outline, shows one way that groups cause individuals to act in accord with norms.

A manufacturer wanted to induce a retailer to buy his fashionable ties. The retailer had always liked and bought conservative neckties, even though market surveys indicated he was probably losing business doing so. The manufacturer, instead of trying to talk the retailer into buying less conservative styles, invited him to see a new collection of ties and to give his advice regarding whether the collection was well balanced. The retailer was asked to bring along his wife, his buyer, and the head salesman of the men's department.

When the four arrived at the presentation, the manufacturer first showed the group a conservative tie and, knowing the retailer would like it, asked for his opinion. Then, to show his regard for the others, he also asked for their opinions. Next, the manufacturer brought out a less conservative tie, but this time scanned the faces to look for nonverbal signs of approval. The retailer frowned a bit and the salesman looked neutral, but the wife and the buyer leaned forward and nodded their heads. So the manufacturer first asked the buyer for his opinion and, when the buyer said he liked the tie, asked why. Then the manufacturer asked the wife, who of course said she liked it, too. The salesman was now showing signs of moving toward approval, so he was asked for his opinion and expressed a positive one.

The retailer, now faced with a majority opinion of three, went along with the others. The manufacturer wanted to get stronger commitment from the retailer, so he repeated his previous procedure several times and even included questions asking the retailer why he liked the less conservative ties. The retailer, faced with such questions, said things like "Times are changing" and "Some people will wear anything." And finally, when the issue of buying was raised, the retailer indeed chose to buy ties less conservative than he ever had.

In the following chapters we shall be considering in more detail the conditions under

which people take action in accord with majority opinions and with shared norms.

ROLES

Roles are a special case of norms. They are
shared expectations about subsets of individuals in the group rather than expectations about
everyone in the group. These expectations
govern how the subsets should be defined, who
should occupy positions in them, and what the
behavior or belief of the persons in those
positions should be. Everyone is familiar with
roles; most of us occupy several. There are
family roles such as wife, husband, son,
daughter; there are organizational roles such
as president, foreman, salesman; there are
informal roles such as task leader, socio-
emotional leader, and gadfly (Bales, 1970). As
with norms governing the group as a whole,
roles may consist of explicit rules and policy
or simply implicit agreements about who does
what. And, as with general norms, roles are
useful in a variety of ways. There are obvious
uses, such as efficient division of labor in
work groups, and there are uses less visible,
but no less necessary, such as insuring that
members act in a manner appropriate to their
power.
    When roles function to keep people in their
place, they are no more illogical or calculating in the psychological sense than are roles
used to divide up tasks according to merit.
Robert Merton (1948) explains, for example,
that among the Trobriand Islanders sexual
prowess is a positive value, conferring honor
and prestige. But if a rank-and-file Trobiander
male is too successful with women, winning as
many as is appropriate to men of rank, he becomes a scandal and an object of contempt. In
this way, the chiefs retain their prestige and
distinction, justifying their power by superior
role definition. The rejection of a man who

defies his role requirements is not contrived
or purposeful; it is an emotional response to
the person who threatens the orderly maintenance of the group's structure and makes intragroup conflict more likely.

The concept of role is helpful in understanding why people assigned to different tasks
or given different things to do seem to act in
much the same way, regardless of their own
personal predilections. Because roles are
normative, they tell people how their position
in the group should be enacted. For example,
in 1943, William Whyte wrote about a boy's
gang which he had observed for some time.
There was one boy who bowled very well when he
was alone, but scored poorly when he was with
his buddies. They had assigned him a low status
position in the group, a role that required
him to act inferior to others. In similar
fashion, the officer of a company may be influenced by the role requirement to act superior.
The president is expected to drive a prestigious car, to make important decisions, even to
talk with a certain force of manner. Everyone
will notice if the president steps out of role
by acting subserviently or admitting weakness
of any kind.

Violating one's role signals disagreement
and dissatisfaction with the group. When a member of the Cabinet in the White House begins
disagreeing publicly with the President, for
instance, the person is assumed by others to
be on the way out. Indeed, people sometimes
intentionally violate roles to make known that
they are leaving the group. Those group members
who want to stay in the group usually have to
fulfill their role expectations. Sometimes this
demand is hard on people because the requirements of the role are out of date, are too
rigid, or are inconsistent with efficiency and
success at work. In that event, the individual
experiences "role strain" (Secord and Backman,
1974).

ROLE STRAIN

Roles can become outmoded when situations, tasks, or group objectives change but group members maintain their old beliefs. For example, there is the late adolescent whose parents insist that he or she ask permission to go out, that is, remain in the outmoded child role. And there is the supervisor who requires the bookkeepers to keep rigid work hours even though computers have changed their role from nine-to-five clerk to on-call technician.

Sometimes an individual likes the old role requirements, but the group redefines the role. For instance, universities that have recently modified their objectives in line with a business model of productivity conflict with faculty groups whose objectives continue to be defined within the traditional model of scholarship. The professors insist upon a role that permits freedom without the counting of credits and hours; administrators claim new levels of accountability are needed.

Another source of role strain arises from the arbitrary way that some roles are filled. Many roles are assigned to people by virtue of their ancestry, age, sex, race, or religion. These roles appear to have value for the group but are hard on people whose interests diverge from the usual. For example, full professors are expected to look elderly, dignified, and intellectual, if a bit seedy. Their social role is wise man, and if they look the part people judge them to be successful (Ellis and Keedy, 1960). Unfortunately, the role-defined dress and demeanor is incompatible with the desire of many professors to look young, unconventional, fashionable, or feminine!

Individuals whose competence, interests, or beliefs do not fit with arbitrary role expectations can suffer. In the past, these included upwardly mobile blacks expected to choose

entertainment or athletic careers, ambitious
women expected to be wives and mothers exclusively, and shy, retiring men expected to
enter highly competitive occupations.

Role strain can exist because task requirements do not match role requirements. For example, assume we know that solving a problem will require equal input from two women,
each an expert in her field. Suppose, however,
that one of the women is chairing the group and
the other is officially her deputy. The role
of chair may require that its occupant participate more in problem solving, and have greater
weight in choosing a solution. Consequently,
the opinions of the expert who is in the
deputy role are ignored more than they should,
or her performance is too conservative. It
must be said, nonetheless, that this type of
role strain is not inevitably experienced as a
bad thing, for people sometimes use it as an
excuse for their own failures and to protect
their sense of esteem and competence.

ROLE CONFLICT

Many situations require a person to enact
more than one role. The head of a federal
agency, for example, must be an administrator
of the agency, a political negotiator with
Congress and the White House budget office, a
public relations expert for taxpayers, and a
special pleader for the agency's constituencies. Sometimes the requirements of one role
are inconsistent with the demands of another.
The agency official who as manager must effect
a smoothly running organization, but as politician must shake up the operation, is in this
predicament. The general term used to describe
the experience of simultaneous but inconsistent
roles is "role conflict." Role conflict, to
some extent, occurs whenever a person occupies
more than one role or whenever a person's role
carries with it competing role expectations.

Role conflict receives the blame for many personal and organizational problems (even ulcers). A recent study of university and college presidents by Michael Cohen and James March (1974), however, suggests that multiple roles held by leaders, although time-consuming, may be less conflictful and more personally satisfying than is sometimes claimed. Cohen and March identified three roles held by most college presidents; the administrator (dealing with subordinates), the political leader (dealing with constituents), and the entrepreneur (dealing with bankers, customers, and suppliers). Most presidents divided their time about equally among the three roles. A daily role schedule might look like this:

8-10 A.M.	Administrator
10-12 A.M.	Administrator and entrepreneur
12- 2 P.M.	Entrepreneur
2- 4 P.M.	Administrator and entrepreneur
4- 6 P.M.	Administrator and political leader
6- 8 P.M.	Political leader

To live up to their roles, presidents worked long hours. Many said they were tired. Many complained that too many people asked too much of them. But how conflicting were the roles? Cohen and March found that the college presidents moved from role to role with relative ease. Presidents expected, and believed others expected, that they would be administrators, politicans, and entrepreneurs. They were able to separate their roles into separate time segments. Their hours were regular. They did not act to change their roles. In fact, they used their several roles to demonstrate their status and competence. Having to fill several roles made them look as though they were putting a great deal of effort into their jobs, and this effort gave proof of their executive success.

Consciously or not, presidents organize their time in such a way as to maintain a sense of personal competence

and importance in a situation in which that is potentially rather difficult. They make themselves
available to a large number of people whose primary
claim is simply that they want to see the "president."
Counter to most evidence, such interactions remind the
president that he is the boss. Similarly, presidents
preside over otherwise pointless meetings, for the
process of presiding involves a subtle reassertion
of primacy.

   We also believe that presidents work long hours in
large part because they enjoy them [and] . . . because they are successful, not the other way around
(p. 151).

Cohen and March conclude:

   It is a mistake to see the pattern of presidential
attention as a burden imposed on a reluctant leader
by an unreasonable group of associates. . . . We see
very little evidence in the calendar data or in our
interviews that the overload on the president is related in any consistent way to the apparent complexity
of the problems facing the institution, to the size
of the staff available to the president, or to the
organization of the presidency (p. 152).

We see, then, that role conflict does not
necessarily imply personal or social conflict,
and indeed that multiple roles may afford the
individual considerable opportunity to be as-
sertive and to exert influence over others.

SOCIAL PRESSURE

   The effectiveness of a norm or role expectation in controlling a person's behavior and belief, clearly, is partly determined by the advantages to the person enacting the norm or
role of conforming (e.g., the college president
as political leader, say). Nevertheless, it is
equally important to focus on how powerfully
the norm or role expectation is transmitted
and enforced by members of the group. The
degree to which a norm is clearly and forcefully transmitted is not perfectly correlated

with norm adherence, but neither is it likely
that someone will conform to norms that are
poorly comprehended and never enforced. Group
members must come to realize what others expect of them and what may occur if they fail
to conform.

Members of a group verbally express their
judgment about what others should do or think,
and they even discuss what norms should be. Expectations are communicated more subtly too. If
everyone else in the group expresses a certain
opinion or acts with a degree of uniformity,
the individual member will assume that a norm
exists and that others expect him or her to
think or do the same. Because the person will
have learned (if unconsciously) the value of
norms and their obligatory quality, he or she
will adhere to them. The recognition of a norm,
therefore, carries with it social pressure to
conform, if only overtly, even when the norm
is never explicitly discussed.

Social pressure, then, is a psychological
force operating upon a person to fulfill the
group's shared expectations, including those
expectations regarding the person's roles (c.f.
Kiesler and Kiesler, 1969). This psychological
force may be explicitly transmitted, as when an
individual is urged by others to go along with
the group. Or it may be implicitly communicated, as when an individual sees that a person
who holds a minority opinion is being ignored
by the others, or it may be transmitted indirectly, as through biased information from
the group.

DEVIATING FROM NORMS

A deviant is someone who inadvertently or
purposely fails to conform to group norms.
Since even informal norms carry with them an
obligation to behave appropriately, group members are likely to be upset when someone fails
to enact a norm properly. Discomfort occurs
not only when the deviance actually hurts the

group, but also when deviance is inconsequential. The reason may be found in the uses that norms serve. Remember that norms help to define reality and make social interaction predictable. A norm or role violation that does not actually reduce material rewards or threaten people's interests may still be stressful for others because group members are made less certain or because their emotional commitments are shaken.

There are several experiments that demonstrate how group members react to a deviant. One of these is a famous study by Stanley Schachter (1951), conducted in a group setting with college undergraduates. Groups were given human relations cases to discuss and analyze. One case involved Johnny Rocco, an adolescent delinquent. The experimenters knew, by pretesting attitudes, that few subjects would be predisposed toward harsh punishment for the boy when there was still a possibility that a loving home would help. Knowing this, the experimenters assumed that the groups would agree upon loving care or just moderate punishment for him. They placed three confederates in each group, two of whom publicly advocated very harsh punishment for Johnny. (The third confederate conformed to the group's less severe opinion.)

In the face of deviance, the group tried to persuade the two confederates to change. By prearrangement, one of the confederates, the "slider," came around to the group's way of thinking. Communication to the slider subsided as the group concentrated on the other deviant, but he refused to budge. Finally, the group just ignored him, a powerful form of social rejection. Further, when the group was asked later to vote each person into a subcommittee, the deviant was assigned to the least desirable.

The conclusion one may draw from this study is that people face the violation of norms with distaste and react to deviants negatively. They may ignore or contradict the deviant, withdraw their affection, assign the deviant a less rewarding role, or otherwise show their disapproval. Some groups punish deviants by physical aggression (Freedman and Doob, 1968) or use deviants as scapegoats during crises (Allport, 1954). In work organizations people are fired, promoted "upstairs," demoted, or simply ignored for violating norms — even seemingly inconsequential ones having to do with what theories of management are "in" or whether one wears a suit.

One realizes how important norms and roles are when one sees how deviance affects people. It is obvious from the discussion above, for example, that the norm violator's interactions with other group members will be less than satisfactory. People may even assume that one deviant characteristic is associated with others and that the deviant has problems beyond those that are actually in evidence.

Being thought generally deviant is especially unpleasant. For instance, a blind person (whose deviance lies in the fact of a single physical difference) is often assumed to have trouble hearing and so may not be offered a job requiring oral interaction. A businessman who does not want to join a company athletic program is perceived as disloyal in general. An employee who is cold toward people is viewed as indifferent towards the job, too. These deviants may be forced to sacrifice some strongly held beliefs or preferences to reestablish the group's respect, and they might have little choice except to do so. A person who is middle-aged, faces a poor job market, and is saddled with fixed high costs of having a family, feels monstrous pressure to conform. Reactions to deviance, then, can have far-reaching effects on the individual deviant's life.

A deviant's difficulties in interacting with other members of the group are made worse by the tendency for people to avoid deviants. Researchers Kleck, Ono, and Hastorf (1966) have

shown, for example, that people feel uncomfortable and talk less with the handicapped than
with physically normal individuals. People also
disclose fewer feelings to them. Such behavior can prevent the correction of misattri-
butions and the development of close relationships.

Norm violators are likely to feel forced to
interact in a manner that reinforces others'
opinions of them as different. A boy who is
shunned by friends may ignore them to salvage
his pride, and in reciprocating, reinforce his
isolation. The woman who insists on her point
of view may receive disdain, and if she argues
to achieve reconsideration, reinforce the
notion that her behavior is merely argumenta-
tive.

Norm violators eventually may be placed in a
position whereby acting out their deviant role
is the only means to receive attention; but
then the attention is rewarding and reinforces
the deviance. Some neurotic behaviors, such as
working compulsively, are maintined in this
manner; there are also perfectly normal actions
that become a problem through this mechanism.
For instance, a person who takes an unpopular
position in a group might be labeled a trouble-
maker (Becker, 1963). The label redefines the
person as a member of an outgroup, who can now
demand attention only by complaining (if the
person does anything else, no one cares). The
individual must now complain and to find support, join other complainers. Suddenly there
exists a demanding minority group comprised of
former majority members who disagreed with the
group on a single issue. Predictably, the
minority discovers a rationale for itself and
perpetuates the gulf between it and the majority.

CHANGING NORMS

If deviance makes people uncomfortable, it
is not for want of a reason. Deviance does increase uncertainty and unpredictability; it

does change the nature of relationships in
the group. Deviance thus alters the group, and
in so doing causes norms and roles to change.
Think of a restaurant, a smoothly running operation until the owner breaks an unwritten
rule—a norm—and hires a former waitress as
manager. The status hierarchy is upset; the
employees become more informal with each other
regardless of level. This informality results
in greater intimacy, which in turn creates new
expectations regarding the distribution and
sharing of work.

Sociology is the principle discipline in
which changes in norms and roles have been
studied (e.g., Cloward and Ohlin, 1960). One
finding is that old norms decline when
the environment renders them unrewarding.
For instance, a boys' club in the ghetto may
abandon its interest in sports and turn to
delinquency because the boys lose their games
but win their fights (cf. Secord and Backman,
1974).

Some norms fade very slowly indeed. Examples
can be observed in everyday manners, as when
men are still expected to walk on the street
side of a woman (originally to protect her
from horses). In 1952, black and white miners
in West Virginia were integrated below the
ground, but continued to be completely
segregated above the ground (Minard, 1952).
(Sixty percent of the West Virginia miners
behaved consistently tolerant below the ground
and consistently intolerant above the ground.)
In Nashville, citizens accepted school integration but not integration of lunch counters.

One receives an impression from the research
in sociology (cf. Havelock, 1976) that many
social innovations are deviations that died of
success. That is, innovations begin as a new
way of doing things (e.g., crop rotation in
farming) or as inappropriate social behavior
(e.g., living with a person of the opposite sex
to whom one is not married). These new behaviors provoke either rejection of the deviant

actors and those who support deviance, or
adoption of the new behavior because it is attractive, rewarding and useful. (Sometimes some
people reject the deviant while other people
imitate the deviant behavior.) If the new behavior continues to attract people, a social
innovation is the outcome.

Social innovations are not merely inventions
of the social elite, who decide to change
things and advertise their preferences to the
majority. It is true that the richest, best
educated, and highest in social status do
originate many ideas which alter society.
Further, doing so is normative. They influence
ideas about changing our system of government,
about the length of skirts, about the financing
of social security programs, and about the
attractiveness of the stock market as an
investment. Nonetheless, new ideas come from
all sectors of society.

Whatever their origin, new ideas need support
from within reference groups if they are to
gather wide acceptance. This within-group
support is most likely to arise when opinion
leaders in the group adopt an innovation
(Katz, 1957). The social elite, experts, and
other people outside of the group will be
successful to the extent that they can influence the opinion leaders in the group. Much
of the Department of Agriculture's success
in persuading farmers to adopt modern techniques of conservation can be traced to its extension agents, who were able to influence
opinion leaders in the farming communities
through personal contacts and demonstration
projects.

In conclusion, groups need both conformity
to norms and roles and they need deviance. We
saw that conformity provides stability, including predictable degrees of change, structure, and meaning. Deviance is a source of
growth. A minority of people in groups function as pioneers in new behavioral territory

by braving deviance and testing the value of
ideas that defy acceptable ways of thinking.
These pioneers cannot act in highly controlled
groups or societies, so those groups will tend
to have relatively stable norms. In groups,
organizations and societies that are looser and
more accepting of nonconformity, there will be
more social innovation as well as more rapidly
changing fads and fashions and more unstable
relations among people.

Summary

Norms are shared expectations which guide
many behaviors and beliefs in groups. Groups
develop, enact, and enforce norms through
social pressure because norms are useful for
regulating social interaction. Norms act as
implicit agreements for guiding social tradeoffs; they provide information for reducing
uncertainty; they are a vehicle for gaining
social rewards such as liking and respect.

Roles are norms which apply to subsets of
individuals in groups, and are especially useful for dividing up tasks, power, and resources. Each person has many roles, some of
which may not fit the person very well (role
strain) or may require conflicting behaviors
and attitudes (role conflict). The latter condition can afford a person considerable lever-
age, however.

In assessing the effectiveness of a norm or
role expectation in controlling a person's
behavior or belief, it is important to focus
on social pressure from the group, a psychological force (implicit or explicit) to fulfill the group's shared expectations. A person
who ignores or rebels against social pressure,
that is, who deviates from norms and roles, is
likely to be rejected by the group. Deviance
has many ramifications, some quite unpleasant.
Being thought an outsider, for example, im-

pedes normal social interaction with one's group. On the other hand, deviance is also a source of social innovation—of social change in groups, organizations, and society.

5

Theories of Interpersonal Processes

Norms and roles provide a set of acceptable alternative behaviors for people. They guide and provide explanations for behavior and generally simplify everyday life. But there are so many norms, with so many functions, that it is not easy to specify which norms will be salient in a situation and whether norms, if salient, will cause a person to act. Suppose, for example, a business executive receives a letter asking for a political contribution. Will the norm he attends to be "God helps those who help themselves," or "Be thy brother's keeper?" If he does make a contribution, is it because an altruistic norm caused him to do so, or is the norm merely used to justify his behavior (cf. Darley and Latané, 1970)? These questions make clear that we need theory. Theory is what helps one understand which interpersonal processes occur in various situations.

This chapter covers four theories of interpersonal processes. These are relatively well
researched theories, but they are not the only
ones. For example, there is attribution theory
(which is reviewed in Chapter 2), reactance
theory (to be discussed in Chapter 6), and
Wicklund's [1972] theory of objective self-
awareness). The theories included in this
chapter were chosen as appropriate examples of
a framework for predicting and explaining interpersonal behavior in groups and organizations.

Whereas attribution theory focuses primarily
upon interpersonal perceptions and explanations, the four theoretical developments described in this chapter are primarily concerned with behavior and attitude change.
The theories are (1) social exchange theory,
a theory of how people make decisions which
are in accord with their power to gain rewards
and avoid costs; (2) equity theory, a theory
of behavior and attitude changes which occur
in response to inequitable distributions of
rewards and costs; (3) dissonance theory, a
theory of behavior and attitude changes which
restore consistency between behavior and attitudes; and (4) commitment theory, a theory
about the behavior and attitude changes that
maintain or restore the consistency between
personal commitment and attitudes or behavior.

SOCIAL EXCHANGE THEORY

ASSUMPTIONS OF SOCIAL EXCHANGE THEORY

We owe social exchange theory to sociologists
George Homans (1961) and Peter Blau (1964) and
to social psychologists John Thibaut and Harold
Kelley (1961). As did their forebears, economic
and mathematical game theorists, they assume,
first, that people want to maximize their
satisfactions and minimize their dissatisfac-
tions. Alternatively stated, people are selfish
and attempt in social relationships to gain as

positive an outcome as possible. Their outcome
equals the rewards they gain in interaction
minus the costs of that interaction. A second
assumption is that people make choices, or decisions, based upon a subjective weighing of
the rewards and costs associated with their alternatives. Social exchange theory is a form of
decision theory where the emphasis is upon the
utility, or value, of alternative strategies or
behaviors (rather than upon the probability
that a particular alternative is possible).

The third important assumption of social exchange theory is that people's alternatives are
limited by their control or influence over
their own and others' rewards and costs. The
theory is, therefore, a theory not only of decisions, but also of power, where power is defined as the ability to control or influence
the rewards and costs of oneself and others.

POWER INTERACTIONS

The distribution of power in a group can be
described by an interaction matrix, such as
the ones employed in the previous chapter. Each
person's perceived alternative behaviors are
represented along one row or column of the
matrix, and at the intersection of each combination of alternatives is listed the outcome
of that interaction for each person. The extent to which one person, A, can control the
outcomes of another, B, is clearly seen by
examining the matrix. It is also possible to
see whether A can make it desirable for B to
vary his behavior. It is the distribution of
these two kinds of power, called "fate control" and "behavior control" by Kelley and
Thibaut (1961), in which we are interested.
Figure 5.1 shows an interaction matrix for one
hypothetical dyad which presents the basic
characteristics of social exchange and shows
both fate and behavior control.

Suppose that A is a woman who owns a small
shop and employs B as a clerk. The matrix describes each person's alternative behaviors

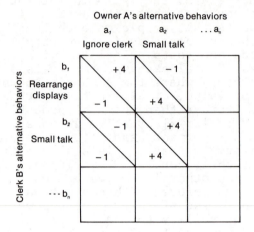

Note: Integer in the upper right corner of each cell equals A's outcomes; integer in the lower left corner of each cell equals B's outcomes.

FIGURE 5.1 Alternative Behaviors, and Their Associated Outcomes, Available to the Owner of a Store (A) and to a Clerk (B) when They Begin Work

when they begin work. The owner might ignore the clerk (a_1) or might engage in small talk (a_2) or might give instructions for rearranging displays (a_3). The clerk also has a repertoire of behaviors, represented by b_1, b_2, and up to b_n. The degree of satisfaction or dissatisfaction—that is, the value of the outcomes—that they derive from their own behavior is represented by positive (or negative) integers in each cell of the matrix. Because the owner is reserved, for example, she receives an outcome equaling +4 from ignoring the employee (a_1) when the employee rearranges the displays (b_1). If the employee tries to engage in small talk while the owner is ignoring him (a_1, b_2), the owner derives some dissatisfaction from that exchange (-1). Looking now at the more sociable clerk we see that he gets some dissatisfaction

(-1) from being ignored when he either begins rearranging displays (a_1, b_1) or when he tries to engage in small talk (a_1, b_2).

Note that no matter what the clerk does, his outcomes are determined entirely by the owner's behavior, i.e., -1 if the owner ignores him and +4 if the owner talks with him. This is called "fate control," which is defined as a person's having the ability to control another's outcomes. But the clerk has power, too. If the clerk shifts his behavior, he will motivate the owner to change her behavior. That is, by changing from b_1 to b_2 he can motivate the owner to change from a_1 to a_2 because what he does affects the owner's outcomes. The clerk's power is termed "behavior control," defined as the ability to influence another's outcomes by changing one's own behavior. (But remember that a clerk who provides negative outcomes to an employer may not always count on being allowed to play that game.)

To complicate matters more, note that the owner can convert her fate control to behavior control. If she wishes, she can employ a matching strategy whereby every time the employee engages in b_1, she matches it with a_2, and every time the employee engages in b_2, she matches it with a_1, thereby motivating the clerk to always perform b_1. Given the employer's own outcomes, however, you might ask why she would employ such a strategy. If she were to do so, she would simply penalize herself (the result of matching b_1 with a_2 is an unpleasant outcome for her). The answer is that she probably would not do so for long. Her power is not wholly usable, assuming the matrix does not change.

USABLE POWER

It is the distribution of usable power, in combination with perceived rewards and costs, that determines decisions in social exchange. We turn now to a consideration of the factors that influence usable power.

THE DISTRIBUTION OF RELATIVE OUTCOMES. The previous example showed how usable power depends not just upon the size of rewards and costs associated with alternative behaviors, but also by whether one is penalized for using particular strategies. In assessing such penalties, one must look at the array of outcomes for each person relative to the other's. One important question is whether outcomes are positively correlated or not. Figure 5.1 represents a case in which outcomes are indeed positively correlated—that is, one can find a combination in which each person receives positive outcomes and both will be satisfied (a_2, b_2). Figure 5.2 shows a situation in which outcomes are not positively correlated. If A performs a_1, B will choose b_2, which will motivate A to perform a_2, which in turn will induce B to do b_1. Although each has behavior control, neither has enough usable power to achieve a positive outcome that sticks. The participants will have to change the matrix itself or come to some understanding for a tradeoff.

INFORMATION. The ability to anticipate another's behavior increases one's usable power. This ability is gained in part by knowing what is satisfying and dissatisfying to the other. But even with complete information about the other's and one's own outcomes, one still may not be able to predict how the other will behave. To do so, you must have more complete information about the characteristics of the other, the context, and the other's interaction goals. The classic situation in which information about outcomes is of little help is the so-called "prisoner's dilemma," depicted in Figure 5.3.

Suppose the matrix represents two men suspected of a crime. Some circumstantial evidence exists so that they can both be linked with it. Theoretically, each has behavior control over the other, and maximum joint outcomes can be obtained if each keeps silent. Previous agreement

A's alternative behaviors

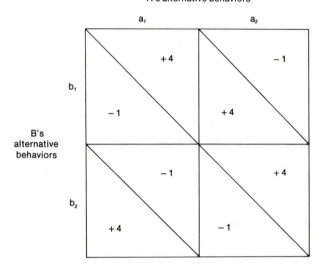

Note: Integer in the upper right corner of each cell equals A's outcomes; integer in the lower left corner of each cell equals B's outcomes.

FIGURE 5.2 Matrix representing the case in which A and B have behavior control and outcomes are negatively correlated

may be reached between the two of them, in fact, to do so. In that case, if each can be sure of predicting the other's behavior, usable power is very high and equal between the two.

Now enters the District Attorney who, with his circumstantial evidence in hand, separates the two prisoners and explains to each that his punishment will be reduced for confessing (the D.A. will press lesser charges). Each of the prisoners knows the consequences of his and the other's behavior. If either one confesses, the confessor will get off with a light sentence, whereas the other will receive

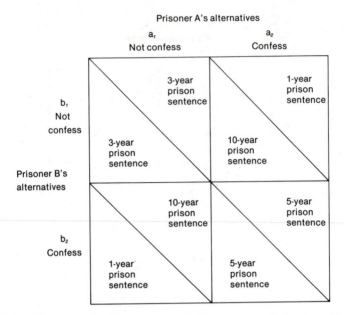

Note: Integer in the upper right corner of each cell equals A's outcomes; integer in the lower left corner of each cell equals B's outcomes.

FIGURE 5.3 The Prisoner's Dilemma

the maximum sentence (a_1b_2) or (a_2b_1). If both confess, they will receive heavy, but not maximum sentences. Once they are separated, the prisoners cannot really be sure of each other. Will the other guy confess, taking advantage of you? Each prisoner's usable power is so reduced that both confess in self-defense. This strategy is called the "minimax strategy," whereby each acts so as to minimize the chance for loss as well as maximize the chance for gain.

More complete information about the other's trustworthiness and the constraints of the setting could increase the likelihood of being able to remain silent in the prisoner's dilemma situation. For example, if one prisoner has friends who will punish a squealer, he can be more certain that the other will resist confessing. Anticipating future interaction with the other would also help.

SEQUENCE. In everyday life people often do not act simultaneously, as our previous matrices have assumed, but act in sequence, responding to the actions of another and acting in anticipation of another's response. If we continue to assume that individuals act in order to maximize their positive outcomes, a strategy that may result in satisfaction is one in which people stick with a behavior that has been rewarded in the past and shift their behavior if they are punished or if expected rewards do not follow. This win-stay/lose-shift strategy is like a personal reinforcement theory. The problem in many situations, however, is that having to depend upon such a strategy may considerably reduce one's usable power, since past rewards and punishments may be misleading (Gergen, 1969). Figure 5.4 illustrates this point by showing (a) an outcome matrix, (b) the result of simultaneous actions, and (c) the result of sequential actions for a situation in which a union is bargaining for wage increases with management. The matrix indicates that both the union and management can achieve satisfaction if each compromises. Assuming they act simultaneously and maintain a win-stay/lose-shift strategy, they will reach this compromise, since not compromising will be punished and result in a shift. But if they must act in sequence, rewards and punishments will be so misleading that a compromise cannot be reached. This example demonstrates how sequencing of interaction can prevent power from being usable. (Does the example remind you of the communication spiral?)

THE COMPARISON LEVEL FOR ALTERNATIVES. Usable power also depends upon whether the outcomes one can control or influence are high enough

A. The outcome matrix

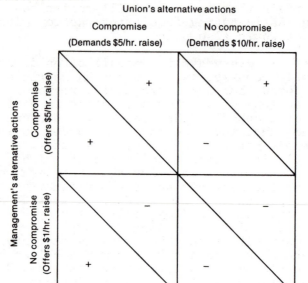

Explanation: It is assumed here that satisfaction is gained by: (1) compelling the other to compromise, and (2) achieving an agreement. In this distribution of outcome it is not possible to obtain agreement without compromise on both sides.

B. Simultaneous actions

	Union's action	Management's action
Step 1	Demands $10 −	Offers $1 −
Step 2	Demands $5 +	Offers $5 +

Explanation: Step 1—Each tries most favored alternative and loses. Step 2—Shift results in mutual compromise, maximizing available outcomes.

FIGURE 5.4. The Effect of Sequence on the Ability to Reach a Compromise

C. Sequential actions

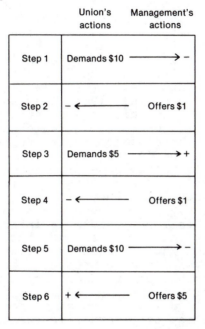

Explanation: Step 1—Initial demand of union results in loss for management. Step 2—Initial offer of management results in loss for union. Step 3—Union shifts, resulting in win for management. Step 4—Management stays, resulting in loss for union. Step 5—Union shifts, resulting in loss for management. (This step returns parties to Step 1.)

FIGURE 5.4 (Continued) The effect of Sequence on the Ability to Reach a Compromise

to maintain the relationship. In considering this point, we need to introduce a concept of Thibaut and Kelley's called "the comparison level for alternatives." This level is defined as the standard a member of a relationship uses

in deciding whether to remain in it or leave.
Each time a person weighs his outcomes in an
exchange, he will consider whether they fall
above or below outcomes he could obtain in
another relationship. If the outcomes are
equal to or above those he would obtain in
interaction with someone else, they will be
felt as satisfactory. But if they fall below
his comparison level for alternatives—if they
appear to be less than he "deserves"—then he
will, if he can, leave the relationship.

Thibaut and Kelley (1961) discuss the role
of the expert in this regard. An expert has
special skills or knowledge which can improve
or worsen others' outcomes if, respectively,
the information is provided or withheld. But
the expert's usable power is reduced to the
extent that he or she gives away information
and is replaceable. They cite a study by
Wilensky (1956), who found that the staff
specialist in labor unions is influential in
decision making to the extent that he is ir-
replaceable. Thus, the lower the union's comparison level for alternatives, the higher the
expert's usable power. There are a number of
ways in which people may maintain or increase
their usable power by reducing the relative
attractiveness of alternative relationships.
For example, they may offer additional rewards
—in particular, unique ones—to the other, as
suggested by Blau's (1954) finding that less
competent government bureaucrats were friendli-
er to employees. They can overreward others,
promise that future rewards will increase, or
even form a coalition with the competing party.

APPLICATIONS AND LIMITATIONS OF SOCIAL EXCHANGE THEORY

The value of any theory lies principally in
its ability to predict. This section examines
social exchange theory's predictive usefulness
and its limitations.

ARE PEOPLE RATIONAL? Social exchange theory

assumes that behavior follows very rational
strategies. People are said to be rational if,
their behavior is consistent with what they
logically should have done to maximize their
outcomes.

A recent experiment by Michael Enzle, Ranald
Hansen, and Charles Lowe at the University of
Connecticut (1975) is typical of studies testing
social exchange theory, and it bears on the
question. In this study, pairs of female students
were tested together, so that each student
would believe that the other subject was actually responding to her. Each subject was provided
with a typical apparatus used in gaming experiments consisting of a black button, a red
button, and four lenses to display a payoff
matrix. The subjects were told that the experiment was a study of dyadic interaction and that
they should try to accummulate as many points as
possible. (In this study no money was paid for
points, but in some studies subjects may win
small amounts of cash.) Two different matrices
were used in this study in order to evaluate
the subject's own strategy and perceptions of
her partner.

One matrix was designed to encourage competition; it was similar to the prisoner's dilemma matrix discussed earlier. The other matrix
was designed to reduce competition. This matrix
was predicted to do so because of high punishment for a competitive choice that was matched
by a competitive choice. The two matrices are
given in Figure 5.5. Note here that the structures of the matrices are identical in that
the partners can maximize outcomes by picking
black, the cooperative choice; but choosing
black entails the risk that the other will
choose red, the competitive choice. In the
upper matrix the minimum outcome for Person 1
(-4) can occur when she picks black, while in
the lower matrix the minimum value occurs only
when she picks red. If the minimax strategy
is employed, subjects given the top matrix will
be competitive (picking red) more often than
will subjects given the lower matrix.

Payoff matrices presented to subjects		Results: Average cooperative choices by subjects.*	
Competition facilitating matrix		Cooperative partner	Competitive partner

Person 2

		Black	Red
Person 1	Black	Your pts. = 6 Her pts. = 6	Your pts. = − 4 Her pts. = 6
	Red	Your pts. = 6 Her pts. = − 4	Your pts. = 0 Her pts. = 0

4.43	2.86

Competition inhibiting matrix		Cooperative partner	Competitive partner

Person 2

		Black	Red
Person 1	Black	Your pts. = 6 Her pts. = 6	Your pts. = 0 Her pts. = 6
	Red	Yours pts. = 6 Her pts. = 0	Your pts. = − 4 Her pts. = − 4

6.05	3.86

* The higher the number, the greater the cooperation. The highest possible cooperative score: 10.

FIGURE 5.5 Payoff Matrices in the Enzle, Hansen, and Lowe Study (1975) Displayed to Subjects from the Point of View of Person 1, and Average Number of Cooperative (Black) Choices in Each Experimental Condition

This experiment involved a variation in the partner's behavior. For each matrix,

half the subjects had a partner who made 100
percent black, or cooperative, choices. The
remaining half of the subjects received 100
percent red, or competitive, choices. Subjects'
choices were influenced both by the matrix
type and the other subjects' apparent choices.
More competitive choices were made with the
competition facilitating matrix than with the
competition inhibiting matrix. Choices were
also more competitive when the other subject
competed. Private ratings showed that subjects
trusted the other more when she cooperated.
In addition, the subjects were more likely to
perceive that the other's strategy was caused
by personal factors, rather than environmental
forces, when her actions were inconsistent
with the most rational strategy.

This study provides support for the rationality of social exchange within a limited situation. When people are forced to make an explicit choice, when the alternatives are sep-
arately and clearly specified, when the subjects are strangers who will never see each
other again, and when no interests are at stake
other than accumulating points, winning a game,
and satisfying the experimenter's requirements,
behavior is reasonably consistent with the
theory. Yet the subjects in such an experiment
have no reason to be other than "rational."

Turning to more complex situations, we find
that the question of rationality is actually
moot because we can no longer specify in advance what is objectively rational and what is
not.

For example, Robert Cialdini and his colleagues (Cialdini et al., 1975) did a series
of field experiments in which the subjects
were pedestrians on a university campus. In
the first, an experimenter approached each
pedestrian and asked him or her to donate two
hours a week for two years to work with disadvantaged youths. Naturally, almost every
subject refused. Then the experimenter asked
the subject to donate two hours just once to

take some of the youngsters to the zoo. He
found that 50 percent of the subjects who were
first asked the large, then the small, favor
complied with the smaller request. In contrast,
just 16.7 percent of those asked only a small
favor complied. Only 25 percent of a group
given a choice between the large and small
favors complied. Objectively, there is no
reason why people should be more likely to do
a small favor if first they have turned down a
large favor. But psychologically there is a
very good reason. People are rewarded not
simply by events that increase their material
resources, but also (perhaps primarily) by
feeling good about themselves and by satisfying social needs. Treating another equitably
by, for example, reciprocating a concession
is one way to obtain such rewards. The behavior of those subjects who complied with a
small request after turning down the large
request was psychologically reasonable. By
agreeing to the small request, subjects reciprocated what looked like a big concession by
the other person, and gained the rewards of
feeling fair and altruistic. Who is to say they
acted nonrationally?

WHAT IS A POSITIVE OUTCOME? The experiment just
described makes a clear serious theoretical
problem in social exchange theory and, in fact,
in all decision making models in which predictions depend on specifying the utilities or
values of various acts. That is, how can we
know beforehand what will be rewarding or
costly, if rewards and costs include such a
multitude of things as social approval, power,
self-esteem, freedom, and the need to conform
to norms? From whose point of view is the
value of an alternative to be defined? For example, how rewarding is a material gain if the
other can respond by taking it away? Remember
that one must specify not only the utility of
each behavior, but also the rewards and costs
to the other person as well as each person's
alternatives.

The problem is very apparent when we observe
behaviors that are altruistic. On the face of
it, altruism involves giving up positive outcomes for the benefit of others. Exchange
theorists contend that altruism is actually rewarding, but admit that it is more likely to
occur when the costs are low. They have demonstrated that the chances of a potential donor
helping another person increase when the recipient has valuable resources (Pruitt, 1968)
or is liked (Daniels and Berkowitz, 1963) and
when the donor's costs for helping are low
(Schopler and Bateson, 1965). How can we
predict before the fact whether the rewards of
altruism will be greater (and the costs lower)
than the rewards of selfishness? The researcher
is often compelled to ask people what is rewarding and what is costly (or to hold everything constant except one potential reward).
This, itself, is a problem because one's predictions then depend upon collecting a large
amount of information about each specific alternative or controlling its effects. In addition, the likelihood increases that "experimental demand" (pressure to comply with the
experimenter's wishes) will cause people to
prefer a behavior that they think the researcher considers rewarding. For this reason, many
social psychologists (including researchers of
social exchange processes) have become more
interested in identifying perceptions of different situations and the motives that are
aroused in them. For example, investigations of
the types of situations in which people desire
social approval (i.e., under what conditions
approval is or is not satisfying) may lead to
better predictions of behavior than attempts
to discover the utility of approval (and its
probability) in each specific situation in
which someone makes a choice.

DO PEOPLE MAKE DECISIONS? Research studies
employing a game such as Enzle, Hansen, and
Lowe (1975) used, while intended to simulate
decision making behavior in everyday life, force

subjects to make a decision and, further, induce them to carefully consider their alternatives before they do so. But the assumption
that all behavior follows a decision, including
marriage, having children, changing jobs, accepting innovation, and making promises, is
actually open to question. Studies that test,
rather than assume, whether people act on decisions show a considerable lack of conscious
forethought for many important behaviors.
Other studies, by showing how people can be induced to behave with only the illusion of
choice, illustrate how readily behavior is influenced by external forces, even though the
individual believes he or she has made a decision. Let us examine two important behaviors
as examples: the donation of a kidney, and the
bearing of a child

Twenty kidney donors as well as some people
who were potential donors were interviewed for
two and a half to three and a half hours by
researchers Carl Fellner and John Marshall
(1970), who wondered at what point in the long,
drawn-out process (which included special physical examinations and tests, evaluation by a
transplant team, a short hospitalization, and
repeated briefings) the donor actually made his
or her decision. This is what the researchers
concluded (p. 272):

> It appeared that not one of the donors weighed the
> alternatives and decided rationally. Fourteen of the
> donors and five of the prospective donors waiting for
> surgery stated that they had made their decision im-
> mediately when the subject of the kidney transplant
> was first mentioned over the telephone "in a split
> second," "instantaneously," "right away." Five said
> they just went along with the tests hoping it would
> be someone else. They could not recall ever really
> having made a clear decision, yet they never con-
> sidered refusing to go along either, and as it became
> clear toward the end of the selection process that
> they were going to be the person most suited to be
> the donor, they finally committed themselves to the
> act. However, this decision, too, still occurred

before the session with the team doctors in which all
the relevant information and statistics were put before them and they were finally asked to decide.

A study of the intention to have children
was conducted by Linda Silka and Sara Kiesler
(1977). Couples who intended to have children,
intended not to have children, or were unsure
were interviewed at home. One series of questions asked how long and how often the couples
had considered and discussed their childbearing
intentions. The answers to these questions
showed that people who intended to have children were least likely to have carefully considered the alternatives, had discussed it
least, and were least likely to change their
minds.

Why might this have occurred? Those who intended to have children anticipated many rewards, but few costs. Long ago, they had developed a good feeling about having children
or simply assumed they would have children.
They never had to make a decision because
their intentions were perfectly compatible with
social norms, their lack of awareness of costs,
and their life style. In general, people do not
actively consider the merits of specific behaviors that are consistent with social norms
and, without really thinking about it, become
gradually committed to them.

Would kidney donors and child bearers act
differently if they were told the complete reward-cost story? Some might, for awareness of
costs, in particular, is known to change intentions. Some might not, for their needs might
not be as well satisfied by other behaviors.
Either way, an explicit decision still might
not be made.

EQUITY THEORY

The three theories to follow stand in contrast to social exchange theory, primarily in
that they more specifically focus upon processes

that follow rather than precede decisions or
actions. Equity theory, the theory we examine
next, was first developed by J. Stacy Adams
and subsequently has received important attention from Edward Lawler, Elaine and G. William
Walster, Ellen Berscheid, and many others who
have applied its predictions to behavior in
business and social relationships (cf. Lawler,
1971; Walster, Walster, and Berscheid, 1978).

ASSUMPTIONS OF EQUITY THEORY

Equity theory, like social exchange theory,
assumes that people are selfish. Nevertheless,
equity theorists point out that people cannot
and do not invariably act in their own interest. One reason for this is that they learn
they will be punished if they do, but will be
rewarded in the long run for acting equitably
or fairly toward others. The theory, then, proposes that individuals have learned to behave
equitably, expect others to act equitably,
punish others for not acting equitably, and
feel distressed if they themselves do not act
equitably.

RECOGNIZING, MAINTAINING, AND RESTORING EQUITY

How do we and others know what is equitable
and what is not? The theory specifies that a
relationship is equitable when participants
are perceived to be receiving relatively equal
outcomes (rewards minus costs) in comparison to
their inputs. Inputs are the contributions they
make to an exchange entitling them to rewards
or costs. Positive inputs include power, effort, capital assets, physical beauty, status,
and favors. Some negative inputs are socially
undesirable behavior, poor qualifications, reduced effort, and ugliness. Equity depends upon
their receiving deserved outcomes (rewards and
costs) in correct ratio to their inputs.

The equity equation is expressed as:

$$\frac{(\text{Outcomes}_{person\ a} - \text{Inputs}_{person\ a})}{\left|\text{Inputs}_{person\ a}\right|}$$

$$= $$

$$\frac{(\text{Outcomes}_{person\ b} - \text{Inputs}_{person\ b})}{\left|\text{Inputs}_{person\ b}\right|}$$

This equation (abridged) defines the theory. Its terms are the considerations that people are assumed to make when judging their relationship to others. (See Walster, Walster, and Berscheid [1978].)

The theory allows for the fact that people will differ in the extent to which they perceive a particular input or outcome to be good or bad. For example, a worker may feel that his West European origin is a valued input in a worker-employer relationship, whereas the employer or an observer may not. In addition, people differ according to their perceptions of who is a comparable other (*person b* in the equation). The possibility of divergent perceptions of the "facts" in the equation makes possible, in turn, that people will inadvertently act inequitably in the eyes of others. Nevertheless, social norms insure that many relationships will be commonly interpreted as equitable or inequitable.

Given that individuals recognize equity in relationships according to prescribed rules and learn to act equitably, the theory predicts that they will engage in equitable behavior so long as it maximizes their outcomes. In other words, sometimes people act inequitably because it is to their advantage to do so. This proposition weakens the predictive power of the theory (because people are not always trying to balance the equity equation). Nevertheless, equity theorists have had to recognize that people are more likely to insist that they

receive equitable shares of reward than they
are to give up rewards in order to share them
equitably with others.

Now we turn to inequity. An inequitable relationship is one in which the equation depicted above does not hold. This may occur when
one's own inputs or outcomes are relatively too
low or too high, or when the comparison person's (or group's) inputs or outcomes are relatively too low or high. Because distress is assumed to result from inequity, the theory predicts that individuals in an inequitable relationship will attempt to restore equity. This
can be accomplished in either of two ways: (1)
by increasing actual equity—that is, by in
fact increasing or decreasing the person's or
the other's inputs or outcomes—or (2) by increasing psychological equity—that is, by distorting the person's or other's inputs or outcomes. The choice of equity restoring mechanism
will depend upon which one more completely restores equity and requires less material or
psychological cost. These predictions have been
tested in a number of studies, some of which
are described in the next section. (A more
complete review of these may be found in
Walster, Berscheid, and Walster, 1973, or in
Walster et al., 1978).

APPLICATIONS AND LIMITATIONS OF EQUITY THEORY

Equity is a complex concept. For example,
there are many ways to increase or decrease
equity. Suppose we want to predict the behavior
of a female typist who feels her organization
is underpaying her. She can restore actual
equity by typing more slowly or not trying as
hard to be careful (lowering her inputs); she
can force her bosses to make the coffee or to
run their own errands, thereby increasing their
work lead (increasing their inputs); she can
join a union which demands a raise (increasing
her outcomes); or she can steal pencils, paper,
and other equipment from the office (lowering
her bosses' outcomes).

Alternatively, the typist may restore psychological equity. She might believe that typing is an easy job anyone can do (minimizing her inputs); she night focus on her bosses' long hours (maximizing their inputs); she might feel she had good friends in the office (exaggerating her own outcomes); or she could opine that people in higher salaried positions are headed for ulcers and heart attacks (minimizing their outcomes).

Equity theorists have responded to the obvious complexity of the concept by studying just a few categories of equity restoring techniques and by doing research that controls all but a few (or one) of the factors in the equity equation. They have studied, in particular, relationships in which one party has reduced another's outcomes (by harming or exploiting the other person) and relationships in which one party has increased another's outcomes (by helping or materially rewarding the other person).

EXPLOITIVE RELATIONSHIPS. If we suppose that two parties are in an equitable relationship and that one of them then harms the other, the theory predicts that the harm-doer, as well as the victim, will feel inequity. Suppose your supervisor absently leaves you out of an important meeting. You, as the victim, respond with distress because your outcomes are unfairly reduced; the supervisor, as harm-doer, is distressed because you may retaliate and also because the action violates the harm-doer's expectations (called "self-concept distress"). Let us see how equity theorists have increased our understanding of the behavior of harm-doers (the behavior of victims is much more obvious).

In one of the early papers on equity, Elaine Walster and Perry Prestholdt (1966) proposed that harm-doers' responses generally fall into two distinct categories: compensation given to the victim (restoring actual equity) or justification of their own harmful behavior (restoring

psychological equity). From the victims' point
of view, the distinction is likely to be crucial since compensation is the response that
will restore their own equity (unless they
think that they deserve punishment). From the
harm-doers' point of view, however, justification is probably the easiest response for them;
if they can convince themselves that the victim
deserved the harm, then they can restore equity
without having to take action or to incur
costs. Further, compensation is difficult because it has to be just the right amount; insufficient compensation or too much compensation unbalances the equation in other ways.
Justification, being a distortion, can more
easily be made to match the harm done; it just
needs to be plausible and unlikely to be chal-
lenged directly.

To test the viability of these distinctions,
Walster and Prestholdt induced social work
trainees to misjudge a client and thereby harm
her by giving the trainees only one side of
the client's case before they had to make their
initial evaluation. The trainees were then
given the other side of the story, which made
clear that they had evaluated the client more
negatively than she deserved. Trainees were
then given two alternatives to restore equity.
They could compensate the client by volunteering to help her, or they could justify their
misjudgment by derogating her (e.g., feeling
she deserved her fate or was of low social
worth). The researchers found, first, that
subjects either compensated or justified their
harm (not both). Second, subjects were more
likely to justify their initial behavior when
they had committed themselves in public to
their initial judgments. Derogation of the
victim was therefore consistent with their
previous actions.

Later studies have more clearly drawn the
line between compensation and justification:

1. Compensation, rather than justification, is
   likely to occur when it can be just adequate

to· restore equity. For example, Berscheid and Walster (1967) induced women from various church organizations to deprive others of trading stamps. When the women were given an opportunity to compensate the others at no cost, they were more likely to do so if they could restore the exact number of stamps the others had lost than if either they could not give enough stamps, or could only give more than they had taken.

Walster, Berscheid, and Walster (1973) contend that this phenomenon helps explain the negative or apathetic public reaction to demands for compensation that can never be adequate, as in the case of the demands of native Americans for their land. These researchers speculate on the value of a strategy in such cases to temporarily lower the perceived injury that the minority has suffered in the eyes of the majority so that the majority comes to believe that "adequate" compensation can be made. Greater injuries can be discussed later.

2. Compensation, rather than justification, is more likely to occur the lower the cost of doing so. Experimental research makes clear that the psychological cost, as well as the actual cost, of compensating the other must be assessed. First, it is psychologically costly (as we shall see in the next two sections) to act inconsistently with one's previous behaviors. Thus is explained the Walster and Prestholdt (1966) finding that one tends to justify, not compensate, a harmful behavior that one has made publicly or is otherwise committed to. Second, it is psychologically costly to act in a way that makes one look bad in one's own or others' eyes. To compensate another may cause one to lose face, especially if one's responsibility for the harm would have gone unrecognized without an attempt to compensate. Alternatively, psychological costs may result if

one justifies, rather than compensates, another. If one is committed to interacting
in the future with someone, for example, derogating the person will be inconsistent with
that commitment and, further, will cause one
to feel discomfort and embarrassment. Some
researchers have found that justification is
employed less, and compensation more, when
one is committed to interaction with another. Davis and Jones (1960) found that subjects induced to ridicule a peer publicly,
later derogated that peer only when they
did not anticipate meeting him.

3. When the victim (or an intervening agency)
   restores equity, the harm-doer is less likely to do so—either by compensating the victim or by justifying the harm-doing behavior. Berscheid, Boye, and Walster (1968),
   for example, hired subjects to administer
   electric shocks to another person. If the
   victim was known to be unable to retaliate
   (administer electric shocks in return), the
   harm-doer subject derogated him. But if the
   victim could retaliate, no justification occurred.
      Walster, Berscheid, and Walster (1973) note
   that it is in almost everyone's best interest
   if harm-doers compensate their victims. If not,
   victims are likely to retaliate or an outside
   agency may have to step in (as, for example,
   in the prison system). They pose this question:
   Would it not be best in some circumstances for
   victims to retaliate or force restitution before harm-doers justify their behavior? For
   if harm-doers do justify their harm, the
   probability that they will do even more harm
   is increased.

In summary, justification of harm is more
probable when (1) exact compensation is not
possible, (2) the harm-doer is committed to the
harmful act, (3) no future interaction with
the victim is anticipated, and (4) the victim

cannot retaliate. Compensation is more probable
when these conditions are reversed.

BENEVOLENT RELATIONSHIPS. Imagine an equitable
relationship between two co-workers, each of
whom has equivalent social assets, works about
the same number of hours, and receives equal
pay. Then one worker's machinery breaks down
and the other spends a week helping out. Equity
theory clearly predicts that the previously
equitable relationship has become inequitable.
How do the benefactor and the recipient of help
respond?

Researchers have focused again on two kinds
of responses: reciprocation (i.e., compensation
to the benefactor) and justification. Thus, a
benefactor may alternatively demand or expect
reciprocation from the recipient, or a benefactor may justify the help through increasing
regard for the recipient. Recipients may
respond to help by reciprocating in kind, or
they may psychologically restore equity by
convincing themselves that they deserved the
help, or by derogating the derogating the
benefactor.

Two factors seem to affect responses. First,
the more intentional a gift or help is, the
more inequity distress is felt, and the greater
the desire to restore equity. Subjects partici-
pated in one study, for example, that supposedly
would identify characteristics important for
"success in the business world" (Greenberg and
Frisch, 1972). Each subject discovered, however, that he would need graphs from a partner
in order to complete the task. In a high intentionality condition, the partner helped the
subject and sent along a note making clear he
intended to help ("I'm sending them over since
you can probably use them"). In the low intentionality condition, the partner sent the
graphs, but the accompanying note made clear
he did not realize he was helping. As predicted, subjects were much more eager to restore equity (by reciprocating) when the help

had been intentional. (Intentionality, by the
way, probably has a similar effect in exploita-
tive relationships.)

The ability to repay a benefactor is another
important factor influencing the response to
help, just as the adequacy of compensation
influences the response to harm. Benefactors
are much less distressed when they know a recipient can pay them back. Recipients are much
more likely to return help when they have the
ability to exactly repay a benefactor (and they
are more likely to respond with derogation of
the benefactor when they cannot). One of the
more interesting implications of this hypothesis is that aid to foreign countries should be
appreciated (and repaid either in kind or in
favorable policy agreements) to the extent that
aid is tied to clearly stated obligations that
can be met by the recipient.

Kenneth Gergen and his colleagues have conducted studies of aid. One survey, Gergen (1968)
of citizens in countries that had received aid
from the United States showed that gifts accompanied by clear obligations, rather than unclear or excessive strings, were preferred.
"No strings attached" is a suspicious phrase
to people. In a field experiment (Gergen,
personal communication), Kenneth and Mary
Gergen tried to give away a basket of money on
the street of a Scandinavian city; most people
refused. In the sophisticated confidence game,
suspicion of something for nothing is lowered
by convincing the mark that he or she really
will have to incur costs (albeit very low
ones).

In the laboratory, the studies show also that
perceived obligations affect responses to aid.
For example, Gergen et al. (1975) arranged for
subjects to receive monetary aid from another
member of an experimental group that was
wagering money in games of chance. For half the
subjects the donor appeared to be the person
who had won the most money, while the remaining
half believed the donor had little money remaining. Written communications established

expected levels of obligation. One-third of the subjects were told that nothing need be returned (low obligation); the next third were told that the donor wished his money returned after the experiment (equal obligation); the last third, that the donor wished his money returned with interest. Subjects in three countries (Japan, Sweden, and the United States) responded in much the same way: attraction was highest for the poor donor, who had shown his good will by giving up valued resources, and for the donor who expected equal obligation.

Another interesting ramification of the reciprocation hypothesis concerns employer-employee relationships. We can readily predict that underpaid workers will feel distress from inequity, but the theory predicts that overpaid workers will also experience inequity. According to equity theory, they will feel distressed and will reciprocate if they can. One might think that psychological restoration would be easier; the worker need simply convince himself or herself that the high pay is deserved. Sometimes, however, this avenue of equity restoration is not plausible. The experiments of J. Stacy Adams and his colleagues show what happens when it is not.

In one experiment (Adams and Rosenbaum, 1962), students were hired through an employment office to do some public opinion interviewing. Each was paid $3.50 per hour. Half the subjects were made to feel unqualified and overpaid because of their lack of interviewer training and experience; the other half were made to feel qualified and equitably paid because of their high education and intelligence. Measuring the number of interviews per unit of time, the researchers found that the equitably paid group averaged just .19 interviews per minute, whereas the overpaid group averaged .27 per minute. Thus, persons overpaid by the hour by virtue of insufficient inputs appear to feel inequity and may work harder.

And what of people paid for piecework? Adams

was intrigued by this question because producing more cannot restore equity when one is paid more for greater amounts of work. He predicted that persons overpaid for piecework would instead increase their quality of work, and in 1963 he published an experiment that supported this prediction.

Before you rush out to proselytize the virtues of overpayment, however, remember that these studies were performed to test a theory, not to demonstrate a practical technique. In testing the theory, avenues of equity restoration other than changes in quality or quantity of work were controlled or made difficult. Thus in the experiment described above, students in the overpaid condition were paid enough more than the going rate and were so explicitly reminded of their lack of qualifications that they could not restore equity psychologically. But in everyday work situations this may not be the case. Overpaid workers may be very well able to convince themselves they are worth their pay, and unions often reinforce this opinion.

Lyman Porter and Edward Lawler (1968) have concluded that the most practical strategy is to pay employees commensurate with their performance, so that those who perform less well will receive less and those who do well will be rewarded. They contend, however, that unless employees are aware of others' pay and everyone's performance ratings, perceptions of inequity may occur.

WHO FEELS INEQUITY? Equity theory obviously has a number of practical, as well as theoretical, applications. Certainly, the student of organizations, in which harmful and benevolent decisions are made almost every day, will want to know, for example, the conditions under which a person who negatively affects another may go on to derogate that person, the conditions under which help will be appreciated rather than resented, and the conditions under

which pay should be clearly tied to performance
or effort. Nonetheless, equity thoery, having
so specifically identified a major motivation
in individuals, is not so highly developed that
one can be sure when people feel inequity.

Inequity has many different sources. Inequity can result from relative differences in
inputs, rewards, and costs, all of which may
be difficult to specify (just as rewards and
costs are difficult to specify in advance in
social exchange theory). Further, it is not
always clear who the "comparable other" is.
Recently, William Austin and Elaine Walster
(1974) demonstrated that participants in a
relationship may willingly sacrifice equity
when they know that the other is trying to restore "equity with the world"—that is, to restore equity that was previously taken away or
sacrificed in other relationships. Finally,
since equity is learned, its perception is influenced by one's culture. Presumably, cultures
in which fair play and justice are emphasized
will socialize children to be especially at-
tuned to equity. Cultures in which the saving
of face is important should produce individuals
for whom public equity is essential.

An example of cultural effects (which we at
this point must recognize as changing the
degree but not the pattern of equity responses)
is provided by the Gergen et al. (1975) experiment described earlier and represented in
Figure 5.6. This graph shows that in Japan, a
country famous for face saving, attraction was
very high for the donor who wanted to be paid
equally and very low for donors who asked for
nothing in return or for a return plus interest. In the United States these same results
were considerably weaker; for example, attraction to the donor who asked for no return was
fairly high. In Sweden, the curvilinear trend
was flatter; for example, returns with interest were not regarded so poorly.

In conclusion, practical application of
equity theory will depend upon the degree of
one's understanding of the perceptions and

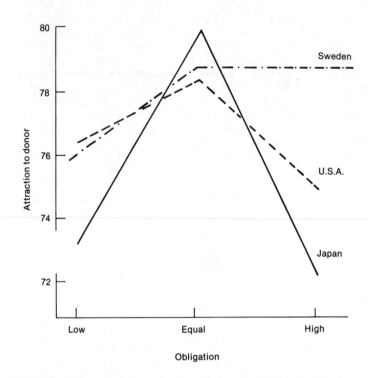

FIGURE 5.6 Attraction to the Donor in Three Nations
As a Function of Obligation Level (Reprinted from
Gergen et al., 1975, by permission from American Psycho-
logical Association)

cultural background of others, and the number
of psychologically valid options open to them.

DISSONANCE THEORY

That people are motivated to be consistent,
and like a consistent world, is assumed in
nearly every social psychological theory. One
theory in particular, famous for its nonobvious
predictions based on the consistency principle,

is now familiar to (but not necessarily understood by) many people. Dissonance theory was
developed by Leon Festinger, his students and
colleagues. Since 1957 over four hundred experiments have been published. An intense con-
troversy between "dissonance theorists" and
theorists from other traditions has flourished
and died down; the theory has been refined
considerably, and we are left with a somewhat
narrower but more useful set of propositions.
(For a brief review see Jabes, 1978, in this
series. See also Festinger, 1957, for the
original dissonance theory and Brehm and Cohen,
1962, for a later version. Abelson et al., 1968,
describe all of the major consistency theories,
and Kiesler, Collins, and Miller, 1969, review
and evaluate them as well as other theories of
attitude change.)

Assumptions and Propositions of Dissonance Theory

"Dissonance" is defined as an uncomfortable
psychological state whereby one or more cognitions about oneself are inconsistent with (or
do not follow from) other cognitions about oneself. This state is likely to occur in two
kinds of situations: (1) when one makes a decision or (2) when one is induced to comply
with another's request or demand. For example,
if I decide to work for someone (cognition
about my behavior) even though I do not like
that person (cognition about my initial attitude) I will experience dissonance because the
two cognitions about myself—the attitude and
the behavior—are inconsistent. Or, if I agree
to comply with a group's request (cognition
about my present behavior) in spite of my previous objections (cognition about my previous
behavior), I will experience dissonance because
the two behaviors are inconsistent.

Two important assumptions are made here. The
first assumption is that the cognitions must
be clearly inconsistent. The second assumption
is that dissonance is aroused only when cogni-

tions about the self are involved—that is, when the inconsistency has implications for the actor. Dissonance is aroused when you realize that you are eating yogurt but have always objected to its being served (the behavior has implications for your own consistency); dissonance is not aroused if you do not like yogurt and see someone else eating it (no implications for self). Dissonance is aroused if you are persuaded to buy a car that was not your first choice; it is not aroused if you do buy your first choice (your decision is consistent) or if someone else buys the car (no implication for self).

These distinctions are crucial because only when we can be sure that dissonance is aroused, can we make clear predictions from the theory. Unfortunately, the term "dissonance" has come to be used rather loosely. I have heard, for example, a person described as "feeling dissonance" when he perceives someone else acting inconsistently; the theory does not make predictions for this situation, nor does it make predictions for the situation in which one person's attitudes are inconsistent with another person's behavior or attitudes. Dissonance arises from inconsistencies in oneself, not from inconsistencies in the rest of the world.

Now we come to two propositions of the theory: (1) individuals are motivated to reduce dissonance by changing one or more cognitions about themselves, and (2) they will reduce dissonance by changing the cognitive element(s) least resistant to change. If I agree to work for a person whom I have not liked, I can change the first cognition by revoking my decision or I can change the second by liking the person more. Either way I will have reduced dissonance by reducing the inconsistency between my behavior and my attitudes. Since I agreed to accept the job, however, that decision is relatively harder to change than my attitudes. Therefore, I will probably reduce dissonance by starting to see more and more positive qualities in my prospective employer.

In fact, the difficulty of reversing explicit decisions or of taking back behavior means that, practically speaking, dissonance will most often be resolved by our changing our attitudes. The theory is thus known as a theory of attitude change, although behavior change is another means by which people reduce dissonance (and should be considered by any practitioner interested in applying the theory).

It is very difficult to make predictions from the theory unless one can specify which elements are most and least resistant to change. Therefore, an unequivocal prediction from the theory will be obtained when we know one source of the dissonance is difficult to change such as an explicit behavior or decision. It is nearly impossible to make clear predictions when merely inconsistent attitudes create dissonance. The theory, as it has come to be used, predicts that people change their attitudes to make them more consistent with explicit acts or decisions they have taken. Those acts or decisions must be inconsistent with initial attitudes, with their views of themselves, or with prior behaviors and decisions. We cannot predict attitude change when the act or decision in question is not explicit (i.e., not resistant to change or distortion), or when no inconsistency is generated.

So far, we have been discussing the arousal and reduction of dissonance as if only two cognitions were involved. Of course, this is an oversimplification. Usually, people have a number of thoughts and beliefs about their decisions and their actions; it is therefore appropriate to consider the relationship among sets of cognitions. In doing so, we come to a third proposition in the theory. This proposition states that the fewer the number of cognitions consistent with a behavior or decision, the greater the dissonance and the greater the attitude change. This has also been stated in another way: that is, the less justification there is for a decision or act, the greater the dissonance and the greater the subsequent atti-

tude change to justify the act or decision. For
example:

High dissonance	Low dissonance
I sign a petition favoring an expensive new high school that requires higher taxes. I have always been against tax increases. My neighbors did not pressure me to sign. I received no public approval for signing.	I sign a petition favoring an expensive new high school that requirers higher taxes. I have always been against tax increases. My neighbors pestered me until I signed. I received public approval for signing.

In the previous example there is a difference
in the degree of dissonance because in the high
dissonance situation I have no cognitions consistent with, or justifying, my having signed
the petition, whereas in the low dissonance
situation I have at least two. Public pressure
justifies my signature (I can tell myself, "I
did it because they would have hounded me if I
did not"), and public approval justifies it
("I did it because I needed the good publicity"). With high dissonance, I have no avenue
of dissonance reduction open other than attitude change (e.g., "Tax increases are sometimes
necessary" or "The old high school is much
worse than I ever realized before").

This third proposition, then, allows us to
predict the degree to which attitudes will
change following a behavior or decision. You
will find more applications of the theory to
interpersonal situations in the following section.

APPLICATIONS AND LIMITATIONS
OF DISSONANCE THEORY

Researchers have identified a number of situations in which people act or make decisions
that are insufficiently justified, and have
demonstrated how the theory can predict their
subsequent attitude change.

LOWER INCENTIVE, HIGHER DISSONANCE. The more a person is paid or rewarded for a decision or action, the more justification he or she has for doing it. If justification is ample, then even an act that is inconsistent with previous attitudes will not arouse dissonance. For example, if I pay someone $20.00 to tell a white lie (and give the person other good reasons for doing so), there are no cognitive elements inconsistent with the lie other than the person's belief in telling the truth. If, on the other hand, I pay the person just $1.00 to tell a lie, then there is less justification for doing so and more inconsistent cognitive elements; the person will have higher dissonance.

A classic experiment by Leon Festinger and J. Merrill Carlsmith (1959) demonstrates how low incentives produce high dissonance and its subsequent reduction via attitude change. Male undergraduates at Stanford University obtained credit in an introductory course by participating in a study of "Measures of Performance." For one hour each individual worked alone at two boring and repetitive tasks (e.g., filling and refilling a tray of spools). When the experiment was presumably over (it really wasn't), the experimenter explained that the study had been conducted to investigate the effect of expectations on performance. He told each subject that he had been part of the "control group," where expectations had not been manipulated. He then said that the subjects in the other group, the "experimental group," met a confederate who gave them specific expectations about their tasks before they worked on them. This statement introduced the fiction necessary to induce the subject to act inconsistently by telling another person that the tasks on which he had worked were not boring.

The experimenter showed the subject a sheet of paper on which the so-called confederate's statements about the boring tasks were written. These statements were clearly false, for example, "The task was very enjoyable," "I had a lot of fun." Now the experimenter began to act upset and asked the subject to do a favor for him before he left. "The fellow (the confederate) who normally does this for us couldn't do it today," he said. "We've got another subject (in the experimental group) waiting." He then asked the subject if he would mind being the confederate, that is, telling the next subject that the tasks had been interesting, fun, and enjoyable.

All the subjects were asked to the same thing—to lie—except that some were offered $1.00 for doing this favor (and for being on call to do it again) and some were offered $20.00. If a subject hesitated, the experimenter said just enough to obtain agreement, such as "It will take only a few minutes." Every subject agreed. Each subject was then introduced to the supposed "other subject," actually the only real confederate in the experiment. The subject then gave his positive comments about the task to this confederate and went on to complete a private questionnaire, presumably distributed by people teaching introductory psychology. The questionnaire was purposely not connected in any way with the present experiment except that in asking about psychology experiments, it included questions about the tasks the subjects had just completed. One item asked, for example, "Were the tasks interesting and enjoyable?" Answers were, of course, to be private and anonymous.

Here are the results obtained from this questionnaire. The subjects who lied to another person for $20.00 still thought the tasks were relatively unenjoyable. The averate private rating of the tasks on a scale of -5 to +5 was -.05, nearly equal to ratings given by subjects in a control group who were not asked to do the favor (-.45). But subjects who were paid $1.00 had changed their attitudes to a statistically significant degree. Their average on the scale was +1.35, which meant that they felt the tasks were more enjoyable than when they worked on them.

These results have provocative implications.

They suggest that the less you pay people or otherwise reward them for an inconsistent act, the more they will come to believe that the act is a good one. (This goes for social rewards as well as monetary ones.)

Practitioners must understand the difficulty of carrying out such a plan, however. To change someone's attitudes, you must induce the person to act or make an explicit decision, for without that, you cannot expect attitude change. To appropriately induce someone to act or make a decision, however, may require some sensitivity to the person's perceptions and individual inclinations because you are trying to employ just enough pressure or incentive to obtain the behavior, and no more. It is true that higher incentives would increase the probability of the person's acting or making a decision, but higher incentives would also decrease the probability of attitude change because of the low dissonance. (Remember, if incentives sufficiently justify the person's act, there is little dissonance and little attitude change.) You need enough incentive or pressure to induce the behavior in question, but that incentive or pressure must be insufficient to psychologically justify the behavior.

Anthony Doob, J. Merrill Carlsmith, and Jonathan Freedman (1969) conducted a series of experiments that provided the opportunity to test this dissonance theory prediction and to resolve a marketing problem of a business. The issue was whether the technique of introductory low prices results in higher eventual sales. The dissonance prediction is that a very low introductory price will not raise sales in the long run, for the low price sufficiently justifies the initial purchase by the consumer. According to the theory, a somewhat higher price will attract fewer persons, but those who buy will psychologically justify their purchase and feel greater long-term brand loyalty. Five experiments were performed to test the theory in a group of discount stores that were introducing some in-house brands of common products.

In some stores a very low introductory price was employed for a week or so; in others the regular discount price was posted throughout. Sales were measured over a period of months. The results for all products were consistent. That is, the low introductory price helped sales while it was in effect, but seemed to have discouraged sales after it was withdrawn.

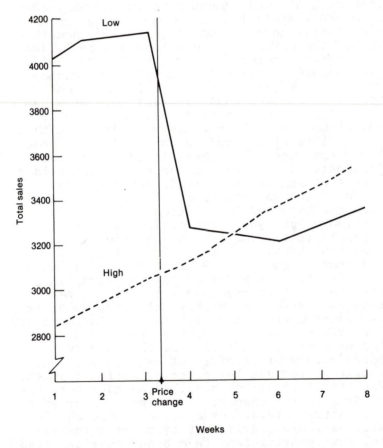

FIGURE 5.7 Aluminum Foil Sales in Two Sets of Stores Before and After an Introductory Low Price (Low) in one set was changed to the regular price (High) (Reprinted by Permission from Doob et al., 1969)

Figure 5.7 illustrates the sales of aluminum foil, demonstrating that lower incentives may produce greater attitude change (and subsequent behavior change).

LOWER THREAT, HIGHER DISSONANCE. Just as lower incentives to perform an inconsistent act or make an inconsistent decision increase dissonance and attitude change to reduce the dissonance, lower threat also increases dissonance and attitude change. Another way of stating this hypothesis is that if people are threatened with high costs or punishment unless they perform an inconsistent act, dissonance is low. To illustrate, if a prisoner of war confesses his allegiance to the enemy while tortured or threatened with death, he will experience little dissonance—the threat sufficiently justifies his behavior. He need feel little guilt about why he has confessed. But if he can be induced to confess on penalty of losing his cigarette privileges, he is likely to experience high dissonance and to reduce it by changing his attitudes (e.g., "Perhaps their system of government isn't so bad after all").

GREATER PERSONAL RESPONSIBILITY, HIGHER DISSONANCE. With high incentive or threat, people feel more pressure to make a discrepant (inconsistent) decision or act. This external pressure reduces their perceived freedom of choice, and with low choice they can tell themselves that they acted because of the situation or because others forced them to do so. In other words, high pressure reduces personal responsibility. Dissonance theorists have conducted a great number of experiments in which freedom of choice or personal attributions of responsibility were varied independently of incentive or threat. The results of these studies suggest that high dissonance and resultant change depend upon a person's feeling personally responsible for the discrepant action or decision.

Joel Cooper (1971), for example, induced subjects (i.e., did not force them) to choose

to work with a partner with a negative personal
characteristic that eventually resulted in
their both failing on a task. Cooper found that
the subjects increased the perceived attractiveness of the partner when they felt high
choice and when the negative trait had been
foreseeable. Attitudes about the partner became more positive, the more negative his
trait (i.e., the more dissonance engendered
by choosing to work with him). Michael Pallak
and his colleagues (1974) found much the same
kind of effect. In their study, negative consequences of a task performance increased the
positive evaluation of the task when subjects
had freely chosen that task and felt personally
responsible for their choice. Finally, in Joel
Cooper and Stephen Worchel's (1970) replication
of the Festinger and Carlsmith (1959) study,
the subjects who changed their attitudes most
favorably toward the boring tasks were those
who thought their lie to the confederates had
been believed, i.e., who had to take personal
responsibility for the consequences of their
actions.

   You may be reminded here of equity, and, in
fact, the responses of people to their own inequitable behavior may be seen as a case of
dissonance reduction. That is, if people choose
to hurt or benefit another inequitably, then
they should experience dissonance. Their distress will be reduced by changing their behavior (compensation) or their attitudes
justification).

HIGHER NEGATIVE CONSEQUENCES, HIGHER DISSO-
NANCE, Remember that attitude change to reduce
dissonance depends upon the occurrence of a
discrepant act or decision. It has been suggested that some discrepant elements may be
introduced after the act or decision. For example, one might carry out a decision and then
find that it had very bad effects, as when one
buys a car that turns out to be a lemon. In
this case, having produced negative consequences is dissonant with having made the de-

cision. George Goethals and Joel Cooper (1972), for example, studied the effect on people of different levels of choice and different consequences of a choice. In one study, they found that if a person chose to make a counter-attitudinal speech and convinced a listener, then the speaker changed his attitude to fit with his speech. In a second study, the same phenomenon occurred even though the audience impact was unintended. (These results are not inconsistent with the data on personal responsibility, since one can feel personally responsible for unintended acts.)

In conclusion, dissonance theory is highly useful, but it is complex; to predict dissonance one needs to meet a series of conditions (such as high perceived choice). The effect one desires (e.g., changes of attitude) may occur in few situations of interest to you. For example, in two different studies (Collins and Hoyt, 1972; Frey and Irle, 1972) attitude change in accord with an initially discrepant essay that subjects were induced to write was obtained only under (1) low financial incentive, (2) high personal responsibility, and (3) serious consequences.

A person who can induce others to behave or make decisions inconsistent with their original attitudes may be in a good position to induce a change in beliefs as well. But here is a warning. If compliance with the desired act is not obtained in the first place and if, in addition, the people take responsibility for their refusing to comply, then they may become even more negative toward the act or decision desired. That negative change would be greater, the greater the pressure that had been used to try to obtain compliance.

In a study demonstrating just such an effect, John Darley and Joel Cooper (1972) offered subjects $1.50 or $.50 to write an essay against their beliefs. They managed to induce every subject to refuse to write the essay. Those who in refusing gave up $1.50 became significantly more opposed to the position espoused

in the essay. This result is what we would
have expected: The more one gives up in order
to do something, the more one justifies one's
action. This goes for refusals to act, as well
as for positive actions.

COMMITMENT THEORY

Many of Leon Festinger's colleagues have
developed other theories in social psychology,
for example, Stanley Schachter and his students
(and their students), the theory of emotion.
Some of these theories, such as equity theory,
were derived from dissonance theory. Others
were not, yet ended up addressing some issues
raised by it. The theory we turn to now,
commitment theory, falls into the latter category. Two questions it addresses follow:

1. Is there a parsimonious psychological explanation for why low incentive, low threat,
high choice and personal responsibility, personal sacrifice, and negative consequences produce attitude change following discrepant acts?
2. If so, does this explanation have implications for other kinds of situations?
Charles Kiesler (cf. Kiesler, 1971) answered
both questions in the affirmative. First, what
the factors listed in question 1 produce is a
psychological state in which a person cannot
deny or take back an action or decision. A person who is "bound" to a decision or an act must
deal with its implications. In doing so, the
person will change less resistant aspects of
the self (e.g., private attitudes).
Second, when there exists a psychological
state that binds or commits a person to a behavior, that state affects the person whether
or not the behavior is inconsistent with attitudes. If the commitment to behavior is initially consistent with attitudes, then commitment should solidify those attitudes and make
them more resistant to change. With this hypothesis, commitment theory was made to apply

to many situations not addressed in dissonance theory.

ASSUMPTIONS OF COMMITMENT THEORY

Kiesler has defined "commitment" as a pledging or binding of an individual to behavioral acts (Kiesler, 1971). What this means, psychologically, is that when someone performs a behavior or makes a decision that is explicit (e.g., public), relatively important, irrevocable, and freely chosen, that behavior or decision becomes less changeable, that is, more resistant to revocation or denial. The lower the incentive or threat (pressure) and the higher the personal responsibility, the greater is commitment.

As we have seen in examining dissonance experiments, the person who is committed to an inconsistent act cannot easily change it or take it back (psychologically). In order to restore the feeling of consistency, the person must either do something that modifies or neutralizes the action, which is often difficult, or must change the attitudes that cause the feeling of inconsistency. That is, the person must justify the behavior or decision.

What if a person is committed to an act or decision that is consistent with prior attitudes? Suppose, for example, a man is induced to give a public speech espousing a view that he already holds. Since committing oneself makes an act less changeable, the prediction is quite clear. The man who agrees to give the consistent speech will be more resistant to change in or attacks on his attitudes in the future than if he initially has the same views but is never required to commit himself.

APPLICATIONS AND LIMITATIONS OF COMMITMENT THEORY

Let us examine one of the early commitment experiments (Kiesler and Sakamura, 1966). Students at Ohio State University were asked to tape-record a speech for a study of regional accents. The speech was to favor lowering the voting age to 18 (this was before the law was changed), and students were very much in favor of such a law. Half the subjects were paid just $1.00 for making the speech; the remaining half were paid $5.00. Then, in ostensibly a second experiment, half of each of the previous two groups read a countercommunication attacking the view that the voting age should be lowered. Finally, the subjects completed a final, private attitude questionnaire. The results are presented in Table 5.1. Notice first

TABLE 5.1 Results of the Kiesler and Sakamura Experiment (1966)

Condition	Payment	
	$1.00	$5.00
Experimental group	.14	.76
Control group	-.025	-.15

Note: Integers in the table represent mean attitude changes in the direction advocated in the countercommunication.

averages for subjects in the control group, who did not read the countercommunication. These subjects would not be expected to change, since they simply made a speech consistent with their previous beliefs, and, except for a slight intensification of attitude, they did not change. Moreover, there was no difference between those paid $1.00 and those paid $5.00.

Now examine what happened to experimental subjects who, after making the speech (committing themselves), read an attack on their attitudes—that is, a countercommunication. Those who were paid more ($5.00) for making the speech were affected quite a bit by the countercommunication and changed their attitudes in its direction. (They became less favorable toward lowering the voting age.) But those who were paid only $1.00 (those who had less incentive to make the speech) were much less convinced by the attack. In Kiesler's words (1971, pp. 41-42), "The more money accepted, the easier it would be for the subject to discard the meaning and implications of his behavior, by simply telling himself that he did it for the money." Those paid just $1.00 could not accept the opinion expressed by the countercommunication since they would then have had "an opinion that conflicts with undeniable behavior."

DEALING WITH THE IMPLICATIONS OF BEHAVIOR. The most interesting results in both dissonance and equity research are obtained when people are forced to contend with the implications of their own behavior for their self-concept or for their future interactions (as when someone harms another with little justification). Having to deal with the implications of one's own behavior is a crucial facet of commitment theory. According to the theory, commitment by itself does not motivate people to change their private opinions or feelings about others, nor do external incentives or pressures. It is the combination of high commitment and awareness of a behavior's relevance to self (as produced, say, by a later attack) that produces change or increased resistance to change. Otherwise, people can simply ignore their behavior probably the most common reaction in everyday life.

The effects of commitment therefore depend on action and on awareness. Forms of persuasion (e.g., political campaign work) and advertising (e.g., coupons) which require action depend on this principle, as in the following example.

Charles Kiesler (1971) conducted a field experiment to identify those conditions that would maximize volunteering and attitudes favorable to the dissemination of birth control information in high schools. The first day was devoted to obtaining signatures for a group called "Yale Wives," on a petition favoring such dissemination, from half of a sample of young married women. This was the "commitment condition." In a "no-commitment condition" for the other half of the sample, the women were not asked to sign a petition. On the second day, half the respondents in the commitment condition and half in the no-commitment condition, received on their doorstep an emotional pamphlet attacking birth control information for teenagers. On the third day, all of the women were polled, ostensibly by a market research organization. The poll was to obtain names and phone numbers of women who would like to volunteer for any of 6 community organizations, one of which advocated disseminating birth control information.

The percentages of women volunteering were: 19 percent of the uncommitted subjects who did not receive the anti-birth control pamphlet and just 6 percent of the uncommitted who did receive the pamphlet volunteered. Only 10.5 percent of those who were committed to favor birth control, but did not receive the pamphlet, volunteered. But *41 percent* of the women who were both committed to favor birth control and received the pamphlet against it volunteered. Thus, the women were most likely to act in accordance with their beliefs when they were committed and then were exposed to an opposing view forced to consider the implications of their behavior.

SUMMARY

The four theories described in this chapter focus on the processes which lead to attitude and behavior change in groups and organizations. Social exchange theory and equity theory show how people exchange resources and handle problems with the distribution of resources. Dissonance and commitment theory show how people adjust their own attitudes and behavior in the context of interpersonal exchanges.

The major features of these theories are as follows:

(1) Social exchange theory assumes that people act to maximize their outcomes (rewards minus costs). These outcomes depend on the amount of usable power people have, including control over others' outcomes, the ability to influence others' behavior, and information. The theory predicts behavior by identifying rational choices given certain preferred outcomes, various levels of reward and cost, and the distribution of power.

(2) Equity theory assumes that people learn to desire a fair and equitable distribution of outcomes and that they experience discomfort when they or others (especially others) act inequitably. To restore equity, people either take certain actions, such as compensating a victim of inequity, or they change their attitudes to justify the inequity.

(3) Dissonance theory assumes that people desire consistency between their own behavior and their attitudes, and that they experience dissonance when they act explicitly in a manner discrepant with their attitudes. Usually, people change their attitudes in the direction of the behavior to reduce dissonance. The conditions that bring about the dissonant behavior affect its resolution. The lower the pressure or justification to act inconsistently and the greater the personal responsibility, the higher the dissonance and the greater the subsequent attitude change.

(4) Commitment theory assumes that when people act explicitly, especially under low pressure or justification, with publicity, and with high personal responsibility, they become committed or bound to their behavior. When people are forced through circumstance or action to reflect on their commitments, their attitudes change to become consistent with these commitments or, if already consistent, they become more resistant to attack.

6

Social Influence

> It took me six months to convince my boss to make one
> obvious administrative change. It took her two days
> to deny that she had ever opposed the change.—A
> government project coordinator (Studs Terkel, 1975)

By its broadest definition, social influence
is what this book is all about—the effect of
people on other people. In its more usual,
narrow use, social influence is defined as a
change in the behavior and attitudes of people
that occurs as a result of interpersonal, or
social, pressure. In the quotation above are
illustrated the two major types of social influence: a change in overt behavior and a change
in private attitudes. Thus, because of an employee's persuasive pressure an employer raises
the employee's salary (behavior change) and
then comes to believe it was her idea all along
(attitude change). It is these two kinds of
social influence that this chapter addresses.
But, first, a caveat is in order.

The broad principles governing change of behavior and attitudes in response to social
pressure are not difficult to understand. They
have been known in a general way for centuries
and have been demonstrated through empirical
experimentation over and over again throughout
the last thirty or forty years. Yet for some
reason the translation of these principles into
teaching programs, management practices, and
other everyday affairs of life has been carried
out carelessly and with a great deal of misunderstanding.

The largest source of misunderstanding about
social influence derives from the confusion of
social influence principles with prescriptions
for management. Good examples of this confusion
can be found in many programs for worker participation and people-oriented job redesign
which are supposedly based in a direct way on
"facts" of human nature.

The danger of moving directly from theoretical principle to advice was recently articulated well by Edgar Schein in remarks he was
making about Douglas McGregor's (1960) "Theory
Y," a set of statements about human relationships and goals (Schein, 1975, pp. 81,83,85).

> Theory Y states, in essence, that man is capable of
> integrating his own needs and goals with those of the
> organization; that he is not inherently lazy and
> indolent; that he is by nature capable of exercising
> self-control and self-direction. [These statements
> have led to the belief that] . . . the essential task
> of management is to arrange organizational conditions
> so that people can achieve their own goals *best* by
> directing *their own* efforts toward organizational
> objectives.
>
> [But] Theory Y is a set of assumptions about human
> nature which a given person holds consciously or uncon-
> sciously inside his own head. It is not a managerial
> philosophy. It is not a management style. It is not
> a property of an organization or a management system.
> It is not a set of external managerial behaviors,
> strategies or tactics.
>
> . . . .

> If workers behave in a demonstrably anti-organiza-
> tional, anti-managerial manner . . . as they do in a
> highly unionized conflict-ridden industry like the
> automobile industry, does this mean that Theory Y
> assumptions are incorrect? If workers feel more
> linked to external reference groups in the community,
> or if they are alienated from their work, or if they
> put family concerns ahead of work concerns, does this
> constitute negative evidence for Theory Y? Clearly
> the answer is no. Such data do constitute negative
> evidence for participative management, but they do
> not constitute negative evidence for Theory Y.

How did this so-called application of behavioral science come about? Knowing about social
influence and doing something about behavior
is not the same thing. Yet confusion of the
two persists to this day. A principle reason
is that the theory of social influence compels
the interest of people concerned with practice.
Its relevance is obvious. This we see easily in
the history of Theory Y, out of which suggestions for practice seemed to flow naturally:

Some thirty years ago, a famous series of
studies was conducted in a factory setting,
the purpose of which was to discover what features of the working environment led to higher
productivity (e.g., Homans, 1950). These
studies, now known as the "Hawthorne studies,"
were especially notable for their revelations
of the importance of social groups in the work
place—a focus that stimulated hundreds of
studies and a whole area of basic and applied
behavioral science called industrial human relations. Among the many findings of the Hawthorne studies was one that since has been
recognized as a major facet of social influence: the closer workers felt to each other
through their membership in social groups, the
more they affected each other's working behavior. Let's consider what this simple finding
means and how it was used and misused by

managers and others when they developed methods of managing employees.

We have seen in the previous chapters that people have a strong need to be liked and respected by others. Because of this need, people seek out groups or particular people in them who will satisfy, as much as possible, their desire for emotional support and approval. Such groups function as well to help people achieve informational and material objectives. The Hawthorne studies, as have many others since, demonstrated that cohesive social groups based on mutual attraction functioned in the work setting (just as they do in other settings) to enable people to achieve both emotional and work-related objectives.

In the "Bank Wiring Room" of the Hawthorne study site, for example, social groups had a major influence on the jobs that workers did. Workers in the same social group traded jobs with each other even though job trading was against a company policy designed to match specific skills with specific jobs. The workers undermined this policy by united efforts to pressure supervisors and build flaws into equipment so supervisors would cooperate with the job-trading practices (Schein, 1975). In such groups, social relationships made possible the achievement of individual and group objectives through the exertion of peer pressure. These data were evidence that workers are not inevitably the passive, lazy creatures depicted in old-fashioned theories of work, but are active, purposive men and women highly involved in the concerns and goals of their group (i.e., they conform to the Theory Y assumptions).

It was perhaps predictable that the next step would involve a search for ways to capitalize on this "real" nature of workers in order to achieve greater efficiency of management. The discovery of two basic interpersonal principles seemed to make this possible. First, it was found that higher participation in group activities leads to higher commitment to the group.

Second, it was discovered that, as commitment based on mutual liking and regard increases, so does the effectiveness of peer pressure.

A number of management programs and reforms in the name of "human relations," "Theory Y," or "group dynamics" were designed. Many of them followed a general formula: (1) induce workers to participate in implementing pro-management decisions about their jobs; (2) redesign jobs to fit better with the desires of workers; and (3) wait for peer pressure, high morale, and individual satisfaction to produce greater productivity (or to achieve other organizational objectives). For example, managers in one factory decided to let employees build components in small cooperative groups of their own choosing (within the practical limits of their training, of course). The idea here was that, by means of free and mutual participation in the distribution of tasks, workers would be more productive. Unfortunately, the employees, though closer together, rejected people who worked "too hard," and later united in militant efforts to press for union demands.

The problem with the formula was not its assumptions—workers *were* involved with their group and influenced to achieve group goals. The problem, instead, was that the goals of the group were not the same as the goals of the larger organization. Workers were involved, yes, but not with the employing organization. Thus, one major barrier to application proved to be the simplistic translation of ideas into practice.

Even when managers were wiser and more sophisticated about the meaning of research, there were failures of application. The major reason was that organizational constraints and external conditions mitigated against the assumptions and objectives of the programs. Consider, for example, Volvo's experiments in work redesign carried out in car and truck factories near Gothenburg, Sweden. The results claimed by Volvo for the Gothenburg program include lower labor turnover and greater

employee satisfaction. Yet neither labor intensity nor productivity along the assembly
line was improved. These were fixed by agreement with the union. Mitigating constraints,
are a major barrier to research (cf. Walton,
1975).

The existence of barriers does not mean that
one cannot try to use social influence principles, or, more generally, behavioral science,
in management. It does mean that any program
must be based on a firm respect for the difference between ideas and practice and a good
deal of common sense about the constraints of
the situation. Richard Walton (1975) has recently described several programs of this sort.
One of them, a job redesign employed in a pet
food factory in Topeka, Kansas, illustrates
some of the subtleties of a successful application of knowledge about how people change
their behavior and attitudes (pp. 118-119):

THE TOPEKA PLANT
This plant, in which General Foods produces pet foods,
has been in operation since January, 1971.* To date
this experiment in work restructuring has more than
met the objectives of the designers in terms of productivity and human satisfaction with the quality of
work-life. The effectiveness of the Topeka plant results from a number of features which combine to create an internally consistent work culture.

Self-managing work teams assume collective respon--
sibility for large segments of the production process.
The teams have from seven to fourteen members. They
are large neough to embrace a set of interrelated
tasks and small enough to allow effective face-to-
face meetings for decision making and coordination.

Activities typically performed by functional units
—that is, by departments of maintenance, quality
control, industrial engineering and personnel—were
built into the operating team's responsibilities.
For example, team members perform what is normally a

*
My latest information on the Topeka plant is based on
a visit in October 1973 and more recent discussions
with plant management.

personnel function when they screen job applicants for replacements in their own team.

An attempt was made to design every set of tasks in a way that would include functions requiring higher human abilities and responsibilities, such as planning, diagnosing mechanical problems, and liaison work. The aim was to make all sets of tasks equally challenging although each set would comprise unique skill demands. Consistent with this aim was a single job classification for all operators, with pay increases geared to mastering an increasing number of jobs, first within the team and then in the total plant. Because there were no limits on how many team members could qualify for higher pay brackets, employees were encouraged to teach each other. Within several years nearly half of the employees had earned the top rate for mastering all of the jobs in the plant.

In lieu of a "foreman" whose responsibilities typically are to plan, direct, and control subordinates, a "team leader" position was created with the responsibility for facilitating team development and decision making. After several years, the self-management capacities of teams were sufficiently well-developed that these team leader positions had become unnecessary and were being eliminated.

Operators were provided information and decision rules that enabled them to make production decisions ordinarily made by higher levels of supervision. Management refrained from specifying in advance any plant rules. Rather, rules have evolved over time from collective experience.

Differential status symbols that characterize traditional work organizations were minimized—for example, by a single office-plant entrance and a common decor throughout office, cafeteria and locker room. The technology and architecture were designed to facilitate rather than discourage the congregating of workers during working hours. These ad hoc gatherings not only have afforded enjoyable exchanges but also have provided opportunities to coordinate work and to learn about other jobs.

The initial work force of 70 was selected from among more than 600 applicants. Thus management was able to hire a relatively qualified work force. More important

than the actual selectivity permitted, however, was
the social and psychological effect of the rigorous
screening and orientation activities. They helped create a sense of excitement about the new plant culture.

Employees generally praise the variety, dignity,
and influence which they enjoy; and they like the team
spirit, open communication, and mastery of new skills
which are fostered by the work organization. They certainly don't see the work system as without imperfec-
tions; for example, the pay scheme has been a matter
of concern and is still evolving, but they are satisfied that the work system as a whole is better than
any other they know about.

Plant management reports favorably on the capacities
and sense of responsibilities that the work force has
developed. The plant has been manned with 35% fewer
employees than if the work had been organized along
traditional lines. Even more important economic benefits include improved yields, minimum waste, avoidance
of shutdowns, lower absenteeism, and lower turnover.

Some managers at higher levels in the corporation
have mixed feelings about Topeka. Generally they are
favorably impressed with the results, but they observe
that a plant as deviant as Topeka creates some new
tensions in the corporation affecting both central
staff groups and superiors in the line organization.
Nevertheless, Topeka has inspired efforts in many
forms within the corporation to diffuse the restructuring of work. The eventual success of the diffusion
effort as well as the long-run viability of Topeka
itself remains to be seen.

Walton notes a number of respects in which
this program differs from traditional applications of human relations theory in industry. A
few of them follow:

1. Traditionally, the focus and values have
   been primarily on productivity. In the
   Topeka program, there was a more explicit
   concern for improving the quality of working
   life as well as productivity. Workers have
   responded, in general, far better to innovations in which improvement in their work
   life is an objective of equal importance

to productivity of the organization.

2. Traditionally, management has not informed employees of the manipulations they intend to carry out or of their real purposes. Innovators at Topeka, however, were completely candid and were viewed by workers as far more sincere than in other programs.

3. In traditional programs, group purposes are often found to be at variance with organizational objectives. In Topeka, it was assumed that innovations would be effective only to the extent that workers' group objectives overlapped with organizational objectives and rationales. (In practice, successful innovators have emphasized the overlap in superordinate goals and have worked to build tradeoffs that are useful to both management and worker groups. Where organizations are not at all responsive to worker needs, their approaches tend to fail.)

4. The traditional approach in many industrial programs has viewed salaries and wages as something one has to use to induce people to do work they would not do otherwise. At Topeka, pay incentives were viewed as a means of achieving equity—the matching of worker inputs to their outcomes. Although learning new skills was considered intrinsically gratifying, the mastery of them for more difficult jobs was rewarded with high pay, particularly when it increased flexibility and self-management capabilities.

The Topeka experiment illustrates that a flexible, carefully thought out attempt to achieve objectives of an organization *and* its employees can have positive value. Similarly motivated innovations will be carried out in the years to come. Some will be designed to satisfy the needs of clients and consumers as well as employees. The values of our nation have changed greatly in the last half century. Better ideas about how work can be structured to fit with them is inevitable. Basic to these ideas will be a better understanding of the

social influence processes which lead people
to change. We turn now to their major properties and dynamics.

THE MECHANISMS OF SOCIAL INFLUENCE

Mechanisms for influencing people (intentionally or not) vary so much that it is useful to
classify them into four categories. These are
explicit pressure, implicit pressure, environmental pressure, and persuasive pressure. Each
of these constitutes a variant or part of
social pressure, the more general term for the
psychological forces that operate on people to
fulfill others' expectations of them.

The most obvious attempts to influence others
use explicit pressure, such as incentives
(e.g., money), threats, requests, or demands.
These kinds of pressure can be especially effective in obtaining overt compliance with
expectations, especially if the pressure is
strong. For example, in a well-known study of
obedience, Stanley Milgram (1965) told people
who had volunteered for a scientific experiment
that electrically shocking another subject was
a "necessary" facet of his research on punishment and learning. By insisting that shock was
necessary, he was able to induce individuals
from all walks of life to appreciably harm
another person with electric shock (by all
appearance).

The second way that social influence is
transmitted is through implicit pressure. Implicit pressure is pressure that people feel
even though nothing specific has happened to
them. They feel pressured because of what they
think others expect.

Expectations that others have are communicated in various ways. For example, people
might observe that others in the group are all
acting in a particular way or expressing the
same opinions. This makes them feel that everyone expects the same behavior of them. For implicit pressure to work this way, a person must

perceive that he or she is expected to change.
Subtlety rests in the fact that the group makes
no explicit move to persuade or influence, nor
need group members intend to influence the target. Of course, the situation is less subtle if
everyone sees deviants being snubbed or expects
other kinds of rejection for deviance.

A third mechanism of social influence is the
physical environment—that is, influence can be
channeled through the physical structure of the
setting. Seating arrangements in schools, for
example, can be changed so as to alter student
participation rates. Office arrangements in organizations can be altered to influence perceptions of status and power. (Remember how the
Topeka plant was designed to minimize status
differences.) Institutions can be placed in
certain geographical locations to influence how
people perceive its role or goals.

The fourth way that social influence is
transmitted is by persuasive pressure. Persuasive pressure is, broadly, the use of words to
influence another's opinions or feelings. Persuasion combines information with implicit or
explicit social pressure. That is, the target
person is given information to justify change,
while at the same time he or she is led to believe that attitude change is desired by the
group and will be rewarded.

These categories of social influence mechanisms are by no means independent although
scholars have sometimes treated them as such.
For example, Raven's (1965) and Gamson's (1968)
typologies of power differentiate between persuasive or informational power (which uses
persuasive pressure) and coercive or reward
power (which uses explicit pressure). Persuasive or informational power transmits ideas;
reward power uses incentives such as respect or
a salary raise; and coercive power uses threats
of punishments such as a demotion. There is
little evidence that any of these exist in a
pure state. For example, Herbert Simons (1974,
p. 179) has argued that "practically all acts
that seem on the surface to be instances of

coercive or reward influence also involve persuasive elements. . . . Protestors, in particular, frequently attempt to persuade by actions
that others pejoratively label as 'coercive.'"
Such coercive acts as sit-ins, strikes, or
threats of firing people make clear to the
audience that the issue is important and that
discussion of the issue is desired—coercion
is thus used to facilitate persuasion.

The reverse is true, too. Acts that superficially seem merely persuasive often are accompanied by incentives or threats to give the
communicator and the message credibility. The
communicator, for example, may establish greater legitimacy or authority (through which respect for ideas can be enhanced) by stressing
his or her power to use coercion or reward if
necessary. Thus, for example, when a boss reasons with an employee, it is not just the message but the authority of the boss that convinces the employee to change.

Most people are not aware of how great an impact the combination of persuasion and legitimacy or authority can be. For example, picking
up poisonous snakes and (seemingly) throwing
nitric acid in another person's face may seem
farfetched for anyone to do, but in laboratory
experiments volunteers have done these things
when asked to do so by authoritative-sounding
researchers (Orne and Evans, 1965).

WHAT IS CHANGED?

To repeat a point made earlier, it is important for practical and theoretical purposes to
distinguish between two kinds of change that
occur as a result of social pressure. The first
is compliance, or overt behavior change. We
infer compliance when a person does what others
expect or ask; compliance may or may not be
accompanied by a change in private beliefs.
Since in everyday life we ordinarily cannot
know what a person's private attitudes are, but
must instead infer them from behavior, compliance

is often the initial goal of social influence.
In fact, it may be the only goal, for sometimes
a person's overt behavior is the only thing
that really matters.

Nevertheless, private attitude change may be
more important in the long run. Take, for example, an employee who desires a raise in
salary. The employee may induce the employer to
give the raise by threatening to quit, by going
on strike, or by promising to increase future
work output. Probably the raise in salary (compliance) is an important objective. But
wouldn't the employee be better off if the employer's private attitudes changed as well—if
the employer wanted to reward the employee with
a well-deserved raise? On the one hand, the employee would experience high self-esteem and
would have a better chance of obtaining salary
increases in the future without having to plot
or use explicit power. On the other hand, the
employer would not feel loss of freedom and
the need to constantly watch the employee. In
sum, compliance accompanied by private attitude
change often has the advantage of increasing
satisfaction in both parties and of decreasing
the need for surveillance and the depletion of
usable power.

OBTAINING COMPLIANCE

The question we now address has been considered by scholars and practitioners for
centuries. That is, under what conditions are
compliance and attitude change most effectively
produced? The answer is simplest when we are
speaking of compliance alone. In general, the
greater the social pressure, the greater the
compliance (although extreme and unwarranted
pressure can produce the reverse—change opposite to that desired, resentment, and rebellion). The general principle of "more pressure,
more compliance" can alternatively be phrased
in the terms of social exchange or equity
theory: compliance is something one has to do

in exchange for something one gets. If one receives more rewards or lower costs, one is expected to give more (compliance) in return. The relationship between pressure and private attitude change is considerably more complicated (because of the lack of surveillance), so we shall consider compliance first.

COMPLIANCE DUE TO EXPLICIT SOCIAL PRESSURE

As we saw, people can obtain compliance from others by requests, demands, threats or promises. The greater the pressure, the more likely is compliance, as long as surveillance over the targets' behavior is maintained. Explicit social pressure is often employed by co-workers or peers. It is certainly not confined to hierarchical relationships. For example, in an organization where workers' positive evaluations of each other are used as a criterion for wage increases, promotions, or other job benefits, workers may use this power to force compliance of peers on other issues.

Explicit and effective use of incentives or threats is not always possible. First, one may be reluctant to exert power. The direct use of power over resources may conflict with one's self-concept or values (as when a manager's goal is to be "democratic"); it may be costly in time or effort; and it may have deleterious side effects. For example, workers who are performing at a high level may be negatively affected when they observe an employer overtly using power to obtain compliance.

Another reason for not using explicit pressure is that one may not have usable power in the first place. An employer, for example, may be restricted in the use of incentives or threat by a union contract that gives employees tenure or has specific rules for conferring job benefits. Or one may not be aware of which rewards or threats are effective. Bennis et al. (1958), for example, found that two major factors limited the influence of hospital supervisors on nursing staff. They had incorrect

perceptions of what rewards the nurses desired,
and they were unable to increase or withhold
rewards.

Finally, the authority system may not be
synchronized with tasks. When this happens,
the person who supposedly has the responsibility may not have the authority to act. Consequently, actions taken tend to backfire,
undermining the position of the person taking
the unacceptable action. With such a "systems"
problem, administrators will be loath to use
the power they do have.

COMPLIANCE DUE TO EXTERNAL THREAT TO THE GROUP

Another way compliance is obtained is indirectly, through external threats to the
group. In nearly every war, there are cases in
which attacks on a city have had the opposite
effect intended. Instead of creating social
disorder, the attack has rendered the victims
more unified and more compliant with the requests of their leaders. This phenomenon also
occurs in social crises, in work groups, and
in organizations. Investigators who have found
increases in compliant, group-oriented behaviors after an external attack include
Prince (1920) in a study of a ship explosion,
Kutak (1938) in a study of the 1937 Louisville
flood, Stouffer et al. (1949) in studies of the
American soldier, and Lanzetta (1955) in a
study of work groups harassed by an experimenter.

The cause of compliance through external
threats lies in perceptual and emotional processes which result in implicit pressures to
comply. Threat from outside a group makes the
group members seem more similar to each other
since they share danger and are being treated
alike in that respect. Increased similarity
facilitates mutual regard of members for each
other and derogation of the attackers. An attack is stressful and causes people to compare
their reactions with each other (the social

comparison process), thus increasing the potential for comforting social interaction. The necessity of dealing with the threat distracts group members from disagreements among themselves and directs their attention to a common goal. All of these factors increase implicit pressure to comply with group expectations.

A classic field study in a boys' summer camp by Sherif et al. (1961) illustrates the impact an outside threat can have. Sherif first created two cohesive groups, the "Rattlers" and the "Eagles," by isolating two groups of boys and having them play together all day. Then he created conflict between the groups by setting up competitive situations, such as baseball and tug-of-war games. Since winning was stressed, the boys who lost games developed a resentment toward the other group. When the Rattlers had won a game, the Eagles retaliated by burning the Rattlers' flag. Negative stereotypes of the other group and name calling developed.

At this point Sherif tried to see what would happen if both groups were exposed to a common threat. The researchers created a series of incidents that seemed to place both groups in danger. For example, on a camping trip the truck stalled and neither group of boys could return home. The two groups had to pull together on a rope to get it started. The result of this common predicament was to markedly reduce intergroup hostility. In working together against common threat, conflict was reduced, the boys cooperated more with each other, and compliance with common objectives increased.

The use of outside threats to obtain compliance will not always work. We can all think of cases in which stress from attack simply disrupts a group. Researchers have found that if failure is inevitable, groups will not draw together following a threat. Nor will a threat increase cooperation and mutual compliance if members can easily leave the group. Instead, noncompliance should be high as each person leaves or attempts to salvage something

from the threatening situation. A study by
Stedry and Kay (1966) in industry is illustrative. Foremen of work groups were given easy,
difficult, or impossible six-month goals by
supervisors. After six months, crews with difficult goals improved significantly more than
those with easy or impossible goals. It thus
appears that outside threat (or a difficult
goal) will unify a group when the group knows
it has a chance, but when the group knows it
will fail, threat simply increases dissent and
conflict.

The quality of leadership would be important
to consider. Sometimes even in "impossible"
situations, an effective leader can promote
hope and guide anxiety in useful directions
(cf. Mulder and Stemerding, 1963). Perhaps the
important variables are common fate and
resolvable problems, not threat per se. True,
threat increases the perception of similarity
and shared losses or rewards—that is, a common
fate. But other events could lead to perceiving
the group's fate as hopeful, and the group will
work together.

A recent study by John Dovidio and William
Morris (1975) demonstrated the importance of
common fate by separating the outside stress
from the commonality of fate that two-person
groups experienced. Their subjects were put in
one of four situations: high stress-common fate
(a subject and a confederate waited together
for an experiment involving electric shock);
low stress-common fate (both waited for an
innocuous work association experiment); high
stress-dissimilar fate (the subject awaited the
shock experiment but the confederate did not);
and low stress-dissimilar fate (the confederate but not the subject waited for the shock
experiment).

In this study, "cooperation" was the proportion of subjects who helped the confederate
pick up 100 pencils that he had "accidentally"
knocked on the floor. As predicted, high stress
caused cooperation when the subject and confederate expected a common fate (both waiting

for the shock experiment). Stress inhibited
helping when they did not expect a common fate.
Over 85 percent helped under high stress and
common fate. Only 27 percent helped under high
stress and dissimilar fate. These compare to
an average of 60 percent helping under low
stress in both fate conditions.

In sum, an outside threat to a group will
tend to increase compliance within a group as
long as the major effect of the threat is to
bring people in the group closer together.
This may be an interesting piece of information, but not very useful for someone trying
to obtain (or resist) compliance as an insider.
It is useful, however, to know how effective
the perception of common fate can be, for factors other than outside threat may enhance it.
The appeal of superordinate goals, for example,
can increase common fate, as can feelings of
emotional interdependence and commitment. The
next section speaks to the latter as a means
for obtaining compliance.

COMPLIANCE TO BE LIKED

An individual's need for approval, liking,
and respect often underlies the willingness to
comply with expectations. The individual
assumes that he or she will be rejected by
the group for deviance; caring whether it
happens, the person complies. No one need make
any demands or request anything; others simply
make it known what is desired and reject people
for failing to comply.

Figure 6.1 illustrates some performance data
of a new employee in a pajama factory, which
was studied by Lester Coch and John French in
1948. The worker was a presser placed with a
work group producing about fifty units per day.
As she learned her job, she began performing at
a higher rate than the others. The other employees, fearful that a new standard of performance
would be set by supervisors, began scapegoating
her (ignoring her, teasing her, blaming her
for problems). Note her compliance with the

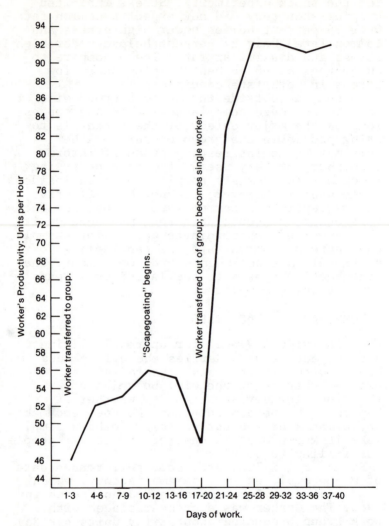

FIGURE 6.1 A Worker's Productivity When Working with and Without a Group Whose Production Norm Is About 50 Units Per Hour (From Coch and French, 1948)

group standard after scapegoating began, and compare it with her eventual performance out of the group. Here, the loss of attraction from others was a powerful inducement to comply.

An individual's desire to be liked by others does not necessarily stem only from a need to feel accepted. The person also may want to ingratiate himself or herself with others in order to obtain material rewards or more power. Michael Hendricks and Philip Brickman (1974), for example, showed that students who were asked to estimate their grades in a course presented themselves in a favorable light (higher grade estimate than actual grade) when their audience was their own teacher, whereas they were more modest with a peer or uninvolved researcher. Presumably, students who exaggerated their ability before a teacher were interested in more than simply being liked; they wanted to impress the person who controlled an important academic outcome.

There is yet another reason for complying in order to be liked: The group as a whole may benefit from mutual attraction. When members of a group like each other—that is, when mutual interpersonal attraction is high—we call the group a "cohesive" one. The greater the cohesiveness, the more likely that group members will wish to stay in the group and to settle conflict by mutual compliance. (Groups with deviant members who refuse to change for the good of the group are likely to split up or lose members.)

The more cohesive the group, the greater the likelihood that individuals will comply with the expectations of others. It is a spiraling effect. The greater the compliance, the greater the potential for increasing cohesiveness, and as cohesiveness increases, members depend more upon each other for obtaining approval and liking, so that more compliance is likely.

The pattern, "We are liked, We like them, We conform, We are liked..." is analogous to one alluded to earlier with reference to the application of human relations theories. Many have incorrectly assumed that if they can promote cohesiveness, or "morale," they will automati-

cally obtain compliance to productivity goals
(see also Simmons, 1978).

As we have seen, the connection between cohesiveness and productivity is not automatic.
Yet one of the first human relations innovations in industry did produce that effect. It
took place in the pajama factory of the employee
depicted in Figure 6.1 (Coch and French, 1948).
Work groups in the organization had resisted
attempts to increase their productivity by
using more efficient procedures. Subgroups were
cohesive, but organizational cohesiveness
(attraction to the organization as a whole) was
relatively low. The owner, who was a former
student of social psychologist Kurt Lewin, allowed employees increased participation in
decision making to obtain greater commitment to
the organization. The most effective participa-
tive strategy was to engage workers in group
discussions of new work methods. Thus involved
with the new methods, the employees accepted
them more readily and absenteeism and turnover
were reduced.

It is quite possible that this program would
not work today in the same way it did originally, for in the 1970s employees do not accept
change for the goal of productivity with the
same equanimity as they did in the 1930s and
1940s; they are much more sophisticated
bargainers.

The Hawthorne studies taught us that while
nearly any group one wishes to influence is
more likely to act together and inhibit deviance when it is more cohesive, group members
may decide to comply with expectations that are
different from the goals of the intended influence agent.

Suppose a man supervises people who are
supposed to work together. He arranges a meeting of employees for a discussion of cooperative
work methods because he is worried about a few
people who seem isolated from the rest. He has
in mind exactly what work method he wants to
use (cooperative teams that pull in isolates).
Through the participatory technique, he intends

the group to choose that method and no other. With a skilled discussion leader who, for example, induces workers to propose the method themselves, he might obtain the desired effect. But it is also possible that increased interaction among the employees will cause them to agree upon some other goal, such as getting rid of isolates. The point is that cohesiveness increases compliance but, we must consider, compliance to what? A poorly thought out method of leadership or management, based on the assumption that if everyone likes each other, they will work toward one's own goals, may backfire when the group members comply with some other goal.

This point was effectively made again in 1951 by Schachter et al., who induced groups to be more or less cohesive. They found that high cohesiveness heightened group members' susceptibility to social influence from one another. When the direction of influence (what the group wanted) was to increase productivity, cohesiveness increased it more. But when the direction of influence was to restrain production, increased cohesiveness restrained it more. Thus, cohesiveness per se does not necessarily increase or decrease productivity. What it does is to make more possible whatever the group members want to do.

COMPLIANCE DUE TO WORK INTERDEPENDENCE

Traditionally, cohesiveness has been defined as "the resultant of all forces acting on members to remain in the group" (Festinger, 1950). This definition, however, is in some respects too broad, because the forces that cause group members to join or stay in a group vary greatly. Some of these forces affect behavior in special ways.

The reasons people have for joining or remaining in a group may have little to do with personal feelings toward others (at least originally); instead, the group enables the person to attain material rewards, information,

solutions to problems, political support, or
the completion of a task. In such cases, the
group member is dependent upon others' competence, skills, or knowledge, and the group must
work together. This need to work together is
called "work interdependence." Interdependence
increases when group members must rely upon
each other to share knowledge and information,
reduce certainty, or otherwise cooperate to
complete a task or make a decision.

The distinction between compliance based on
attraction and compliance based on work interdependence is sometimes important. In groups
that are primarily feeling (attraction) oriented, the substance of thought or behavior is
often less important than their relation to
group expectations. The group member may not
worry about how correct ideas or acts are as
long as they conform to the normative expectations of the group. But in groups primarily
task oriented and work interdependent, the
group member is likely to care a great deal
about substance—including the quality and
quantity of work and the definition of problems. It matters relatively less to be liked
and relatively more to get the job done—and
done well, if possible.

Compliance detrimental to solving a problem
or accomplishing a task (e.g., goofing off
with friends) will be much easier to obtain
when a group is oriented toward liking people
than when it is work interdependent and oriented toward tasks. In contrast, compliance
that is needed to make decisions or get tasks
completed will be more important in work interdependent groups. These tendencies can overlap.
For example, in a work group that is work
interdependent but also close emotionally,
group members will tend to avoid disagreement
because (1) conflict would delay decision
making and (2) friends could be embarrassed.
Thus they may gloss over conflict that should
be discussed or refuse to back up and reconsider marginal decisions.

Several researchers have emphasized the distinction between work interdependence and attraction based cohesiveness, some using different terminology and operations. The first were probably Morton Deutsch and Harold Gerard who, in 1955, published a paper called "A study of normative and informational social influences upon individual judgment." To Deutsch and Gerard, normative social influence is compliance with the expectations of others because one likes them and wants to be liked. Informational social influence is compliance from a concern for obtaining correct information—that is, compliance due to work interdependence.

Deutsch and Gerard hypothesized that the greater the concern for attraction in a group, the greater would be compliance with group judgments even if they were incorrect. To investigate these hypotheses, they employed a procedure like the one Asch (1956) used (described in Chapter 4): a subject was asked to judge the length of lines after three confederates had done so, sometimes wrongly. Compliance was measured by simply counting the errors that the subject made that duplicated or followed the confederates' errors.

As they had expected, Deutsch and Gerard found that compliance was high in situations where the subjects were relatively concerned about being liked (as when subjects were face to face rather than separated by partitions). Compliance was also high in interdependent groups (as when the whole group could win tickets to a Broadway play if it cooperated and performed better than other groups). But when the subjects could actually see the test stimuli, rather than having to rely on memory, and therefore could see when the confederates were incorrect, compliance was reduced. In these latter circumstances, compliance was reduced even more when the group was interdependent (working for tickets) than when the group was simply concerned with attraction. These data indicate that interdependence inhibits compliance with incorrect group judgments (see also Sakuri, 1975).

COMPLIANCE TO REDUCE UNCERTAINTY

Many problems and decisions have no single correct answer. Groups may be forced to choose an alternative that simply looks right because they have no way to evaluate its merits except through subsequent experience. In these situations, individual uncertainty is relatively high, and unless group members use some objective criteria for ordering their preferences, they will tend to rely upon each other's opinions to do so. In general, the greater the uncertainty, the greater the influence of the group.

Creating uncertainty in order to increase subsequent compliance is a technique that is sometimes deliberately used by administrators and politicians, but more often it is imposed by the situation. Given any task, uncertainty results from inconsistent feedback, from impressions that experts or valued others disagree with the group, from information that shakes the group members' confidence in attributions about others, from unfamiliar settings or emergencies, or even from time pressures that prevent people from searching out relevant information.

The famous radio show by Orson Welles, "The War of the Worlds, produced uncertainty. The show created panic in many who tuned in too late to hear the announcement that the program was fictitious. They thought they heard a news bulletin that the earth had been invaded. Many sought out neighbors and acquaintances for advice (the need for social comparison being maximized under extreme threat and uncertainty). They were certainly open to social influence on a large scale; for example, had an announcer told them to leave the city, they probably would have done so. This kind of dependency on other people's views is common in groups that experience high uncertainty and has very important implications for any person who will be working with groups.

IMPORTANCE OF THE ISSUES INVOLVED

Many people are well aware that the importance of issues affects compliance. In trying to change a group, for example, a leader may play down the implications of compliant behavior for the members themselves (that is, the behavior's potential impact on their future behavior or self-concepts), because if the members think an issue has such implications they may resist change. Or a leader may exaggerate the benefits of compliance to the group. Compliance may be represented as a small favor, which is nonetheless worthwhile to the group. Often, compliance is effected little by little, so that the implications of the total behavior change for individuals is neither recognized nor resisted (see Chapter 4). This step-by-step approach is particularly effective with people who, if faced with the total change required, would resist mightily.

Sometimes step-by-step change seems to be nothing more than a series of unrelated role playing gambits. Terkel's (1975) interview with a female writer and producer of commercials is illustrative. In a few pages are described no fewer than ten instances of compliance with implicit expectations of the traditional female role. For example (pp. 105-107):

"We go to the lounge and have drinks. I can drink with the men but remain a lady. . . . That's sort of my tacit business responsibility."

"If a client will say, 'Are you married?' I will often say yes, because that's the easiest way to deal with him if he needs that category for me."

"He'd say, 'Let's have some coffee, Barbara. Make mine black.' I'm the waitress. I go do it

because it's easier than to protest. If he'd
known that my salary is more than his."

None of these actions was recognized by the
producer as having implications for the kind
of person she was or could become, nor did she
view her "real" self as threatened. Compliance
to social expectations was effected because
it was viewed as unimportant. (You may have
noted that social influence went two ways in
this example. In part, the producer acted in
accord with her company's and client's expectations, but she also managed to manipulate *their*
behavior.)

CLARITY OF EXPECTATIONS

Other factors equal, the clearer a group's
expectations, the more likely it is that group
members will comply with the group. Making expectations clear is as important to compliance
in face-to-face situations as it is in more
impersonal situations, such as in advertising,
political campaigns, and persuasive public
speaking attempts. McGuire (1969) concluded
from his review of the attitude change
literature: A persuader needs to have the audience understand what change is expected, as
well as to motivate the audience to change.
Howard Levanthal's (e.g., Levanthal, Singer,
and Jones, 1965) field studies of compliance
with requests for various health measures
(stopping smoking, obtaining inoculations)
demonstrates the need for clarity convincingly.
When recipients of a message urging them to
take some action were clearly told what was
desired and how to do it (e.g., subjects were
given the address of a clinic where inoculations could be obtained), compliance was much
more likely. In another study, people who were
induced to write down and review their reasons
for future acts of compliance (making expectations clear) increasingly adhered to the decision to do so (Hoyt and Janis, 1975).
Yet those desiring compliance in others often

avoid transmitting clear expectations. Their
messages are unclear or conflicting. Here is an
employer's double message quoted from Terkel's
Working (1975), this time from a copy chief in
an advertising agency (p. 117):

"There's a kind of cool paradox in advertising. There's a pressure toward the safe, tried
and true that has worked in the past. But
there's a tremendous need in the agency business for the fresh and new, to differentiate
this agency from another. Writers are constantly torn between these two goals: selling the
product and selling themselves. If you do what
they tell you, you're screwed. If you don't do
what they tell you, you're fired."

Why does this happen? Often influence agents
or persuaders are themselves in a double
bind—damned if they do and damned if they
don't. They hesitate to make expectations explicit because the clearer they make their expectations, the more likely they are to attract
attention to their intent to influence. If
these intentions are made salient, others may
(1) suspect that the persuader is biased, (2)
suspect that the persuader is motivated only
by self-interest, or (3) become aware of the
implications of compliance for themselves. Such
suspicions and concerns can cause people to react in the opposite way from what is desired.
For example, Kiesler and Kiesler (1964) showed
that an audience which had been forewarned that
attitude influence was the purpose of a message
was much less likely to be convinced by a persuasive speech than was an audience not so informed.

In making expectations clear, therefore, it
is important for an influence agent not to appear to have malicious or manipulative intent
nor to focus too much attention on the act of
compliance. In this regard, a highly attractive, expert, or trustworthy persuader has the
advantage. His or her intent is less likely to
be regarded with suspicion; the appearance of

needing compliance is less salient; the persuader may be assumed to have objective reasons
for urging change. Even if a manipulative intent is clear, the audience may be more than
willing to follow the lead of such a person.
In fact, Judson Mills and Elliot Aronson (1965)
showed that the clear intent to persuade facilitated influence when a very attractive female
student was speaking to male undergraduates.

The communicator low in prestige or credibility has a more difficult problem. The best
strategy is to make expectations clear but
render the intent of the persuasive attempt
benign. One way is to argue against what seems
to be one's own best interests. Walster,
Aronson, and Abrahams (1966), for example,
found that a felon was as effective as a prose-
cutor was in arguing for a more powerful court
system.

In conclusion, the person desiring compliance
must make expectations clear and offer social,
material or informational rewards. But if he
or she is not very powerful, expert, trustworthy, or attractive, the method of communicating social pressure should be subtle. Explicit demands for change would produce suspicion and resistance.

COMPLIANCE AS A COMMITMENT

Compliance begets compliance. That is, if an
influence agent can cause another person's behavior to change, it is likely that the influence agent will be successful again with
the same person. Moreover, the person who has
changed will be more likely in the future to
act along the same lines even without the influence agent.

Compliance is a public behavior that is committing. If it is performed with high perceived
choice and relatively low justification, the
person will change attitudes so that they are
consistent with the compliance. Now having
come to accept or believe in the compliant

act, the person will resist attempts to influence him or her in other directions and in the future will tend to act in the same way.

The commitment *principle* is fairly simple, but to make specific predictions consider that a person who has complied is probably committed to several different things, such as (1) behaving in a particular manner, (2) reacting positively to a particular other person or group, and (3) having been the sort of person who complies with others. Imagine, for example, a man who complies with a co-worker's request for assistance on a job. That assistance may imply to the man that he is committed to working on that particular job, that he is committed to helping the other person, and/or that he is committed to being a charitable type of person. Will he become more favorable toward helping in general, toward the person he helped, or toward the particular job on which he assisted? The answer is that his attitudes about all three may change positively (or he may resist change in the opposite direction), but this will depend on how he justifies his behavior. If he helped "because the co-worker is a good guy," for example, he will tend to help that co-worker again in the future but not necessarily to help anybody else who asks or to work on the job when no help is needed.

THE FOOT-IN-THE-DOOR TECHNIQUE

It will be clear now why a technique called the "foot-in-the-door technique" works rather well. The foot-in-the-door technique involves inducing commitment to a small action, which is then followed by a request for a large action. A study by Jonathan Freedman and Scott Fraser (1966) demonstrates the technique. They hypothesized that once a person has granted a small favor, he or she will be more likely to do a large favor. Freedman and Fraser contacted suburban housewives in their homes and asked them to either sign a petition or place a small sign in their window. The message on each favored either the beautification of California or safe driving. Two weeks later a different person returned and asked each housewife to place a large, unattractive billboard promoting auto safety on her front lawn. A control group was asked only the large favor. The data illustrated the foot-in-the-door effect (here the foot-in-the-door = the small favor). The women who had complied with either of the small requests were much more likely to comply with the larger one than were those just asked the large favor. A similar finding was reported by Mark Snyder and Michael Cunningham (1975), who measured the willingness of people to participate in a lengthy telephone survey of thirty questions after a previous telephone request to answer just eight questions. Both studies illustrate the effectiveness of gaining initial compliance. The person who complies becomes committed to compliant behavior, and subsequent compliance is more likely. Probably, the more similar the small act is to the large, the greater the subsequent compliance because the implications of the small act for the large are clearer.

INTERPERSONAL INTERACTION

Snyder and Cunningham's study of the foot-in-the-door technique included a condition in which people were telephoned and asked a large favor that was so demanding it would certainly be turned down. As were the other subjects, these people were telephoned later by a different person with a request to answer the thirty-question survey. Few people in that condition agreed to the second survey. As expected, producing a commitment to *not comply* reduced the chance of producing later compliance. These data seem inconsistent with the study by Cialdini et al. (1975) that was described in Chapter 5. In that study pedestrians who turned down an experimenter's large request to help out delinquents on a regular basis were even more likely to comply with a smaller request

to take them to the zoo than were pedestrians
just asked the small favor. What produced the
difference between the studies?

Perhaps the answer is that in the telephone
survey the target was committed to turning down
a request, *plus* any felt inequity could be reduced through justification. In the pedestrian
study, however, the target was faced with a
person in the flesh to whom he owed a favor.
The necessity of rectifying inequity by compensation might have overwhelmed the usual effect
of commitment to noncompliance (by justifying
one's noncompliance). The situation created
pressure to comply with the other's more acceptable request and at the same time to restore equity. (The fact that two studies came
out with "opposite" results is a good example
of why research results cannot be used in practice like a formula or a pill. To apply these
studies, you would have to understand the process underlying both results.)

Interaction with others, particularly when
one is committed to extended interaction with
them in the future, is an important variable
to consider. The more people are committed to
interaction with others, the more they will act
so as to make that interaction easier and more
pleasant (by, for example, complying with requests) and the more they will be motivated to
compensate for injury or to provide equitable
benefits.

There is a potential problem with commitments
to interaction, however, that is important
to understand also. Compliance in a group may
reduce commitment to a particular behavior
because the members are committed to each other
rather than to any special way of behaving.
Once people have acted on behalf of a group,
such as traveling a long distance to meet with
it, they have good reasons for being influenced
by the group in the future and need no further
justification for their traveling to meetings.
Yet without this justification of the meetings
per se, positive feelings toward the group may
increase, while the motivation to meet and

work on problems dissipates.

Take another example. Suppose we have a work crew in which all must agree on a work plan. One fellow, who has just been promoted to the group and wants very much to be accepted, listens to their plan to divide up the work. Considering his attraction to the group, he is likely to give up his own ideas and go along. But, having complied with them for good reason (to be accepted), he is unlikely to justify further their plan. He may still think his own ideas are better.

In contrast, consider another fellow who has less incentive to comply with the group because he is disliked. Suppose he cannot leave the group, however, and goes along with their work plan. Ironically, he will feel rather committed to the new plan, for he will have had to justify his compliance by changing his attitudes. In a sense, the first fellow can tell himself, "I went along with the group because they're good guys even though their plan is wrong this time." The second fellow cannot say this, so he must believe, "The plan is good even though the people aren't so great."

The positive effect of compliance on attitude change when there exists low attraction to the group has been demonstrated experimentally by Kiesler and De Salvo (1967). They showed that if we comply with the requests of people we very much like, we are unlikely to change our attitudes about our compliant actions. But if we comply with people we do not like, we change our attitudes about our actions to justify them. In the experiment, groups of subjects were to choose one of two tasks, a "biography" task and a "collating" task. The collating task was deliberately made to seem dull and tedious, but the subjects were told that everyone else in the group had chosen to work on it. In half the groups, the subjects were induced to decide publicly to go along with the group's choice. In the remaining half, a decision would presumably be made later. The experiment also included a difference in group attractiveness. By telling subjects how others felt about them, some groups were made to seem very attractive and others unattractive.

How did compliance and the absence of compliance with the group's choice affect private attitude change? Table 6.1 shows that when the subjects did not have to commit themselves to a nonpreferred task (that is, when the decision

TABLE 6.1 Changes in Perceived Enjoyment and Interest in Two Tasks by Individuals When Groups Choose A Nonpreferred Task (Adapted from Kiesler and DeSalvo, 1967, Table 1, p. 166)

Were the Individual Subjects induced to comply with the Group's Choice of the Non-preferred Task?	How Attractive Was the Group?	
	High	Low
Compliance	Nonpreferred task = +4.24	Nonpreferred task = +4.82
	Preferred task = -.24	Preferred task = -8.74
	Total change toward group choice = +4.48	Total change toward group choice = +13.56
No compliance	Nonpreferred task = +8.53	Nonpreferred task = -1.19
	Preferred task = -4.16	Preferred task = -1.95
	Total change toward group choice = +12.69	Total change toward group choice = -.76

Note: Each score represents the sum of the change in perceived enjoyment and interest in a task. The subjects' nonpreferred task was a collating job, deliberately made to seem dull. Each subject was led to believe that the rest of the group had chosen to work on it. The subjects' preferred task involved constructing a biography of a famous person. See text for discussion.

would be made later), those who liked the group
better evaluated the group's proposal to work
on the nonpreferred task more favorably. But
if compliance with the group's choice of the
nonpreferred task was actually obtained, attitudes about that choice were more favorable,
the *lower* the group's attractiveness. Thus,
with compliance, commitment to the group's
choice, attitude change favoring the initially
least preferred task was greater when the
group was unattractive than when it was attractive. This principle should hold whether the
initial incentive for compliance is group attractiveness, material rewards, threat, or
whatever. If compliance is obtained, the greater the external pressure or incentive to do
so, the less the attitude change. (See the
discussion of dissonance and commitment in
Chap. 5.)

The dilemma of the person who desires to influence others is this: If one wants to change
private attitudes as well as overt behavior,
strong attempts to influence or raising one's
attractiveness and credibility or high pressure and incentives will be successful in obtaining compliance, but these tactics tend to
lower the probability of private attitude
change. A lower degree of external pressure or
less information favoring compliance lowers
the chances of obtaining compliance, but if
compliance does occur, attitude change is
likely to occur also. The general form of the
relationship between compliance and attitude
change is depicted in Figure 6.2, which shows
that attitude change is most likely if the
group (or person) desiring influence uses just
enough pressure to produce compliance and no
more. Under that circumstance, attitude change
will be maximized.

OBTAINING PRIVATE ATTITUDE CHANGE

Without some minimal level of commitment to
a behavior or to others, we cannot easily

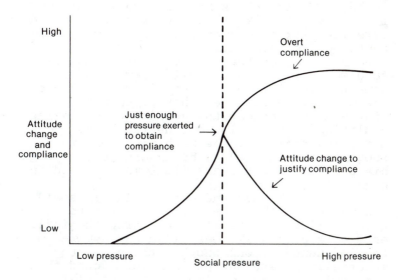

Note: Social pressure includes explicit demands, incentives, and threats, persuasion, as well as implicit or indirect forces on the person.

FIGURE 6.2 Example of Degree of Overt Compliance and Private Attitude Change Obtained with Social Pressure

predict private attitude change as a result of social pressure. But it is possible to change attitudes without commitment, and this may be the change agent's only alternative. In the section below, we assume that the target of social influence is relatively passive and is not yet committed to change.

ATTITUDE CHANGE TO BE LIKE RESPECTED OTHERS

People you admire have the advantage in social influence attempts. Admired people capture one's attention, and by agreeing with their attitudes one feels closer to their competence or status. Private emulation (or

imitation) is motivated partly by hope and
partly by the desire for consistency in the
world, or balance, as Heider (1958) would put
it. For you to like things that people you admire like makes your environment seem consistent and predictable.

Does this mean that if your very competent
auto mechanic praises cauliflower, you will
come to like it? In a sense, it may, because
the mechanic will have a better chance of getting you to consider the advantages of eating
cauliflower than will someone you do not admire. Nevertheless, the mechanic's opinions
about food will tend to be ignored even though
his opinions about spark plugs may be held in
high esteem.

A study by Zander and Curtis (1962) is illustrative of the power of attraction to produce attitude change. They compared the influence of a person who was liked and admired with
the influence of one who had the power to
materially reward and punish. They found that
the admired person was more influential in
motivating a particular standard of achievement
and producing stronger feelings of failure when
the standard was not achieved than the person
with greater reward and coercive power. Field
studies have shown dramatic influences on attitudes produced by people who are admired.
Theodore Newcomb's (1952) studies of students
at Bennington College (and of new fraternity
members) are classics in this area, as is a
study by Alberta Siegel and Sidney Siegel
(1957) of sorority groups.

The field experiment by the Siegels (1957) is
probably the most convincing example of the
influence of admired others. They discovered
that students who admired another group of
residents more than their own maintained many
attitudes like those of the group they admired,
and were relatively resistant to the influence of their own living group. Subjects of the
study were women at Stanford University who
were given attitude tests in two different
years. Some of these women had initially been

assigned to either a large freshman dormitory,
a small house, or one of the former sorority
houses, known as Row Houses. (In spite of
their lack of physical comfort, the Row Houses
were undeniably higher in status than other
accommodations, so random drawings had been
held to assign students to them.) In the first
year, the Siegels found that those preferring
Row Houses scored significantly higher on the
"Ethnocentrism-Fascism"(E-F) Scale, which may
be interpreted as a measure of political conservatism.

A year later the Siegels studied changes in
attitudes as a function of where a student
lived (the membership-reference group) and of
where she wanted to live (the admired-refer-
ence group). To do so, the Siegels compared
attitude change on the E-F Scale among women
who had gained assignment to a Row House and
wanted to stay (Group A), women who had not
gained assignment to a Row House and drew for
a Row House again after having spent the
sophomore year in a non-Row House (Group B),
and women who had not gained assignment to a
Row House and chose to remain in a non-Row
House (Group C). They found that where one had
lived as well as where one wanted to live affected attitudes dramatically. Those who lived
in a dorm had reduced scores on the E-F Scale,
whereas those who lived in Row Houses did not.
But, more interestingly, those who lived in a
non-Row House but admired those in Row Houses
and wanted to move there changed only half as
much as those who did not want to move to a
Row House. This is a remarkable effect of a
reference group to which one does not even
belong.

ATTITUDE CHANGE TO BE LIKE LIKED OTHERS

We change our attitudes so that they are
similar to those of people we like. But the
question why is unanswered. Evidence for the
heightened influence of people we like has already been cited in this book. For example, the

Kiesler and DeSalvo (1967) study showed that before a commitment was required, group members who were attracted to others in the group were more likely to privately favor the group's choice than were group members who were less attracted to the group. Indeed, one wonders why people would stay in a friendship group if their attitudes did not agree with those of the others.

Some researchers have argued that people have a need for uniqueness as well as for similarity to those they like. In this regard, they have suggested that while there is an acceptable range of similarity, one does not want to be identical to one's friends and family. Therefore, they hypothesize, a person who must interact with people whose attitudes are nearly identical to their own will change some attitudes away from those of the others (e.g., Smith, 1975). Being similar but not being identical is not inconsistent. We all know, for example, of friends whose similarity in life style, beliefs, and opinions makes us feel comfortable with them, but whom we would not emulate in every respect.

Attitude Change to Reduce Uncertainty

Besides attempting to maximize perceived prestige, status, and likableness, an influence agent will probably try to produce uncertainty among an audience or group and offer ways to reduce it. People want to be correct and they want to feel their attitudes are consistent with their values and goals. To produce attitude change, one can shake their confidence in extant opinions and provide proof that another attitude is the more correct. At the same time, the influence agent can try to show how his or her own goals, the goals of the group, and the superordinate goals of both overlap. Until the last ten years, this kind of social influence was the focus of more research than any other. The outcome of this research was to show that people who are uncertain

seek out others' opinions and that they are
most likely to believe people who are seen as
competent, or as having expertise on the issue,
and whose motives are trustworthy. Persuasive
information can be presented effectively by
tailoring the content of communications to the
audience, especially to their interests and objectives.

One basis of the discovery that susceptibility to influence derives from uncertainty was
Stanley Schachter's (1959) studies of stress
and affiliation. In several experiments, students were told by a "Dr. Zilstein" of an impending severe electric shock. These students,
rather than those expecting mild shocks, tended
to want to wait with others in the same boat.
The studies showed that people who are anxious
and uncertain about the future will seek out
others; presumably, such people, in seeking
reassurance, would be open to social influence.

Roland Radloff's study in 1961 was designed
to test whether people would seek others to
evaluate opinions about which they were unsure.
Radloff proposed that uncertainty leads us to
seek out the most expert advice and information
available. To test this idea, he told college
students about the opinions of other people
which contradicted their own opinions on college tuition costs. Then the students were
asked if they would like to join a discussion
group with these people. Two results are of
interest. First, those who were asked to join
a group of peers (other college students) were
more interested than those asked to join a
group of younger people (high school students), and
those asked to join a group of experts (economists) were more interested than either of the
other two groups. Second, those who were more
unsure of their opinions were more interested
in joining any group.

According to Radloff's research, people will
be most influenced by experts, yet we know,
also, that one's peers are a major source of
influence (Chapter 2). How do we resolve the
discrepancy between these two principles?

Are we more interested in whether our peers agree with us than whether some dissimilar (albeit expert) group does? The answer, perhaps, depends upon our interests at the time. If we want to be correct, maybe we will seek out experts. Experts may be perceived as sources of the objective information that reduces uncertainly. But sometimes we want to evaluate how we stand in comparison with others. Then, we will seek out the opinions of friends or information about peers.

Different sources serve different functions. Swimmers observe the performance of the Olympic champion to see what really excellent performance is like, but when they evaluate their own performance, comparison with the swimming times of those of the same age, sex, and training is more informative. Athletes who compete within a particular category need to know all they can about their immediate competition. But those seeking to move up in a category must also attend to what the more proficient do.

Zanna, Goethals, and Hill (1975) demonstrated the importance of information about one's own category by giving the Miller Analogies Test to sixty Princeton undergraduates and allowing them to choose the groups with which they wanted to compare themselves. They found that 97 percent of the subjects chose people like themselves (rather than excellent others) of the same sex, and most of these subjects preferred to see the scores of students with the same college major or occupational goals.

Given these data, it is not surprising that the most successful persuaders are either peers who arouse the need to compare oneself with similar others or experts who offer to reduce uncertainty about the ultimate correctness or worth of our opinions. Which of these techniques is preferable depends upon the nature of the uncertainty and the purpose of interaction. Advertisers can be observed to use both. We see television commercials using "average" people and those using people with great prestige or expertise. In the laboratory both methods have proven to be effective.

The persuasive leader of an organization in a large industrial or educational setting usually chooses the role of expert authority rather than the role of compatible peer. In that case, what will make a message more believable? The following partial list of techniques culled from the research literature may be helpful. Some of the examples in this section are quoted from Richard Borden's (1935) book on public speaking.

1. The effective communicator obtains the willing attention of the audience. One way to do so is to make a startling statement that, nevertheless, stresses the speaker's similarity in values or sympathy with the audience (e.g., Burnstein, Stotland, and Zander, 1961; Brock, 1965). From Borden, for example, here is an opening to a speech urging business expansion during the depression. Note the use of "us" (p. 16):

   "Fifty years ago an old gentleman resigned from the Patent Office because he felt his job had no future; he felt sure there was nothing more to be invented.

   "A great many of us today, standing in the shadow of the world depression, feel like that old man of the Patent Office. For us the wheels of the world have creaked to a stop. . . . Actually, *there was never a time when the prosperity-creating forces of science and invention were as active as today!*"

2. The effective communicator presents a discrepant message that is not so far away from the audience's opinions that they derogate the speaker. Highly prestigious sources can afford to give the most discrepant speeches (Aronson, Turner, Carlsmith, 1963). For example, the expert educator talking to parents may begin with (Borden, 1935, p. 55):

   "Ladies and Gentlemen, the birch rod of 'Don't'. 'Don't! is a poor child-trainer. A positive psychological approach is a much more effective weapon."

The lay speaker might more effectively begin less forcefully:

"Are you, perhaps, too busy to talk with your children today?"

3. The effective communicator uses arguments that are easily understood (Eagly, 1974). Thus, for a key sentence in a political speech, the following is too complicated.

"Even though the municipal sales tax will give us the discretionary funds which our city needs at this moment, it is basically unsound as a tax principle and we should not forsake fundamental principle to expedite momentary cash flow requirements."

These are better (cf. Borden, 1935, pp. 23-25):

"The sales tax should be defeated. Expediency should not be permitted to defeat principle."

Or (if we assume examples follow) one could say,

"Defeat the sales tax. Don't sell the day to serve the hour! We should not tie ourselves to an unsound tax just to solve a momentary financial problem."

4. The effective communicator arouses the audience. Arousal may distract the audience from counterarguing. Arousal may also cause the audience to attribute good feelings to the positive features of the persuasive message (e.g., Worchel and Arnold, 1974; Harris and Jellison, 1971; Darley, 1966; French, 1944). Researchers have used movies, music, pictures, and even fire engines to arouse audiences. Hitler used flags and storm troopers. The ordinary speaker can use words. Of course, the technique may backfire if there are negative features of the speech; bad feelings would be attributed to the speech.

5. The effective communicator forcefully demonstrates the usefulness of the arguments,

for audiences are most eager to listen to
what they can use (e.g., Freedman, 1965).
To illustrate, hear this psychologist speaking to parents (Borden, 1935, p. 7):

"I invite you parents to consider the subject of
insanity, because *you* have most at stake. *Your*
child, today, has almost one chance in twenty of
being confined."

Or a businessman urging others to lobby:

"I bring up this subject of an apparently remote war
because the war in reality is not remote. . . .
Through its influence on Latin American trade, it
affects the number of dollars in *your* pocket."

These examples give the flavor of effective
persuasion. It is forceful. It is clear. It is
relevant.

FROM ATTITUDE CHANGE TO BEHAVIOR CHANGE

Many who persuade others hope that action
will follow. Often it does not. Bickman (1972),
for example, reported that 94 percent of five
hundred people he interviewed agreed they were
responsible for disposing of litter when they
saw it. Yet less than 2 percent of his respondents actually picked up a piece of planted
litter as they departed from the interview.
There are good reasons why. First, action
takes more effort and is riskier than attitude change. Second, action has more implications for the future. Third, believing in
something is not the same as believing one
should *act* on that something. With respect to
the latter point, overt behavior tends to be
more highly correlated with attitudes about
acting than with attitudes about the issue
(cf. Ajzen and Fishbein, 1972). Rokeach and
Kliejunas(1972), for example, found that attitudes favorable to cutting class were a better predictor of that behavior than were attitudes toward the instructor.
Success in producing behavior change with
persuasive messages has been achieved with two
techniques that change attitudes about action.

The first technique is to personally involve the target with action. Sherif et al. (1973) showed that personal feelings of involvement in an issue or group (not specific attitudes about the issue) predicted whether subjects could be persuaded to attend a meeting. Sixty-three percent of subjects who were highly involved attended the meeting. How to get people involved? Lin (1974-75) studied the Reverend Carl McIntire's recruitment of people to join a pro-Vietnam War "March for Victory" in 1970. She found that ordinary persuasive attempts through the mass media were relatively ineffective and that attitudes about the war did not correlate with participation. In contrast, personal interaction with McIntire or some experience with activism (even on different issues) was highly effective.

A second technique for producing behavior change through persuasive messages is one that convinces the target that he or she is an effective person. Many people who have a favorable attitude about something and want to act may not do so because they believe they are incompetent or they expect negative results from their actions. If one can cause a change in their attitudes about themselves, behavior change often follows and is longer lasting.

Following is an extract describing an experiment by Miller, Brickman, and Bolen (1975), who tried such a strategy to teach fifth graders to clean up after others and not to litter. They compared the usual persuasive approach ("Here are all the reasons why you should be neat and tidy") with an attribution approach ("You *are* neat and tidy"). Teachers in different classes were the communicators; they either verbally supported ecology and gave demonstrations favoring it, or they "noticed" neatness and repeatedly commended the class for being ecology conscious. The results of each program are clear (see Figure 6.3): The attribution group, which kept hearing how ecology conscious it was, picked up the most litter (and continued to do so), whereas the

Method and Results of an Experiment on Reattribution
and Behavior Change (Reprinted by permission from
Miller, Brickman, and Bolen, 1975, pp. 431-433)

Method

Participants

The research took place in three fifth-grade classrooms in an inner-city Chicago public school. Two
fifth-grade classrooms were randomly assigned to the
experimental conditions, while a third was designated
a control group. Three female experimenters, all
undergraduate psychology majors at Northwestern
University, were randomly assigned to a different
classroom for each test.

Experimental Manipulations

There were a total of 8 days of attribution and
persuasion treatments dealing with littering, with
discussion intended to average about 45 minutes per
day.

Attribution condition. On Day 1, the teacher commended the class for being ecology minded and not throwing candy wrappers on the auditorium floor during
that day's school assembly. Also on Day 1, the teacher passed on a comment ostensibly made by the janitor
that their class was one of the cleanest in the
building. On Day 2, after a visiting class had left
the classroom, the teacher commented that paper had
been left on the floor but point out that "our class
is clean and would not do that." The students at this
point disagreed pointedly and remarked that they
would and did indeed litter. On Day 3, one student
picked up some paper discarded on the floor by another and after disposing it in the wastebasket was
commended by the teacher for her ecology consciousness. On Day 4, Row 1 was pointed out as being the
exceptionally neat row in the room by the teacher.
Also on Day 4, the principal visited the class and
commented briefly on how orderly it appeared. After
the principal left the room, the students castigated
the teacher for her desk being the only messy one
in the room. On Day 5, a large poster of a Peanuts

character saying, "We are Andersen's Litter-Conscious
Class" was pinned to the class bulletin board. Also
on Day 5, the teacher gave a lesson on ecology and
talked about what we "the class" are doing to help.
On Day 6, the principal sent the following letter to
the class: "As I talked to your teacher, I could not
help but notice how very clean and orderly your room
appeared. A young lady near the teacher's desk was
seen picking up around her desk. It is quite evident
that each of you are very careful in your section."
On Day 7, the teacher talked about why "our class"
was so much neater. In the interchange the students
made a number of positive self-attributions concerning littering. On Day 8, the janitors washed the
floor and ostensibly left a note on the blackboard
saying that it was easy to clean.

Persuasion condition. On Day 1 during a field trip
the children were told about ecology, the dangers of
pollution, and the contribution of littering to
pollution. They were then asked to role play being a
trash collector and to pick up litter as they came
across it. On Day 2, inside the school lunchroom the
teacher talked about garbage left by students and
gave reasons why it should be thrown away: it looked
terrible, drew flies, and was a danger to health. On
Day 3, the teacher gave a lecture on ecology, pollution, and litter and discussed with the class how the
situation could be improved. Also on Day 3, the teacher passed on a comment ostensibly from the school
janitor that they needed help from the students in
keeping the floors clean, implying here as elsewhere
that nonlittering would lead to approval and commenda-
tion by various adult authorities. On Day 4, the
teacher told the students that everyone should be
neat, mentioning aesthetics among other reasons for
neatness. Also on Day 4, the principal visited the
class and commented briefly about the need for clean
and tidy classrooms. On Day 5, the teacher told the
students that they should not throw candy wrappers
on the floor or the playground but should dispose of
them in trash cans. Also on Day 5, a large poster of
a Peanuts character saying "Don't be a litterbug"
with "Be neat" and "Don't litter" bordering it was
pinned to the class bulletin board. On Day 6, the

principal sent the following letter to the class: "As I talked to your teacher, I could not help but notice that your room was in need of some cleaning. It is very important that we be neat and orderly in the upkeep of our school and classrooms. I hope each of you in your section will be very careful about litter." On Day 7, the teacher appointed several children in each row to watch and see if people were neat outside the building as well as in the classroom. On Day 8, a note was left on the board ostensibly from the janitors to remind the children to pick up papers off the floor.

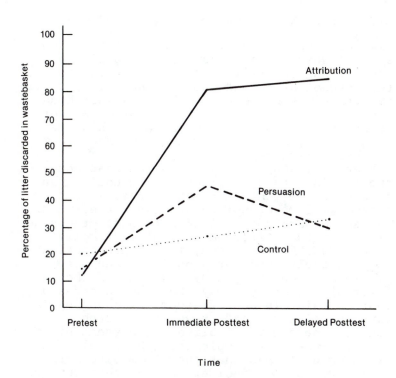

FIGURE 6.3 Nonlittering Behavior of the Attribution, Persuasion, and Control Groups over Time

traditionally persuaded group changed only a little and after some time was no tidier than a control group.

The same technique has been applied in other circumstances. Miller, Brickman, and Bolen (1975) reported much improvement in math achievement among students to whom math ability (or motivation) was attributed. Dweck (1975) showed that positive attributions improved the performance of very poor students; and Loftis and Ross (1974) showed that emotional behavior could be changed in much the same way. The attribution technique seems promising.

ATTITUDE CHANGE, BEHAVIOR CHANGE, AND FREEDOM

We all know of people who do just the opposite of what we ask, who prefer clothing or food we suggest is in bad taste, who want what they cannot have, and who take positions on issues that are opposite to what has just been proposed by others. There is a large body of research to help show why and when this phenomenon occurs, mostly stimulated by Jack Brehm and his colleagues.

Brehm's (1966) theory is called reactance theory. This theory builds on the notion that people desire freedom. Brehm's thesis is that people will make choices or change their attitudes that are not in line with what others desire when their freedom of choice or belief is threatened. For instance, if you are considering two applicants for a position and heavy pressure is put on you by a friend of the first applicant, you may pick the second applicant to maintain your freedom. By changing in ways opposite to that urged or expected by others, one can reestablish one's sense of choice. Sometimes people even choose alternatives or do things that they themselves ordinarily would not consider just so that they can restore their freedom.

There are at least two situations when people become concerned about their freedom. First,

they become concerned when it seems they might
have to commit themselves to positions or decisions that will have further, unforeseen consequences. (Kiesler, Roth, and Pallak, 1974,
have shown that people who are induced to make
commitments will avoid thinking about their
implications if given the opportunity to do so.
Kanfer et al., 1974, demonstrated that people
will avoid making commitments in the first
place when it is likely they may have to follow
them up with action.) Second, a concern with
freedom is aroused when situations or other
people seem to threaten the view that people
have of themselves as choosing to react to the
environment rather than as determined by it
(or by their own personality traits).

In Brehm's works (e.g., 1966) are described
a number of studies demonstrating reactions to
real or threatened losses of freedom. In one
study, people refused to acknowledge and reciprocate a favor because the favor might bias
judgments they had to make objectively about
the favor-doer. In another, people refused free
bread in a supermarket because they were practically ordered to take it. In a third study,
people changed their minds, deciding they really liked a mediocre consumer item that had been
offered but then withdrawn from them. In still
another, people increased their liking for an
old alternative when a new one was introduced
(Brehm and Rozen, 1971). All these studies
point to a similar process whereby reactance
is aroused through some purposeful or natural
threat to freedom of choice or action, and then
is reduced by attempts to restore the threatened alternatives or behaviors.

Reactance theory has undergone some successful tests of its generality in recent years.
For example, Michael Mazis (1975) studied reactions by Miami homemakers to the imposition
of an antiphosphate detergent law in 1972. According to reactance theory, Miami homemakers
should feel a loss of freedom and an increased
desire to have the forbidden detergent, especially if they must switch brands.

That phenomenon is what Mazis reports.
People in Miami, as compared to those in Tampa
where no law was enacted, especially those in
Miami who had had to change brands, felt that
the newly banned phosphate detergents were more
effective than other detergents and they more
often disagreed with statements favoring a
government role in ecology. Other attitudes
that changed to favor the banned detergents included underestimates of their relative cost
and of the amount necessary to use in each
wash. Thus, attitude change occurred, but in
the direction opposite to that desired by
policy makers

These reactance studies raise the issue of
how to predict (much less control) the direction people will go in response to strong or
institutionalized social influence attempts
(including legislation and regulation). That
is, what are the conditions under which people
will conform or change their attitudes favorably instead of acting to restore freedom or
changing in ways opposite to those proposed?
There is some empirical evidence regarding this
question, but mostly we have to rely on con-
jecture. For instance, it seems reasonable that
reactance will substitute for conformity when
the pressure to change is so overdone or inappropriate in the situation that people's consuming interest becomes the process of influence being used. Such is the case when influence is attempted through authoritarian demands ("Do it!"), flat prohibitions unsanc-
tioned by norms ("You can't have that any-
more."), and impolite remarks ("Wouldja get
out of my way!").

We are on firmer empirical ground with respect to the sources of social pressures. Both
experimental and field (or survey) research
have indicated that either strong resistance
or reactance is likely to occur when the people
attempting influence are (1) strangers or
foreigners, and therefore not a member of the
reference group, (2) competitors and others
whose interests are questionable, (3) people

who are either incompetent or relatively low
in social desirability, and (4) people who have
power or status but not enough to establish or
demand their legitimacy in the area under discussion (cf. McGuire, 1969; Wicklund, 1974).
In contrast, reactance is much less probable
when the sources of influence attempts are
peers and others with whom people expect to
interact closely (Grabitz-Gniech, 1971; Pallak
and Heller, 1971; Worchel and Brehm, 1971) or
people with about the same degree of power or
competence (Wicklund and Brehm, 1968; Biondo
and MacDonald, 1971), or, as in the case of
school integration and some strikes, are people
who are recognized as the legitimate, final
arbitrators of a conflict (e.g., the Supreme
Court).

Another situation in which reactance is a
likely alternative to conformity arises when
people are made aware that they are going to
have low choice in a situation. *Awareness* of low
choice is crucial. In everyday life, people do
a lot of things about which they have little
choice, but their lack of choice is not notice-
able to them or they have long before accepted
an implied loss of freedom (Sullivan and Pallak, 1971). It is when individuals are forced
to focus on a loss of freedom that reactance
occurs. Many new laws, court decisions and
regulations have this effect, overriding in
some people's eyes the positive social purposes
meant by the change. Witness reactions of some
groups to water fluoridation, to motorcycle
helmet laws, to smoking bans, to abortion decisions, to civil rights.

Two social psychologists who have examined
reactions to low choice are Steven Worchel and
Joel Cooper (1976). Describing public responses
to various desegregation laws and decisions in
this country, they point out that in some highly publicized cases, protests and resistance
followed desegregation laws ensuing from the
1954 Supreme Court ruling (Brown vs. Topeka
Board of Education). In most places, however,
the legitimacy of the source of low choice,

that is, the Supreme Court, was accepted even
if the decision was not pleasant. Further, a
few states, in permitting discussion and con-
troversy prior to passing desegregation laws,
raised the degree to which choice was perceived to exist. In North Carolina, the state
legislature inadvertently increased perceived
choice even more. The legislature desegregated
schools but offered tuition loan grants to any
parents who wanted to put their children in
private schools. Parents did not take up this
offer, and the public schools were desegregated quickly and quietly. By offering a
choice, reactance was avoided.

We conclude that perceived freedom—as well
as the stature of the influence agent—is a
crucial element of social influence in groups,
organizations, and society.

Summary

Social influence is a change of (1) overt behavior, or (2) private attitudes which occur
as a result of social pressure. This chapter
describes the general principles governing the
effectiveness of social influence attempts, but
warns that the basic principles of influence
should not be viewed as infallible prescriptions for effecting organizational change. For
example, the fact that people work harder for
their own goals and their own groups is not
synonymous with their working for organizational goals.

To understand social influence it must be
recognized that overt behavioral compliance
with social pressure, because it is under
surveillance, is much easier to obtain with
strong pressure (such as monetary incentives)
than is private attitude change. In general,
the stronger the pressure on people, the more
they will outwardly comply. This pressure need
not be direct or explicit. For example, people
may feel pressure to comply with others in the
group when the whole group is threatened by

outsiders, or when the group is a serious
source of affection, or when the group is highly interdependent. These pressures are increased if the issues of interest grow in importance or if the people under pressure feel
highly uncertain.

Low social pressure is an advantage in bringing about private attitude change, however.
To obtain attitude change, it is useful to
employ *just enough* pressure to induce people to
take action or make an explicit decision, but
not enough pressure to fully justify their action or decision. With insufficient justification from outside, private attitudes change in
order to psychologically rationalize what the
person has done. Compliance is a commitment
which causes changes in attitudes (or resistance to change) if the compliance can be obtained with a minimum of pressure. For example, the foot-in-the-door technique is successful because people are induced to comply
with small requests, which psychologically commits them to change later.

Attitude change in response to persuasion,
education, laws and regulations is not easy to
effect, especially if one is interested in behavior change too. Taking all the research
together, three factors seem particularly important: (1) that the audience or targets of
influence feel uncertain and need information,
(2) that the communicator or source of influence be highly credible (either high in status,
expert, attractive, and a legitimate authority;
or similar, a member of one's own group, a
competent and respected peer), and (3) that
the process of influence produce as much perceived choice as possible. Attempts to influence which create the reverse of these factors
(e.g., awareness of low choice) can cause reactance, which in turn arouses attempts to restore freedom of choice and behavior, for instance, by opposing the positions or alternatives that are advocated by others.

7

Interpersonal Attraction

JOB APPLICANTS SAY:

I prepare for interviews by pulling out my only suit and getting my hair cut.

I write down all the questions I might be asked and think about how I'll answer to make a good impression.

I had my résumé redone when I saw what the competition was doing.

INTERVIEWERS SAY:

I do not judge people by their appearance.

My personal likes and dislikes have nothing to do with my recommendations.

We listen to the kinds of questions the person asks and look at actual accomplishments.

The two sets of people speaking above are approaching a common situation with divergent perspectives. One set is intent upon making a

good impression. The other is trying to look
behind appearances for the real abilities,
skills, and motivations of the other. It is
not difficult to understand why each set of
people has these attitudes; it is also not difficult to demonstrate that in different situations their attitudes would be quite different.

The job applicant would not dream of concen-
trating so much on personal grooming or first
impressions when interacting with family or
close friends. The interviewer would be much
more concerned with issues of interpersonal
attraction, or liking, if the tables were
turned. The same person who, as an interviewer,
disparages the effect of appearances and feelings in interviews is often the very same person who, for the home office, dresses carefully, cares about how co-workers regard him or
her, and advocates such extracurricular activities as retreats where colleagues can "get to
know each other as human beings." People tend
to take an either-or attitude toward interpersonal attraction. In some situations (e.g.,
where they are being evaluated) they over-
emphasize and worry about how much they are
liked; in other situations (e.g., where they
are evaluating someone else) they discount
interpersonal attraction. They tend to see
interactions *either* as related *or* as irrele-
vent to liking or love.

Either-or reasoning about interpersonal attraction has two negative effects. On the one
hand, it causes people to worry too much about
interpersonal attraction (such as how much
others will like them) in situations where
they should emphasize the task at hand or their
skills to deal with problems. It causes some
people to be so shy that they cannot even accomplish their first concern—that is, making
a good impression—and others to be so friendly that decisions do not get made. On the other
hand, either-or reasoning causes people to
think too little about how interpersonal

attraction phenomena may be affecting their
own and others' decisions. Job interviewers,
for example, may neglect to recognize how
their own feelings and impressions (based, say,
on physical attractiveness) are affecting their
evaluations of candidates for jobs.

These effects of either-or thinking happen
not just in different situations, but sometimes in the same situation, with the same person experiencing swings of attention from high
to low concern with interpersonal attraction.
A better approach requires a healthy respect
for the complex but not exclusive role that
interpersonal attraction plays in *all* situations. In this chapter is sketched one way of
viewing interpersonal attraction. Beginning
with first impressions and exposure to others,
we trace the outlines of how people come to
like and dislike each other. Then we examine
the impact of this liking and disliking—that
is, interpersonal attraction—on groups and
organizations.

Causes of Interpersonal Attraction

Since interpersonal attraction is essential-
ly an attitude, one might think that the same
factors which cause attitudes about objects,
issues or problems to change also affect attraction in the same way. In one sense this is
so, because the underlying interpersonal processes are similar. But in another sense interpersonal attraction is special. First, feelings
about others usually have stronger emotional
and behavioral implications than feelings
about objects or issues do. It is a lot harder
to ignore your best friend or a job interviewer than an object or an abstract issue, or
even your favorite cause (which, after all,
you can put off doing something about). This
means that feelings about people—interpersonal attraction—are more likely to be tied to
commitments of behavior and emotion than are
attitudes about objects and issues.

Interpersonal attraction is also special because human beings, unlike objects and issues,
talk to each other. We interact with people
rather than act on them. This is a circumstance
that renders unstable much of what we feel
about people; as they respond to us and we to
them, the situation is altered and so are our
feelings. Interpersonal attraction, then, is
an attitude, but it is an attitude that has
more implications for oneself than most attitudes do and is also more changable than most.
In Figure 7.1 are sketched the major factors
involved in attraction.

CHARACTERISTICS OF OTHERS AND
THE DECISION TO INTERACT

When we meet a stranger, our feeling of attraction and the decision to interact further
will necessarily depend to a great extent on
our first impression of the stranger's characteristics and our assessment of the potential
for productive or pleasant interaction. If
she's quiet, how rewarding will that be? If
he's got an axe to grind, how costly will interaction with him be in comparison to interactions with others? If we consider first the
degree to which people are attracted to each
other rather than the intention to interact
further, two general principles are in order.
First, initial liking and regard for a person
will be high if one's similarity to the person
is also high (especially if those involved are
similar to each other in ways that are important to them). Second, liking and regard for a
person will be high if he or she has characteristics and a background which are considered
very desirable in our society.
The first factor, similarity, has been the
focus of more than a hundred experiments, many
of which were conducted by Donn Byrne (1971)
and his colleagues. Typically, the subjects
of these experiments are given attitude
questionnaires to complete. Later, they are

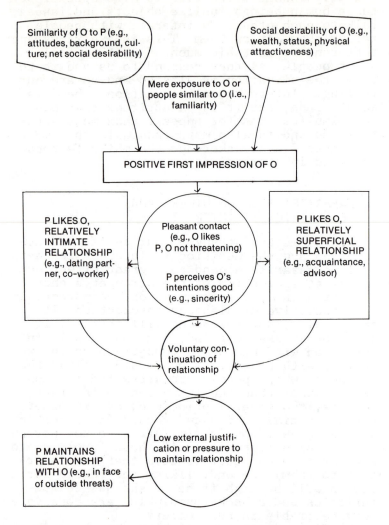

FIGURE 7.1 Simplified Scheme for Some Major Factors
Leading to Person's (P's) Liking of Other (O)

shown a questionnaire that supposedly has been
finished by some other person. The answers
have been especially designed to be more or

less similar to the subjects' previous answers.
If you were a subject in one of these experiments, for instance, you might learn that another person had answered the following item
in the same way you did (Byrne, 1971, p. 419):

21. Money (check one)

__I strongly believe that money is not one of the
most important goals in life.

__I believe that money is not one of the most important goals in life.

__I feel that perhaps money is not one of the most important goals in life.

__I feel that perhaps money is one of the most important goals in life.

__I believe that money is one of the most important goals in life.

__I strongly believe that money is one of the most important goals in life.

Byrne has discovered that when the subjects
are asked to rate their attraction toward the
bogus other person, their answers reflect high
regard for those who are most similar to themselves. Byrne's explanation of this finding is
that people learn and expect that similar people are rewarding. Similar people participate
in social tradeoffs that are low in cost; they
support the validity of one's beliefs; and they
usually affirm the social worth of one's life
style and decisions. Thus, for a first impression of someone, it is not unreasonable that
people base a favorable reaction on similarity.

The second factor of great importance in influencing first impressions is social desirability, also the object of considerable research (cf. Berscheid and Walster, 1978). A
person's social desirability is the net sum of
his or her personal characteristics and background that are considered to be good, valuable
and prestigious in a culture. Many of these
characteristics derive from and contribute to
one's power and status in society (e.g., having
a college degree). Others are subject to
fashion and fad (e.g., owning a poodle). Today,

one's beauty and handsomeness, wealth, intelligence, charm, occupational status, height, weight, and brand of automobile contribute to one's social desirability. If you are good looking in a thin sort of way, and also are rich and well-educated, and in addition have an occupation in which you supervise a great many people, then you are high in social desirability, and people, on first impression, will tend to like and respect you.

Researchers have found that even very young persons are liked more if they have socially desirable characteristics. Teachers and peers, for instance, prefer children who are physically attractive (Dion and Berscheid, 1972). Being socially desirable makes one's motives seem purer to others, because it is assumed that anyone who has such attributes as beauty and status also has high freedom of action. Favors, compliments, or praise from socially desirable people often are assumed to be more sincere than those same social behaviors when they are enacted by people not so socially desirable. (The reasoning behind that perception of sincerity is not difficult to follow: If someone has high prestige and status [social desirability], that person also has power—including the power to say "no" and to ignore others. Therefore, if that same person does say something nice, then it must be sincere.)

One disadvantage of high social desirability is that one is assumed to be personally responsible for one's own fate. (The reasoning here is that if one has prestige and power, then one has control over events.) People high in social desirability are likely to be blamed for their own victimization. For instance, the courts, as you probably know, are more likely to convict people who are low in social desirability; furthermore, people who are convicted are more likely to be punished severely if they have hurt someone high, rather than low, in social desirability. Yet, Edward Jones and Elliot Aronson (1973) have also discovered

that more respectable victims are perceived to
be at greater fault for the harm that has been
done them than are less respectable victims.
So there is a mixture of advantage and disadvantage for those high in social desirability. They are given more credit for their circumstances and their actions, both good and
bad. (Some have argued that heiress Patty
Hearst was punished more severely than she
would have been if she had been poor.)

We may note one other negative outcome of
high social desirability. People who come to
depend upon certain socially desirable attributes as a basis for their relationships with
others may be at a loss if those attributes
fade or are lost. Thus, the man whose money is
the basis for others' attraction to him will
lose friends and self-esteem if he loses his
wealth. The woman whose beauty is the basis
for her relationships will likely be unhappy
as she ages. In one study of beauty and happiness, beautiful women were happier than ugly
or average women until they were middle-aged;
henceforth, they were more unhappy!

All considered, those who have a number of
socially desirable characteristics probably
have an advantage in social interaction. Being
socially desirable causes others to assume they
will like you, commands respect, raises one's
self-esteem, and affords flexibility, for a
person who is everywhere liked can be dis-
criminating in the choice of associates.

Now consider these questions: Since we are
likely to be attracted both to people who are
similar and to people who are socially desirable and since most of us think of ourselves
as average (or a bit better than average), will
we choose to interact with similarly average
people or with dissimilar but highly desirable
people? Will others like us better if we are
similar to them or if we are more socially
desirable than they? In an organization, will
people respect their (similar) peers more than
their supervisors, or will the reverse be true?

To summarize what is probably most correct,

people in relationships which are superficial, distant, and limited in duration will probably like best those who are high in social desirability. In such superficial relationships, people need not fear emotional losses or rejection very much so the costs of association are low, but they can gain from association with a socially desirable person—it makes them look good and reflects well on their own (perhaps hidden) attractions.

In contrast, people who will be relatively close and intimate probably desire association with those who are most similar to themselves. Similarity is not only rewarding in many respects (we have seen that similar people are reaffirmations of our own worth), but it is also a good deal safer than dissimilarity. One is much less likely to be rejected by a person with about the same social advantages than by someone who has many more of them. Thus, we might dance with the handsomest partner, but marry a person who is (safely) only average in attractiveness; we might consult with the most expert person we can find, but work permanently with someone whose expertise is not too much greater than our own. In long lasting relationships, it seems that people are fairly well matched in social desirability.

It is not altogether clear whether the tendency to associate closely with people who are similar stems mostly from the positive aspects of similarity, such as liking to do the same things, or from the negative consequences of dissimilarity, that is, the high probability of being opposed or rejected. Most of the evidence at hand indicates that both motives are strong. People do like other people with similar attitudes and outlooks (as Byrne's work shows). People also fear closeness with those who are much higher than they are in social desirability. Thus, many people prefer closer relationships with others whose *net* social desirability is about the same as theirs. The tendency to seek out people whose social station, on average is equal has been called the "matching

hypothesis" after Goffman's (1952) discussion
of marriage. Goffman claims that the matching
phenomenon applies particularly to marriage
and other long term partnerships. Whereas we
might ideally like to marry a person who has
the highest social desirability, in reality
we do not: "A proposal of marriage in a
society tends to be a way in which a man
sums up his social attributes and suggests to
a woman that hers are not so much better as to
preclude a merger or a partnership in these
matters" (p.456).

In the occupational sphere, the matching
hypothesis applies also. The company hiring
a new employee will usually seek someone who
is similar to those already employed. (Sophisticated personnel selection procedures usually
are designed to do just this, only reli-
ably.)

For the most part, the matching hypothesis
has been tested in dating relationships. In
one of the first tests, Walster et al. (1966)
set up a computer matching dance and studied
which couples were most attracted to each
other. They found that in this one-time-only
situation, high physical attractiveness, not
any sort of similarity, was the best predictor
of liking at the end of the dance. The matching
hypothesis, then, did not predict first impressions of blind dates. Similarly, Kleck and
Rubenstein (1975) discovered that physical attraction was more important than attitude similarity when male subjects were introduced to a
female confederate. Those who met the more attractive woman liked her better and thought
about her more later.

In contrast, net social desirability has been
found to be fairly well correlated with interpersonal choice when future interaction is desired or expected. For example, Kiesler and
Baral (1970) conducted an experimental study
during which bachelors were given positive or
negative feedback regarding their performance
on an ability test. During an experimental in-
termission, the experimenter brought each

subject to a canteen where he accidentally met a female confederate whose physical appearance was either attractive or unattractive. The experimenter arranged to be called away from the canteen, so that after the experiment was presumably called off, observations could be made of the subject's interest in the confederate.

As predicted by the matching hypothesis, men with lower self-concepts wanted to date (match themselves to) the woman whose physical attractiveness was not very high, whereas those with high self-esteem preferred the highly attractive woman. Behavioral measures of interest in the confederate (e.g., length of stay in the canteen, buying her coffee, asking for her telephone number) and in prolonging the relationship (asking her for a date) were highest for the unattractive woman when the man had received negative feedback about his test performance, but highest toward the attractive woman when the man had received positive feedback about his performance.

Exposure and Propinquity in the Development of Interpersonal Attraction

The degree to which exposure and propinquity lead to attraction is an important question for social and organizational policy. Does exposure to people of different cultures make us more favorable toward them? Does school integration decrease prejudice? Should organizations encourage supervisors to join their work groups? Should bargainers with opposing interests meet more or less often, face-to-face or not? The general answer is that while mere exposure of people to each other does seem to enhance their attractiveness, interactions of poor quality may reverse any such positive effect.

If we do not have to worry about the quality of interaction or the particulars of the situation (e.g., how much conflict is inherent in the setting), then increasing exposure will familiarize people with each other and cause them to feel more comfortable, each of which will lead to increased liking. Research on this topic has been conducted by Robert Zajonc (e.g., 1968), who has proposed that unfamiliar stimuli are arousing and that arousal is likely to make people feel uncomfortable (the assumption being that evolutionary processes have made us react to strangeness with alarm). Increasing exposure to a strange stimulus ought to reduce its arousing properties and enhance its attractiveness. This hypothesis, called the "mere exposure hypothesis," is said to apply to people, as well as to music, art, and ideas: Other things equal, repeated exposure to a person (or any other stimulus) enhances attraction. Many studies support this hypothesis (cf. Zajonc, 1974). In one, evaluations of yearbook pictures improved with increases in the frequency of exposure, and in another, liking of actual people increased with greater exposure to them (e.g., Saegert, Swap, and Zajonc, 1973).

There are very good reasons for hoping that exposure, if extended to contact in social groups or organizations, will reduce anxiety and threat, and increase interpersonal attraction. Think what could be accomplished if we could simply throw people together and expect harmonious relationships! The data, however, are mixed. On the positive side there is a report by Festinger, Schachter, and Back (1950) that people who lived close to each other in a housing project (or even had sidewalks in common) were more likely to be in contact with each other and were more attracted to each other than people who lived further apart. Deutsch and Collins (1951) found that blacks and whites who shared a common housing project were less prejudiced toward each other than blacks and whites placed in segregated housing projects. There is also a more recent study by Segal (1974), who studied police at a state training academy. Trainees were assigned rooms and seats in alphabetical order, and their closest friends turned out to be those whose names began with identical or contiguous letters in the alphabet. Exposure and contact, here, led to liking.

On a more pessimistic note, Festinger and Kelley (1951) found that residents of a housing project who thought one another to be "low class" did not like each other in spite of their exposure to each other. When community organizers tried to develop a tenants' organization, that simply intensified antipathies. News reports of protests accompanying forced school integration confirm such pessimism.

What makes the difference? Mainly, it is the degree to which contact and interaction is pleasant and is perceived to be voluntary. With pleasant interaction come the relaxation of anxiety, the realization that others are more similar (or human) than one might have thought, and the growth of interdependence through mutual tradeoffs, obligations, and exchanges. With choice (or the freedom to leave the relationship) come commitment to the relationship and justification of the contact.

Pleasant interaction will have a greater probability of happening in the first place if people have an open or positive attitude. Pleasant interaction will also be more probable if the people involved are more homogeneous in attitudes and goals (if not in personal characteristics). Thus, those who are largely from the same backgrounds and have an occupation in common (such as police trainees) have the best chance; next would come people who work or study in the same place (such as students in the same school); and last, people who live or work near each other but are very different in status and culture (such as those living in adjacent but segregated housing projects).

The problem in many social and organizational settings is that we are most likely to have to *plan* exposure and contact for people who are dissimilar to each other and who have already chosen not to interact. How this can be done successfully requires some subtlety of approach, but that it can be done is evidenced by positive results in most southern communities

after legislated school integration, in com-
panies that have placed executives in work
crews, and in universities that have encouraged
full-time deans to teach undergraduates as
well as to administrate. Some successful approaches involve increasing the perceived
choice of the participants and using just
minimal pressure to induce interaction (as
when there is implicit social pressure but
no overt regulation which forces deans to
teach). Success may require that the physical and social setting be designed so that
common objectives and attitudes will be salient. For example, the supervisor who regularly
puts in a hard day with employees (not doing
the same job necessarily) will be more likely
to empathize with the role of the supervised
than will the supervisor who walks down from
his office for a short tour of the spruced-up
work premises or who pretends to be like everybody else for a few days.

THE "NICE GUY" AND DEVELOPMENT
OF THE RELATIONSHIP

As an acquaintanceship progresses, the
chances for an enduring friendship and increasing intimacy depend less and less on personal characteristics, such as physical attractiveness, agreement on political questions,
or role similarity, and more on the nature of
the interaction itself. (Partly, this is because those who do not make a good first impression never get a chance to interact. (The
book with an unattractive cover is not read,
so we never find out how enjoyable it is.)

As we get used to a person, we notice looks
and labels less and behavior towards us more.
The way the person treats *us* colors our view
of him or her (e.g., we imagine that the person
is always nice). In a sense, another's behavior toward us engulfs our field of perception.

The most important factor in determining the
continuation of a relationship is the perception

that one is liked. People like those who like them, and this correlation is so strong as to be useful in research projects where one wants to study the effect of attraction toward others. For example, in the Kiesler and DeSalvo (1967) study discussed earlier, strong liking for others in a group was created simply by giving subjects feedback that the others liked them. Even the mere anticipation of being liked promotes liking for others.

The politeness of most interaction and the usual assumption that one is a likable person will lead to our typically perceiving that others like us. But there are some kinds of situations in which we will perceive that some-one does not like us, whether true or not. And it is in these situations that friendship and intimacy will not develop. The problematic situation is one in which we suspect the mo-tives of the other person (for example, he seems pleasant, but we know he has a promotion to gain by ingratiating himself). In situations

Where there is a suspicion that anothers' intent is selfish, manipulative, or insincere, we also get the impression that he or she does not really like us, whatever the surface be-havior. What seems to be important is not so much the pleasantness of the behavior itself, but people's impression of its cause. For ex-ample, Garrett and Libby (1973) showed that subjects retaliated for another's doing harm when the other person had acted intentionally, but that the subjects ignored harm when it was perceived as unintentional.

Several bodies of research have illustrated the importance of attributing good intentions and sincerity if people are to like each other. A series of studies by Elliot Aronson, Darwin Linder, and David Mettee, among others, on the so-called "gain-loss effect" is one. These studies were originally stimulated by the biblical phenomenon of the prodigal son: the son who left home and then returned was more beloved than was the son who continually stayed loyal. Aronson and Linder (1965) tried to

discover whether this phenomenon was typical:
do we like someone better who likes us after a
period of indifference or hostility than one
who liked us all along? They and others (e.g.,
Mettee, 1971) found this to be so. The reason
is perhaps that a person who shows liking for
us continuously seems to be undiscerning (we
suspect that such a person likes everyone and
thinks we are nothing really special). The
person also seems not to be reacting to us as
individuals, since there is no change in behavior. In contrast, the person who begins with
some coolness—even hostility—and then shows
increasing regard for us demonstrates a sincere reaction to our own individual qualities.

It is, then, not the total amount of affection that another accords us that is important, but the intentionality, sincerity,
and uniqueness of the affectionate behavior.
The reverse, as we would expect, is also the
case: A person who is hostile to us after a
period of affection is more disliked than one
who was hostile all along because the former
seems more intentional and more personally)
directed.

A second group of studies is also relevant
to the topic of good intentions. These are
studies by Edward Jones, Kenneth Gergen, and
others (e.g., Jones, 1964) on how people
react to ingratiation attempts. What this research shows is that an attribution of ulterior
motives may all but destroy the ordinarily
positive effects of being flattered, listened
to, complied with, done favors for, and generally, dealt with pleasantly. For instance,
subjects who serve in experiments usually like
people who express approval of them, but not if
they suspect the others themselves seek approval (Lowe and Goldstein, 1970).

Even calling a person by name is unsuccessful if it is perceived to be a self-seeking
strategy. Chris Kleinke, Richard Staneski, and
Pam Weaver (1972) conducted two experiments in
which a naive subject was asked to talk to an
individual who called him by name. In the first

experiment, a lovely woman interviewed two men at a time. She called one by his name often, but the other only once. The men whose names she used often liked her more. In the second experiment the result was different. A man and a woman were asked to get to know each other during a fifteen-minute discussion period. The man had been instructed either to call the woman by name frequently or not to use her name at all. In this study, name calling produced a negative reaction. The man who used the woman's name was rated less positively, was viewed as purposely trying to make a good impression, and, further, was viewed less desirable as a future discussion partner. Think about the several reasons why this last result could have occurred; all of them are related to the perception of ulterior motives.

A third group of studies which indicate the importance of intentions was designed to investigate reactions to deviance. If people's intentions are considered more important for liking than their overt behavior, then a person who intends well but violates norms would be more acceptable than a person who behaves well but means to do harm. The data seem to indicate that this is so, if the norm violator is known to have good intentions (cf. Wicklund, 1974; Kiesler, 1973).

Why is intention so important? There is a very good reason. Intention is what explains the present, justifies the past, and predicts the future. If we cannot guess another's motives, we are at a loss in interaction. Consider the assumptions of most social exchanges; one should be able to count on the other person's responding positively to reward and negatively to cost, sticking to agreed tradeoffs and compromises, and being motivated to achieve efficient, regular interaction. But what if the other ignores rewards, breaks agreements, or responds positively to "costs?" What if his or her definition of the situation, as Goffman (1959) calls it, violates our own? Then we should become very uncomfortable, for our frame of reference for the situation is shaken; we do not know what the other will do or really wants, and our future in the interaction is unpredictable. Thus, showing affection for another, acting appropriately in another's presence, treating another equitably: all will go for naught if other people suspect that our private attitudes and feelings are not sincere or if we suspect the same thing of them.

EFFORT, SACRIFICE, AND COMMITMENT TO THE RELATIONSHIP

In Chapter 6, the importance of psychological commitments to people was reviewed. High choice and minimal pressure to interact, providing that there is interaction, will increase one's willing obligation to another and one's liking. Once committed, people reduce inequity in ways promotive of the relationship (e.g., compensation for, rather than justification of, harming the other); they change attitudes to be consistent with the relationship; and they are resistant to attacks on the relationship. Nevertheless, there is a variation on this theme not yet mentioned—suffering for another. Suffering for another person increases commitment even more.

The suffering-love theme has provided the plot of many a story: Romeo and Juliet's love flourished within a climate of feuding and family objections; the trainee who suffered the greatest hardships turned out to be the most loyal Marine. These stories seem to make heroes and heroines of people who love in spite of their sacrifices. But current theory and research suggest that effort and sacrifice nourish affection. Elliot Aronson and Judson Mills (1959) put it like this: The more effort or sacrifice we devote to another, the more we will be motivated to explain the effort and sacrifice. That explanation will often be that we really must like (love) the person for whom we have suffered, or we would not have chosen

to do so. Since we can neither deny nor take
back those efforts and since the other can
never pay us back in the same way, our attitudes must change to justify our costs.

Aronson and Mills' experiment to test this
(dissonance theory) effort hypothesis involved
having young women go through an initiation
procedure before they could join a "sex discussion" (which afterwards turned out to be
very boring). In some cases the initiation was
a mild one, but in others it was rather embarrassing since the women had to pronounce a
list of extremely salacious words in front of
the male experimenter. The data showed that
those who went through the more severe initiation procedure liked the group much more than
those who experienced only the mild initiation.

This experiment was redone by two researchers
(Gerard and Mathewson, 1966), who questioned
whether the Aronson-Mills results were really
due to dissonance reduction. Perhaps, they
said, the so-called "severe initiation" was
sexually arousing and not severe at all. To
find out, they conducted a conceptual replication of the Aronson-Mills study, using electric
shocks instead of obscene words in the initi-
ating procedure. Their results confirmed the
effort-dissonance hypothesis. People who experienced painful shocks in order to become
members of a dull group liked the group better
than those who experienced mild shocks.

Sociologists have documented the same process
in whole societies. Rosabeth Kanter (1972), for
example, found that the more successful utopian
communes have historically been those that required the greatest sacrifices from their members, such as abstaining from dancing, giving
up sex, owning no jewelry or personal property,
not smoking, not drinking, and even refusing
compensation for work. Her data fit well with
commitment and dissonance theory, for sacrifice
is a cost that requires justification and binds
group members to each other.

FULFILLING PERSONAL NEEDS

Having discussed how interpersonal attraction
is affected by the characteristics and behavior
of another, the person's own commitment and
behavior, and the setting, we should consider
one additional—and important—factor; that is,
the extent to which a person's needs are cross-
situational. Does a chronically high or low
level of self-esteem affect regard and affection for others? This section merits some
uncertainty because research and theory in
this area are not well developed. Yet the topic
is important.

Take, for example, a person who is not like
the average people we have so far discussed.
Suppose this person is a woman who thinks she
is not average, but instead, an unworthy, un-
likable sort. It is clear that we might not
expect the same of her as we would of most
people. Will she choose to marry a person she
thinks is like herself, or someone who she
thinks is everything she is not? Will she like
people who like her, or will she avoid them because she thinks their affection must be false?
Will she be committed to someone she suffers
for, or will she simply feel that suffering is
her lot anyway? Our theories do not yet adequately handle this problem of individual
proclivity.

Most research on individual differences in
attraction concerns the ability to love by people who have low self-esteem. The person who
has low self-esteem seems to be at once more in
need of affection and more afraid it will not
be attained (analogous to the employee who
would like to tell his supervisor about a problem but is afraid he will be laughed at).
The resolution of such approach-avoidance conflict would seem to depend on the relative degree of security and love offered by the other
person (cf. Dion and Dion, 1975). Walster's
(1965) study of self-esteem demonstrated that

females with lower self-esteem liked a clearly
accepting male who had requested a date more
than did females with higher self-esteem. In
that study, however, the man proved by his actions that he would not reject the subjects.
Unfortunately, ordinary life does not usually
fit that situation. When people most need affection, support or reassurance, they often act
in ways that make others uncomfortable, thereby
creating a higher probability of being rejected
just when they most dread it.

Whether or not research on self-esteem and
romance can be applied to relationships in
less intimate situations is an open question.
Those who study work adjustment (e.g., Ziller
et al.) argue that individual differences in
self-esteem are extremely important for forming
basic attitudes towards supervisors, co-workers
and others in the organization.

Scientifically, little is known about the
processes involved, but there are many reports
of aberrant interpersonal working relationships
brought about by low self-esteem (sometimes referred to as "insecurity"). For instance, one
study of management (Burns, 1955) uncovered a
clique made up of older men who did not expect
promotion. These men banded together for social
support and intimacy within an unsatisfactory
job setting (as is reasonable). Less fortunately for the company, these men developed a set
of extremely negative norms about relations
with managers who were not members of the
clique. These norms supported feelings of dislike, attitudes unfavorable to the bonus system
and to other aspects of the company which were
favored by most employees, and attempts to
interfere with the activities of management,
such as progress meetings.

The Burns study suggests that low self-esteem
is not beneficial to working groups and organizations, but one could easily go too far in
generalizing its findings. It is unclear whether
chronic feelings about the self really affect
one's work except in highly unusual circumstances (e.g., when they lead to alcoholism).

Probably there are just as many cases of people being unfairly accused of insecurity as there are cases in which low self-esteem has really interfered with the job. Bureaucracies, in fact, are notorious for blaming their failures on individual personality problems like low self-esteem and insecurity.

CONSEQUENCES OF ATTRACTION IN GROUPS

Having considered some of the major factors known (or suspected) to increase and decrease interpersonal attraction, we turn now to the effects of attraction. One hundred years ago people were not very concerned about this issue, whether in application to personal affairs or work. Then, some forty years ago, the tide began to turn toward a concern with "human relations." As mentioned in opening this chapter, it was fashionable to argue that high interpersonal cohesiveness, liking, and regard among people automatically led to all good things: high morale, job satisfaction, high productivity, and conformity to organizational goals. Today, there seem to be more sensible questions, more specific questions, asked about the effects of interpersonal attraction. In part, these derive from empirical evidence collected in many groups and organizations as to the nonglobal effects of human relations programs and policies; in part, they have come from laboratory studies examining how different groups work together.

MEMBERSHIP IN THE GROUP

One question about the effect of interpersonal attraction has to do with how liking affects membership in the group. People who want "in" (e.g., job applicants or low status group members) are concerned about whether they will be attractive to group members. People who are already "in" want the group to stick together. Generally, each side finds that high attraction

to and for others is one reason people stay in
a group and invite outsiders to join them.
Liking and being liked in return is rewarding.
Yet there are at least three factors that may
attenuate or even reverse the relationship
between attraction and staying in, joining, or
being invited to join a group. First, there
are obviously other rewards and costs that may
be more important, such as acquiring skills or
income, mobility potential, and the degree of
responsibility and autonomy (or lack of them)
in a work group. In social exchange terms, attraction to others will lead to creating or
maintaining group membership only when it, in
combination with other rewards and costs, con-
tributes to a net outcome that is as good or
better than other alternatives.

A second factor is the nature of the group
rationale. In a group where friendship is the
reason for membership, attraction will be correlated with joining and staying in the group.
But in many work groups, including formal organizations, getting a job done may be much
more important than friendship, and friendship
may affect group membership much less. (This
does *not* mean that first impressions are unimportant.) Anderson (1975), for example, reported that in the long run the clarity of group
objectives and tasks was a more important determinant of desired membership in experimental
task groups than was interpersonal liking.

A third factor to consider, when maintaining
group membership is the issue, is psychological
commitment. As we have shown in Chapter 6,
psychological commitment to a group increases
as the initial, external overjustifications for
membership decrease. Therefore, in situations
where people perceive they have a large degree
of choice among groups or individuals and join
or choose one of them with minimal justification, they will be more committed and more
likely to remain bound to their decision than
if there is no initial choice and the incentives to join are very high. Among these incentives could be the social desirability of

people in the group. Such factors as this can enhance first impressions but reduce long-term commitment.

Because choice increase commitment, the degree to which one's membership is perceived as voluntary affects the relationship between membership and attraction. If we could draw a rough line between voluntary and involuntary groups, we would find something like this: When membership is viewed as involuntary, a positive relationship between the favorability of first impressions and maintaining membership is likely. In voluntary groups, however, people feel more committed to stay in the group, the more marginally positive the net rewards for *joining*. Very favorable first impressions might have the ironic effect of reducing psychological commitment to the group, because people would feel less pressure to psychologically justify joining the group. This hypothesis will

This hypothesis will not make sense if you read it to mean that liking is unimportant in voluntary groups. Actually it means that *overjustification* for joining a voluntary group because of first impressions tends to reduce one's psychological commitment to the group. Perhaps one stays in the group as long as the people in it are physically attractive or high in status or wealth, but when conflict or unpleasant circumstances occur, one will be inclined to leave. In contrast, a person who has joined a group with less external justification will feel a bond toward the group in spite of negative events and is more likely to maintain the relationship. A simple example is of a woman who joins a company because she is impressed by the wealth and social status of its executives. When hard financial times come, she feels detached and without any reason to stay, while her colleague—for whom social status meant little—stays on. The latter, who perhaps joined the company reluctantly, has been seeking ways since to justify doing so, and now feels more committed to the group and intrinsically motivated to stay on.

PARTICIPATION

Attraction promotes at least a superficial increase in mutual communication, a greater degree of participation in group interaction, and a lower degree of absenteeism from a group (other factors being equal). But with attraction comes the desire not to lose it. People who like each other may withdraw from any group interaction that threatens their relationships, even if that interaction promotes progress toward other group objectives. We sometimes find lower, rather than higher, participation in group interaction among people who like each other. In particular, high interpersonal attraction seems to lower the degree of interaction when conflict or embarrassment is possible. For example, Riecken (1952) studied a work camp where members placed a high value on friendly interaction. Because campers found it difficult to confront each other on issues when someone might have been at fault, they typically apologized for bringing up problems and refused to place blame. Consequently, the group failed to participate in solving some important group problems.

The Brown and Garland study (1971), mentioned in Chapter 2, also demonstrated how attraction may create lower participation. Brown and Garland asked subjects in a laboratory experiment to sing before an audience and found much more abbreviated participation when members of the audience were friends rather than strangers. Furthermore, participation with strangers was brief when subjects expected to interact with them in the future. Attraction may therefore increase participation when things are going well, but decrease it when the consequences are uncertain or likely to be unpleasant, especially when loss of regard from others is a possiblity and a salient concern.

SOCIAL INFLUENCE

The question of whether attraction leads to

increased compliance and attitude change has already been discussed in the previous chapter. Interpersonal attraction encourages compliance with the expectations of others, as well as attitude change, especially when the desired change is perceived as helpful to the group. People who are liked want to do what is expected and what is needed. Interpersonal attraction makes it easier to comply with expectations. People who are liked are perceived by group members as being in compliance with expectations. A good example is cited by Chronbach (1970), who describes a study of department heads and foremen by Stockford and Bissell (1949). These researchers found that when department heads rated foremen, there was a higher correlation between interpersonal attraction and performance ratings than there was between objective measures of productivity and performance ratings. Thus, performance ratings by department heads correlated only .22 with an objective record of the word performance of each crew. The same ratings correlated .59 with how long the rater had known the foreman, and .65 with his liking for the foreman.

SELF-ESTEEM

To be liked is to like oneself. This consequence of attraction, we have seen, may have effects on group interaction and performance because feeling good about oneself can promote personal adjustment to a group. Some people contend that good feelings about oneself and others lower the effect of stress. Evidence in this respect comes from Seashore (1954), whose respondents reported less jumpiness on the job in more cohesive groups, and from Meyers (1962) and Julian, Bishop, and Fiedler (1966), who found that competition between groups (which, as we have seen, increases cohesiveness within groups) heightened member self-esteem and lowered anxiety. Pepitone and Reichling's (1955) study of group cohesiveness showed that highly cohesive groups were more able to express hostility against someone who insulted the group. (This finding stands in contrast to the expected decrease of hostility expressed within the group.) These data, in general, provide support for those who favor maximizing high interpersonal attraction in groups, even though high attraction potentially can reduce the time spent on work and organizational influence.

What might the manager or worker do with all these data? Is it really good to emphasize human relations at work, or is this simply a way to guarantee low productivity? Let us recall an earlier statement about either-or thinking which provides a negative sort of answer: neither alternative is correct. An overemphasis on human relations can, we have seen, reduce conflict so much that good decisions are not made or can cause people to put off decisions they really want to make. On the other hand, there is probably no organization that can survive stress without a moderate degree of personal commitment of employees to each other.

One approach is to accept liking, loving, and respecting, and disliking too, as realities of the workplace. Such acceptance can lead to developing "cooperative productivity," whereby people become committed to working together toward common objectives and respect both their own and others' competence. When attraction is based on a premise of interdependence people will try to take others' perspectives, support overriding rationales, and use criticism productively.

Summary

Interpersonal attraction is the degree to which people like and respect others. People are likely to be concerned about attraction when they are being evaluated or when they are not yet accepted by a group, but attraction affects group interaction even when people are not aware of being concerned about it or do not intend to be influenced by it.

The causes of attraction depend heavily on the type of relationship under consideration. First impressions between strangers are influenced by the social desirability and similarity of their overt characteristics, such as their physical attractiveness. The decision to interact further is affected by other factors too, such as the perceived probability of being rejected or accepted by the others. In situations where there is more exposure and contact, interpersonal attraction depends less on overt characteristics and more on the quality of interaction, especially the perceived sincerity of others and the degree to which rewards are perceived as equitable. As relationships develop and people interact more, commitment to others may enhance attraction (or keep people in a relationship even when attraction is reduced). Commitment to relationships is enhanced if people expend effort for others or sacrifice for them.

Interpersonal attraction has the following consequences for people in groups and organizations. (1) Attraction encourages conformity and the perception of conformity. (2) Attraction encourages participation in the group when doing so is not threatening to the relationship. (Attraction may discourage people from facing conflict or acting in ways that could reduce the level of mutual regard.) (3) Attraction usually encourages people to join and stay in groups, but it is no guarantee. People leave groups, in spite of high attraction, when net outcomes are low or when there is low commitment to the group. (4) Attraction enhances adjustment to the group, which in turn can increase the ability to handle stress.

Aggression
and Conflict

Once there was a president of a small unorganized
company who believed firmly in labor unions. . . .
So when the negotiating committee came in to bargain,
he simply told them that he was prepared to accept
their terms in full and sign a contract at once. Such
a magnanimous attitude, he thought, would establish a
firm basis for harmonious relations. . . . This was
not so. The employer's troubles began as soon as he
had signed the contract. Productivity fell off, there
were wildcat strikes in one department after another,
and it was many months before relations settled down
into the harmonious pattern that the employer's
friendly attitude should have made possible."—W. F.
Whyte, 1967, p. 324.

Like the employer in the case quoted above,
many people would like to wipe out aggression
and conflict. On the other hand, hardly anyone
would advocate a world in which people never
defended their own interests, argued for their
point of view, or compared alternatives

critically. When examined closely, those who
want to reduce aggression and conflict really
desire a reduction in unwarranted hostility,
cruelty, squabbles that lead nowhere, and
fights that end in resentment and failure. If
this aim is ever to be realized, we will have
to understand the causes of aggression and conflict, and learn what can be done to promote
the "good" in it and to reduce the "bad."

Unfortunately, people often do not agree
about the good and the bad in aggression and
conflict. What my side does is for the good;
what your side does is bad. What I feel is
warranted by the facts; what you feel is un-
justified. This disagreement is a major barrier
to understanding. People cannot agree about the
sources of good and bad if they do not have
similar notions of what is being explained. In
labor unions, for example, some may argue that
an "unproductive" strike was caused by the
leadership's demanding too much, because "unproductive," in their minds, is a long strike;
others may contend that business leaders are
simply antiunion—"unproductive," to them,
means lack of respect from the opposition.
Still others may blame members' lack of support, because their concern is low morale in
the union, while yet another group thinks there
never should have been a strike in the first
place because to them, "unproductive" means
not helping company earnings and job security
in the long run. With such wild variation in
objectives, attributions, and accusations, as
is common in serious disagreements, it is no
wonder that people have trouble weeding out the
"bad" in aggression and finding productive solutions to conflict.

Sometimes, simple approaches to aggression
and conflict situations work rather well. These
include, for example, the "let's just sit down
and talk about our differences" and the "if I'm
pleasant and cooperative, you will be, too" approaches. Yet these strategies are doomed to failure in many situations—in the case heading this

chapter, for example. Being nice didn't work
because (1) the employer's too easy capitulation threatened the employees with a loss of
freedom (to bargain for a union) and caused
them to experience reactance, (2) the employer's motives were suspected, (3) the employer
failed to play his social role appropriately
as a bargainer and representative of business
interests, (4) suspicions that the fledgling
union had asked for too little promoted dis-
sension. Maybe a more sophisticated approach
would have worked better; maybe not (often a
certain amount of disharmony is inevitable).
The point is that good intentions and simplistic strategies often do not suffice to resolve
complex issues and disagreements, particularly
when it is assumed that the problem is only one
of economics, rule-making, or technology while
the social aspects of the problem are ignored.

Although people now know more about aggression and conflict in the relative sense than
their ancestors did, the situation is frustrat-
ing. There are still disparate views among
scientists about the fundamental causes of
aggression, strong disagreements about the uses
and misuses of conflict, and much theorizing
that lacks empirical evidence. This chapter,
then, can serve at best as an heuristic device.
The reader will have to use a good deal of
imagination to turn what is now known and
thought to good purpose and practical use.

AGGRESSION

Traditionally, the study of aggression has
been separated from the study of conflict. One
reason for this separation is that aggression
has often been associated with what individuals
do, whereas conflict has been associated mainly with groups. Another reason is that aggression has been identified, in many minds, as a
basic cause of conflict (that is, as a source
of conflict, rather than a part of it). Later

in this chapter we shall bring the two concepts together by showing how aggression can
be used as a tool in the resolution of conflicts. First, we will review the major theories of aggression as they have existed for
many years.

INSTINCT THEORIES

One traditional view of aggression is that it
is caused by instincts. This view still finds
support, particularly in popular books for lay
people. The ideas involved have a long history,
from Aristotle, to Hobbes and Freud, and to
modern times. The assumption, generally, is
that nature (or a deity) has created in humans
a basic aggressive instinct, which is expressed
in behavior because it is incompletely blocked
by the "higher" faculties of reason and spiri-
tuality. In support, theoriests have pointed
to fighting throughout the natural world (e.g.,
Lorenz, 1966), to the "savagery" of primitive
societies (e.g., Hobbes, 1950), to the hostile
dreams and free associations of neurotic
patients (Freud, 1943), and to the destructiveness of animals which can be triggered merely
by electrically stimulating their brain (Moyer,
1971).

The evidence that aggression in humans is
instinctive is not strong, however. People's
aggressiveness is somewhat unlike the predatory and defensive behavior of subhuman species. Many animals fight other species for
food or survival and their own species for
territory and dominance. Aggression between
members of the same species has typically
evolved as a nonfatal ritual, set off by
specific physiological states and situations.
In contrast, people intentionally injure and
kill their own kind, and they do so for a
variety of reasons, social and emotional, political and economic. Theirs is a complex aggression, qualitatively different from that of
lower animals (cf. Tedeschi, Smith, and Brown,
1974).

Nor is human aggression a human constant. There are some primitive cultures, such as that of the Tasaday (Nance, 1975), whose lack of aggression is so complete that they have no words for enemy, kill, bad, or war. Some Eskimo groups will not even defend their own territory when the sure result is starvation and death (Montagu, 1968). Not all neurotics speak of hostility or "death wishes" during therapy; therapists interested in self-esteem, for example, hear patients speak of their concerns about their self-worth and their appeal to others (Rogers, 1967). Finally, electrical stimulation studies do not prove there are innate neural circuits that produce aggression, for electrical stimulation may simply produce pain, which understandably produces an attack reaction (e.g., Azrin, Hutchinson, and Hake, 1963).

Yet the logic of instinct theories is appealing to many: (1) We are animals and like other species, must be naturally aggressive. (2) Aggression is functional (i.e., in benefiting natural selection), so it must be "built-in." (3) We are so aggressive that aggression in humans must be immutable. So saying, instinct theorists have concentrated not on causes but on the question of how to control aggression.

Control strategies have taken three general forms: outlet, constraint, and wit. Aristotle (1951) was in favor of promoting harmless outlets for aggression. He wrote of the tragic play, which "through pity and fear" effected "the proper purgation" of violent emotions. Freud (1943, 1953) favored catharsis, too, through expressive enactment of emotions in therapy and displacement of objectionable impulses by art and intellectual pursuits. In Freud's scheme, the actor was his own audience (Rieff, 1959). Cathartic techniques are still with us, exemplified by psychodrama, implosive therapies, "Give him a punching bag" advice to parents, movies intended to drain the emotions, and drunken office parties in the working world.

Unfortunately, catharsis is often the exact opposite of what actually occurs when outlets for aggression are provided. Dana Bramel's (1969) review of experimental studies on catharsis reveals little support for the hypothesis that catharsis reduces aggression by purging emotionality. Subjects in a variety of studies did not feel less hostile or act less aggressively after (1) attacking an antagonist, or (2) observing someone else attacking an antagonist, or (3) observing an attack having nothing to do with their own source of anger. In many of these studies a catharsis technique caused subjects to act *more* aggressively. For example, DeCharms and Wilkins (1963) designed an experiment in which an egotistical confederate insulted subjects over an intercom system. Some subjects were given a chance to retaliate verbally; others were not. The results indicated that subjects given the chance to retaliate were more likely to later criticize the confederate than were subjects not given the opportunity to retaliate. These data are hardly supportive of the catharsis hypothesis and they lead one to question the value of blowing off steam by being aggressive.

The second control strategy that has appealed to instinct theorists is constraint. The idea is that society can force the repression or control of natural aggression by creating laws, governments, systematic punishment, and, paradoxically, disciplined group aggression (war and rebellion). Hobbes's (1950) social contract, the medieval Church's devil, the divine right of kings, and Marx's (1951) theory of economic exploitation all legitimized the necessity of coercive power to contain the inherent evil in man. Today, the belief in stockpiling weapons, in the effectiveness of capital punishment, and in the advantages of punitive reactions to work stoppages and strikes reflects that traditional view. But as with catharsis strategies, the evidence favoring a strategy of constraint to inhibit aggression is weak. Threats often provoke aggression,

and punishment often teaches it, as we shall
see.

A third control technique suggested by instinct theorists is the use of wit, intelligence, or education. To Machiavelli (1948), for
example, one might deflect the harm of a rival
or the masses by outwitting them. Others have
prescribed education: Educated people, presumably, are more in control of their aggressions
than ignorant people are (their higher faculties are stronger). In still another version
of this approach, the idea is to communicate
more clearly (see Chapter 3) in order to reduce
the misunderstandings that cause aggression.
Yet as Machiavelli discovered, these strategies
are far from ideal for blocking aggression.
Tricks, education or communication may, in
fact, provoke aggression. The person whose
"consciousness," for example, is raised by education may be the person who knows whom he may
attack for gain or revenge, and how power is
acquired. (In fact, some people fear education
too much because they believe it stimulates
aggression against authority. After the 1831
Nat Turner insurrection in Virginia, Alabama
provided that attempting to teach blacks to
read, write, or spell was punishable by fines
of $250 to $500 [Grant, 1968]).

SITUATIONAL THEORIES

Situational theories also go a long way back,
for example to Plato (1964), who believed that
violent drama could water the growth of pas-
sions, and to Rousseau (1950), who believed
that society corrupted the individual. The assumption, in its simplest form, is that human
beings are basically either neutral or good,
but will be aggressive in response to situations that provoke aggression. Situational
theories in the hands of sociologists and psychologists have developed in two directions.
In one, aggression is considered to be a
learned response, most usually through imitation. In the other, aggression is a reaction to

the frustration of goal directed behavior. Both theoretical versions have been employed to explain riots, criminality, and violence (e.g., in the Report of the National Advisory Commission on Civil Disorders, 1968), as well as conflict, bad decisions, and emotionality in the working environment.

Learned aggression has been most thoroughly researched by Albert Bandura and his colleagues, who demonstrated beyond a doubt that children do learn by imitating others. They imitate language and accents; they imitate self-control and self-reward; they imitate helpfulness and generosity (Bandura, 1965). They also imitate aggression, whether it is that of an experimenter hitting a large vinyl doll (Bandura, Ross, and Ross, 1961), a father beating his children (Bandura and Walters, 1959), or characters in a film of violent action (cf. Bandura, 1965). This research, of course, adds to the argument against the catharsis hypothesis and has distinct implications for the effect of violence in the streets and in the mass media. It can be argued (and with some credibility), for example, that one impetus to the union-management conflict presented at the beginning of this chapter could have been the imitation by employees of the kinds of behavior that historically have been associated with the development of unions.

Studies of imitation had an enormous impact on thinking about what we call aggression, but they did not deal adequately with motivation or with thought. They did not explain how the intent to harm is related to aggression; they did not distinguish hurtfulness from play (since it is not at all clear that children intend harm when they hit a doll in imitation of an adult experimenter). Nor did they account for defensive vs. offensive aggression, the use of threats, or the situations under which aggression is inhibited. Some notion of the roles of motives and thinking is necessary to explain these phenomena.

The theory that systematically employed a

concept of motivation was developed by psychologists at Yale University. This motivation oriented theory is called frustration-aggression
theory, for in its original form (Dollard et
al., 1939), frustration was hypothesized to
always cause aggression, and aggression was assumed to invariably result from frustration.
Frustration was defined as an interference or
blocking of behavior toward a goal. Aggression
was any behavior accompanied by the intent to
do harm. The theorists martialed evidence to
show that thwarting movement to a goal (e.g.,
fencing in children from attractive toys)
would cause fighting and other hostile behavior. Instrumental aggression—that is, aggression for purposes other than doing injury (such
as aggression to win a war or to succeed in
business)—was not handled by the theory, nor
was frustration that produced some response
other than aggression (fear or depression, for
example).

In many respects, frustration-aggression
theory overlapped the Freudian (instinct) view
of aggression (in fact, it was intended to
replace sections of Freud's psychoanalytic
theory with a "scientific" model). Frustration,
for example, was assumed to build up in the individual a reserve of excess energy that had to
be drained. If aggression against the frus-
trator was inhibited, aggression would be displaced to the most similar available target.

Most researchers interested in frustration-
aggression theory paid little attention to how
they operationalized either variable. Much more
attention was paid to identifying the target
of aggression, with displacement being the
most popular object of study. Frustration was
usually manipulated by insulting subjects,
delivering electric shocks to them, or arbi-
trarily depriving them of rewards (Buss, 1966).
These are unexpected, inappropriate, and even
unfair, behaviors that doubtless did far more
than simply block goal directed responses.
The dependent measures of aggression in these
studies (i.e., measures of how people reacted

to frustration) included observations of subjects delivering electric shock, evaluating
others negatively, remembering aggressive films,
being late to school, and writing hostile
stories (cf. Tedschi, Smith, and Brown, 1974).
One may question whether these acts were aggressive as defined by the theory. Did the subjects perceive that they were supposed to act
as if they were aggressive?

All together, the data make sense if we take
the liberty of assuming that frustration, as
created in this research, actually aroused
anger because it was inappropriate or unexpected (or possibly it aroused an expectation
that aggression was desired by the experimenter). What the data suggest is that (1) people
who are aribtrarily or unjustly treated get
angry and try to retaliate (e.g., Epstein and
Taylor, 1967); and that (2) when retaliation
toward an attacker is blocked, people are then
most likely to aggress against someone else or
some other group which they are induced to dislike (Berkowitz, 1962). Thus, in regard to the
conditions under which people aggress, it has
looked as if anger in response to inappropriate,
inequitable, or arbitrary attacks (even when
they don't succeed in hurting) is a facilitating condition and as if aggression will result unless it is inhibited by fear or circumstance.

A study by Leonard Berkowitz and James Green
(1962) illustrates how an unfair attack causes
aggression, which when blocked, is displaced.
Berkowitz and Green paired sets of two subjects
with a confederate. The three of them, working
independently, were to design a creative floor
plan for a house. When each had finished, the
experimenter pretended to exchange the plans
so the subjects could evaluate each other's
work. The evaluation was to be delivered by
means of electric shock; one shock meant "very
creative" and more shocks meant less creativity. Half the subjects received only one shock;
the rest received six. Next, the subjects
worked on a second test of creativity, during
which half of them were insulted for no reason

by the experimenter. Finally, the subjects
were allowed to rate the other subject and the
confederate (but not the experimenter, in order
to block aggression toward him).

The results showed no displacement to the confederate, whom the subjects had no reason to dislike, or to the other subject if he had given
a "very creative" rating. But they did show displacement of aggression to the other subject if
he had given six shocks (meaning low creativity) and if the experimenter insulted them.
Thus, a person who could not retaliate directly
displaced hostility to a peer who was disliked.

Experiments testing frustration-aggression
theory, such as the Berkowitz and Green study,
were one stimulus to a new look at aggression
research. They compelled researchers to reconsider the roles of anger and perceived intent
in provocations to aggression.

Meanwhile, two other research efforts were
contributing to changes in ideas about aggression. The first was dissonance and equity research, which suggested that aggression might
be caused or exacerbated by cognitive processes, such as the need for retribution or consistency. The second was research on conflict,
which suggested that a large percentage of
human aggression had been neglected in previous
research: coercive or instrumental aggression
employed in the service of winning conflicts
of interest.

COGNITIVE THEORIES

Cognitive theorists have assumed that the
prediction of behavior that harms others or employs coercion and threats depends upon our
understanding what people are thinking and want
to accomplish in social interaction. The study
of aggression thus falls within the purview of
each of the theories of social behavior presented in Chapter 5.

ATTITUDES AND EMOTIONS. Once aggression researchers began to study hostile thoughts and

feelings in their own right, it became clear
that these are no equivalent to overt aggression. Manning and Taylor (1975), for example,
who employed separate measures of hostility
and aggression in their reexamination of the
catharsis hypothesis, found that the two were
uncorrelated. Nor is anger equivalent to a
hostile attitude toward another. People may
hate when their emotional arousal is very low
(Kahn, 1966) or feel intense rage toward those
they love. The point that anger, hostility and
aggression correlate poorly is important. Aggression can result from a variety of causes
other than anger or hostility, and, in reverse,
anger or hostility can produce many behaviors
other than aggression (such as withdrawal and
depression).

Negative attitudes and emotions, in fact,
rarely cause aggressive behavior by themselves.
People usually have an objective when they aggress, such as "teaching him a lesson," re-
distributing power and resources, or winning in
a competition. Yet in spite of claims that aggressors make for their lack of hostility (as
in "I don't mean this personally"), both victims and observers will tend to attribute hostility to the aggressor. Sometimes this attribution is quite correct.

Hostility and anger could be a contributing
factor. Negative attitudes and emotions do
intensify aggression, make aggression easier
(e.g., by reducing guilt), and justify aggression after the fact. On the other hand, it may
be unproductive to assume that aggression is a
reflection of feelings when one doesn't know
the aggressor. That attribution could obscure
material causes of aggression and render a
victim defensive rather than wise in devising
a strategy to counter the attack.

AGGRESSION TO RESTORE EQUITY. A number of
studies have shown that subjects will retaliate
against a peer who inequitably deprives them
of resources (lowers inputs) or unjustly punishes them (lowers outcomes). Anthony Doob and

Larry Wood (1972), for example, hired a confederate to verbally badger subjects. Subjects who were permitted to punish the confederate were less aggressive later than similarly angered subjects who were not permitted to punish the aggressor. Doob and Wood interpreted their data as demonstrating that the desire to restore equity (through punishment) is a cause of aggression.

In a study by David Holmes (1972), subjects who were made to wait thirty minutes for an experimental partner delivered more shocks to him than did subjects who waited only five minutes. They were also less willing to receive shock, which suggests that once equity was restored they did not want to change the relationship. These studies provide support for a revised catharsis hypothesis, but only under limited conditions: That is, aggression which is just enough to restore equity (i.e., is justified) will tend not to be repeated or intensified.

Small variations in behavior can affect the response to inequity. In one study (Harris, 1974) male and female confederates cut into lines of people waiting at various banks, ticket counters, check-in stands at airports, and stores. The confederates cut in either at the front or rear of the line (which we may interpret as more or less unfair or inequitable); they were dressed well or poorly (that is, had high or low inputs); and the confederates said either "Excuse me" (which would partly redress the harm) or not. The results were consistent with what we would expect. Verbal and nonverbal aggressiveness (e.g., pushing) was higher among people at the front of the line, and among people confronting confederates dressed poorly or who failed to say "Excuse me."

The study of equity in relationships suggests several reasons why people aggress even though they seem to have suffered relatively little. Because equity concerns relative inputs and outcomes, behavior which is good or neutral in the absolute sense may be perceived

as bad. For example, in the case that headed
this chapter, a magnanimous approach on management's part resulted in an aggressive response.
Perceptions of inequity may have been a basic
cause. For example, the president's take-it-or-
leave-it approach, however well-meant, violated
expectations the employees had of a fight (for
which they had prepared) and did not leave them
room for the sorts of face-saving and self-aggrandizing opportunities that negotiating presents. If the employees felt his inputs too
low, the series of wildcat strikes could have
been a tool for reestablishing equity through
reducing the employer's outcomes and increasing
their own (i.e., their power).

DISINHIBITION AND JUSTIFICATION. There is a
norm that permits aggression to redress in-
justice—the norm of reciprocity (Gouldner,
1960). Nevertheless, many people will hesitate
to aggress "legitimately" or to approve of it,
because of a belief in the golden rule, because they have learned not to display their
feelings, or because they fear retaliation or
punishment. These beliefs, habits, or fears are
said to "inhibit" aggression. If a person
or group aggresses in spite of inhibitions,
there is commitment, and the aggressors will
likely try to justify the behavior. In so doing, aggressors are likely to repeat or even
intensify their aggression. Moreover, if aggression has been accomplished with no negative
consequences to the aggressors (e.g., disapproval from peers), the perceptions of risk
associated with aggressive acts will be reduced. These phenomena "disinhibit" aggression.
   Research on aggressive behavior has provided
much support for the disinhibiting consequences
of aggression itself, particularly unpunished
aggression. Certain acts of aggression even
facilitate escalation of aggression after they
have (presumably) restored equity, because the
balance may now be weighted in favor of the
equity restorers, who have to justify their
too aggressive behavior.

One of the best examples of aggression escalation is provided by Jeffrey Goldstein, Roger Davis, and Dennis Herman (1975), who set out to discover why researchers using Buss's aggression machine (a machine that appears to deliver shocks to others) so often reported that subjects increased the mean intensity of their shocks to others over time (e.g., Berkowitz, Lepinski, and Angulo, 1969). Even subjects in control groups, who were neither frustrated, angered, nor subjected to any other emotion-inducing treatment, have delivered increasingly intense shocks (Buss, Booker, and Buss, 1972). Goldstein, Davis, and Herman demonstrated in a teacher-learner situation (like Milgram's [1965]) that escalation of aggression was correlated with justifications for hurting the victims (belittling them and believing they deserved their fate). In addition, there was some evidence that the subjects got accustomed to using the shock machine (maybe their emotionality—and their anxiety—subsided). This example of aggression justification is important because it explains why aggression can spiral, as in the case at the beginning of this chapter, even though objectively the situation doesn't seem to call for more and more aggression.

COERCION. Parents who spank a child do not believe they are aggressive, nor does the doctor who administers a painful injection. A Napoleon setting out to conquer the world, the thief with a gun, and the pilot on a bombing mission do not think their actions are aggressive either. These are acts of coercion, instrumental to the attainment of some primary objective other than injury to the target, although injury may be necessary to reach the objective. Traditionally, these behaviors have been called "instrumental aggression," but some theorists have argued that a more value-free term is appropriate (Tedeschi, 1970). They suggest the word "coercion."

Aggression as a label is important, however.

People certainly react differently to coercion depending upon whether or not they label it aggression. History is replete with examples of warring countries that go to great lengths to rationalize their own use of coercion as legitimate, defensive, or necessary—that is, not "aggressive"—and yet nations also tend to call coercion on the part of other nations, aggression. Having done so, they themselves respond with even greater force. The process, of course, is facilitated by the differing views and interests of each nation.

The use of coercion is most frequently caused by the perception that it is the most effective (or only) means to influence others, to obtain material rewards, or to defend oneself against expected losses. The use of coercion as a means of obtaining compliance has been discussed by political, business, and military experts, as well as by social psychologists. Thus we have Clausewitz's famous definition of war as an extension of diplomacy (1950) and Lasswell's (1965) observation that coercive groups become most active when diplomats, propagandists, and industrialists cannot deal with crises.

The Watergate affair, first announced in 1972, perhaps best illustrates this view of coercion. By many accounts President Nixon and his staff were determined to win an election they felt might not be won by legitimate advertising, speeches, and the advantage of the incumbency position. They wanted to discredit agitators they felt threatened their policies. Their use of force and illegal means to gather political intelligence, their deceptions to put the opposition in disarray, and their secretive decision making may be viewed as strategies employed in the service of obtaining compliance, rewards, and the emasculation of opposing groups.

The union-management case at the beginning of this chapter also illustrated instrumental aggression or coercion. (It is an all-purpose case!) In this instance, the behavior of the employees was probably, in part, a strategy for gaining long-term objectives by convincing the president of the company that they expected to bargain and would not lower their guard even if he seemed to capitulate easily to their demands.

Many different studies of aggression may be alternatively interpreted as studies of instrumental coercion. For example:

1. Milgram's (1965) subjects severely harmed another using electric shocks because they were told to do so by an authority (the scientist-experimenter). They were neither frustrated nor angry, nor was their purpose to inflict injury; instead they were doing what they were told was necessary to study learning and punishment.

2. Toch's (1969) "violence-prone" police, inmates, and parolees were found to have often used physical assaults to enhance their self-image or reputations. Coercion was perceived by violent men as necessary to communicate their importance, fearlessness, integrity, and social position. A majority of these men were deficient in verbal and other social skills for reaching their objectives.

3. Lerner's (1966) review of totalitarian political regimes notes that the mythologies of revolutionary elites are misleading. He says (pp. 463-64):

   The Bolshevik elite was not proletarian; nor was the Nazi elite composed of sturdy German peasants. These interwar regimes of coercive ideology—along with their Fascist and Falangist counterparts—represented no "revolt of the masses." They were, rather, operated by and for . . . the middle classes who had been denied access to what they considered their proper place and organized violent action to gain what they had been denied.

4. Milgram and Toch's (1969) analysis of crowds and social movements makes clear that collective hysteria and violence may be no more irrational than is organized coercion. The members of crowds that become violent

are sometimes self-selected groups of marginal people who have no other means for asserting their needs.

5. Brown's (1965) analysis of panic is perhaps oversimplified, but draws our attention to the compelling facts of reward-cost alternatives in a crisis. Panics, he argues, result only when there is a limited probability of escaping danger; people who have no escape or who have open escape routes do not panic. With limited means of escape, there may be no more rational behavior than the use of coercion. If others might rush for an exit, one's only realistic alternative is to rush, too.

Coercion (and coercive threats), then, may be viewed as a tool for gaining or maintaining power and other objectives, especially in conflicts of interest. In this respect, it has roots in the very same motives—and may have the same objectives—as behavior which involves ingratiation tactics, persuasive speeches, "keeping up with the Joneses," and other strategies of social influence. Coercion is different because we think of it as a last resort.

CONFLICT

"I, John Brown, am not quite *certain* that the crimes of this *guilty land* will never be purged away but with *blood*. I had, as I now think vainly, flattered myself that without very much bloodshed it might be done" (p. 83). This, John Brown's last written statement, in 1859 (Grant, 1968), is another illustration of aggression or coercion used as a means of resolving (winning) a conflict when all else has failed. Why does conflict end this way? What strategies can be used to reduce the need for violence? How can conflict be constructive? In the pages that follow we shall examine these questions.

Conflict is best described as the degree to which people in a common situation have incompatible interests. Since in real life there is never perfect coordination of interests, conflict is always present to one degree or another whenever there is interpersonal interaction. Below are illustrated three types of interpersonal problems, corresponding to Kelley and Thibaut's (1969) classification of problem solving. The first two represent what is commonly investigated in studies of problem solving, group performance, or decision making. The last represents the typical situation studied by conflict researchers.

1. A stock buying club has the problem of deciding how to invest its money. Since each individual has different information (and opinions), the problem the group has is how to distribute information and to decide which is the most useful. This so-called "information distribution" problem poses the question, "Who knows what?"
2. A family sets out to build a cabin in the woods. The problem its members have is to coordinate their efforts and divide labor in order to get the job done. This "response distribution" problem poses the question, "Who does what?"
3. A bowling team has just won a monetary prize, largely due to the skill of one individual. The team's problem is to divide the winnings equitably. This "outcome distribution" problem (more often referred to as a "conflict of interest") poses the question, "Who gets what?"

Intuitively, the first two examples may seem to have little to do with conflict as we ordinarily think of it. But the advantage of beginning with a broad view of interaction problems is that we see how problems of information and response distribution are ~~inex~~- inevitably tricably intertwined with problems of outcome distribution, if not theoretically, then practically. Thus, for instance:

1. The stock buying club may acknowledge the common problem of sharing information, but members may distort the information they provide in the interest of maximizing their own prestige within the group.
2. The family may try to openly discuss who should do the most distasteful jobs, but each member may also rely upon tradition, argument, favors, or displays of weakness to avoid a least desired division of labor.
3. Some members of the bowling team, in discussing their conflict, may fail to share information regarding their best bowler's reluctance to continue with the team, because they want to maximize their own gain in the short run.

These situations are typical. Within groups and between groups we find interconnecting problems of information, response, and outcome distribution. Nevertheless, it is difficult to discuss them at once. In this chapter we shall focus on how groups solve problems of outcome distribution, and leave the major considerations of information and response distribution to the next chapter.

MIXED MOTIVES

All groups (and individuals within groups) have what are called "mixed motives" (Schelling, 1960). That is, there is always some motivation to cooperate with others and some motivation to compete; thus, conflict over outcomes is a matter of degree. Theoretically, groups can have pure motives. Thus, pure cooperation occurs when different groups (or group members) can obtain outcomes that are in perfect correspondence, but even in the highly controlled laboratory situation pure cooperation does not exist. For instance, researchers have required

subjects to choose between cooperative or
competitive moves in a variation of the prisoner's dilemma situation (Chapter 5). In this
variation cooperative choices are the only way
to maximize both mutual and individual gain.
Yet subjects often find it more interesting to
invent a new game in which the object is to
maximize the difference between their own payoffs and those of their opponents (Gallo and
McClintock, 1965).

"Zero-sum," or pure competition rarely exists
either. Theoretically, it occurs when individuals cannot gain without causing an equivalent
loss for their opponents. But there must be at
least some cooperation in a situation if the
relationship is to exist at all. Thus, the conflicting parties must at least agree to fight
or bargain, rather than withdraw, or must be
mutually dependent upon a third party that requires them to remain in the relationship (as
when a mediator instructs them to stay and
bargain). More often, there is even greater cooperation than that. For instance, the bowling
team described earlier might be at great odds
over the sharing of rewards and information,
but might agree on rules for coming to agreement, as by deciding to abide by the decision
of an outside arbitrator, to refrain from verbal insults, or to close off debate after an
arbitrary length of time. Cooperative rules
satisfy the conflicting parties' mutual need
to prevent the prolongation and escalation of
conflict.

Problems of outcome distribution may be described along a dimension measuring the degree
to which the outcomes of each party are positively or negatively correlated, that is, both
gain, or one loses while the other gains. Outcome distributions may also be described along
another dimension—the means-end dimension.
That is, group members may be relatively more
concerned with ends or values that are in conflict, or more with means to the same ends or
interests. Figure 8.1 illustrates a typical
conflict situation, the conflict between

		Selected Questionnaire Items*	Percentage of Respondents Agreeing with Item	
			Business Executives and Owners (N=120)	Labor Union Leaders (N=41)
CONSENSUS	Ends and Values	(1) Not too much is done for the poor.	75	95
		(2) A worker's son doesn't have a chance in the U.S.	8	10
		(3) Third World revolutions are basically national-ist.	72	72
		(4) Rebellious ideas of youth contribute to society.	74	78
	Means and Interests	(1) Cut government spending during a recession.	73	88
		(2) Wage-price controls needed.	69	63
		(3) Reduce defense spending.	62	72
		(4) Legalize marijuana.	27	25
CONFLICT	Ends and Values	(1) The environmental prob-lem is exaggerated.	41	84
		(2) Poverty could be ended in 10 years.	42	95
		(3) FBI threatens civil liberties.	24	65
		(4) The pricing system is competitive.	89	37
	Means and Interests	(1) End oil depletion al-lowance.	32	85
		(2) Enlarge worker's role in management.	12	88
		(3) Compulsory arbitration is needed.	70	12
		(4) Tax polluting industries.	45	88

*Note: In general, business and labor agree on foreign policy and youth, disagree on economic issues.

FIGURE 8.1 Illustration of a Mixed Motive Relationship: Conflict and Consensus on Ends or Values and Means or Interests Between Business Executives and Labor Leaders (1971-72) (Data from Barton, 1974-75)

business and union leaders in late 1971 and
early 1972. On the first dimension of conflict,
outcome correlation, there exist both overlapping interests and some conflict—they agree
on some matters and disagree on others.
Further, conflict occurs on both means and
ends.

Most laboratory studies of conflict employ
games in which values and ends are defined by
experimenter (e.g., the object is to win
money); the conflict resides chiefly in the
fact that means and interests are incompatible
(e.g., two people can't agree on how to split
up the money). Some everyday groups are like
this too. For example, a family may want to
spend some time with each other but disagree
over whether to go ice skating or play Monopoly.
In groups like those described in Figure 8.1,
however, basic values and ends may be just as
much in conflict as the means for reaching
them. For example, business and labor probably
disagreed over the statement, "The environmental problem is exaggerated," because they
value population and economic growth differently. In a sense, they are not even playing
the same game. Keep this in mind as we review
the research on the strategies and outcomes of
conflict; generally speaking, this research
concerns conflicts of means and interests.

STRATEGIES

In recent years, the goal of research has
been to identify strategies which individuals
and groups use to find solutions for conflicts
of interest. Much less attention has been paid
to strategies for creating conflict or insuring that it is not avoided, although it has
been said periodically that organizational and
group ineffectiveness is related to the avoidance of or withdrawal from conflict.

Argyris' (1967) studies within the U.S.
Department of State brought to light social
norms which caused Foreign Service officers to
avoid the discussion of substantive issues. One

norm was that one should not openly discuss disagreements; another was that, in a disagreement, one should withdraw from aggressiveness and evaluate the individual negatively but not tell him. Irving Janis (1972) and his colleagues have included such avoidance of conflict in their discussion of "groupthink" and have identified several major national policy decisions that went wrong because of it (e.g., the Bay of Pigs invasion of Cuba). The phenomenon of groupthink illustrates the necessity of asking more of conflict resolving strategies than simply that they "settle the conflict." The aim must be to use conflict, and the different perspectives it can bring to light, to formulate and carry out good decisions from which many benefit.

STRATEGY 1: KNOW THINE ENEMY. As was pointed out in the discussion of social exchange theory, the individual who is aware of what an opponent is doing and can predict what the opponent is going to do is usually at a distinct advantage. (An exception, sometimes, occurs when the opponent plans to make threatening moves which might cause one to become anxious or defensive.) If one knows the opponent's strategy, one can adjust one's own strategy accordingly or find objectives in common. There are four techniques for increasing one's awareness of an opponent's strategy: (1) observing the opponent's behavior, (2) evaluaating the payoff matrix, (3) observing situational cues, and (4) communication with the opponent. The effects of these are known mostly from game-like experiments of the prisoner's dilemma type.

A strategy people use in conflicts when they cannot communicate with their opponent is to watch the opponent's moves, guess the strategy involved, and adjust their behavior. For instance, subjects in a bargaining situation can discover the "win-stay, lose-change" rule by observing and reacting consistently to their opponent's moves. (It was remarked earlier, however, that whether or not this strategy is successful depends upon the sequencing of responses.) The success of simple adjustment rules which follow observation depend upon the type of relationship involved (Rabinowitz, Kelley, and Rosenblatt, 1966) and upon the complexity of the opponent's strategy (Steinfatt and Miller, 1974). For example, after someone has learned an opponent's strategy and is responding consistently, the opponent may switch tactics (called a "mixed strategy"), and all that observation and planning has gone for naught.

Steinfatt and Miller (1974) have pointed out that in fact many simple adjustment strategies are ineffective. For example, experimenters playing a preprogrammed strategy of either 100 percent cooperative or 100 percent competitive moves in (prisoner's dilemma) games, have little effect upon the subjects' ultimate level of cooperation. In these games the only preprogrammed strategy shown to be consistently effective in increasing cooperation is the tit-for-tat strategy, in which the player matches whatever move the opponent played on the previous go-round (e.g., Solomon, 1960).

A variation of this strategy that works better is the slow-slow strategy. Here the individual has a .6 probability of responding in kind on the first response after the other's move, a .8 probability of responding in kind after the second move, and a 1.00 probability of doing so after the third. Bixenstine and Gaebelein (1971), who compared various tit-for-tat strategies experimentally, conclude that "turning the other cheek (or being slow to compete) is fine, but . . . it is best wed to a cautious exposure of one's cheek to begin with!"

Adjustment rules may also follow observation of the payoff matrix, equivalent in real life to evaluating the objective cost-benefit situation for each side. Obviously, it is an advantage to know what is valuable to one's opponent. The absolute value of payoffs, as well as their structure, has been shown to be important in guiding strategies. For example, the degree of cooperation in some games increases dramatically when the subjects are offered relatively large amounts of money (e.g., Gallo, 1963). When the payoff is crucial, subjects put up with the boredom of making long strings of cooperative responses (and give up the joys of beating out the other).

The problem with evaluating the payoff matrix, even when combined with observation of an opponent's moves, is that as rewards and costs depart from the strictly monetary, it is difficult to judge just how valuable or expensive they will be perceived by an opponent. One may be reduced to guessing whether the opponent's personality is acquisitive, competitive or altruistic. The nature of interaction is such that people are likely to misinterpret the motives of the other when making such guesses. For example, the student in conflict with an instructor over a grade may from one perspective perceive that the instructor is hostile and interpret a conciliatory request for a discussion on the subject to be an attack. The instructor, meeting with resistance, may interpret the student's anxiety as intentional aggressiveness.

A third way that people develop strategies to deal with conflict is by relying upon situational cues that suggest procedures, rules or agreements all parties can accept, and an astonishing large number of conflicts are in fact resolved that way. For example, group members in conflict may agree, without ever really discussing the issue, to divide up resources fifty-fifty because the situation is similar to others they have encountered where they learned such a rule (cf. Kelley and Thibaut, 1969). Strategies that follow imported norms or rules are often successful in producing compromise (but usually not unique solutions). When each party in conflict has had similar experiences and training and when the situation itself has familiar features,

each side can make a fairly good guess as to
what will be acceptable to the other.

Thomas Schelling (e.g., 1960) has called
this strategy of relying upon features of the
situation to produce implicit rules, "tacit
bargaining." He argues that the strategy is
important because it explains how conflict gets
resolved in many situations in which communication is limited: war, legal maneuvers, jockey-
ing in a traffic jam, or even getting along
with a neighbor one does not speak to. Schelling begins his discussion by demonstrating
that, in situations involving little conflict,
implicit rules immediately resolve the difficulties people have in coordinating their responses. Here is a problem, for example, which
he gave to forty-two people: Name "heads" or
"tails." If you and your partner name the
same, you both win a prize. In this sample,
thirty-six persons chose "heads," whereas
only six chose "tails." Obviously, people can
coordinate their expectations by relying on
what they already know about similar situations.

Schelling argues that implicit rules are
used to settle serious conflicts of interest
as well. Suppose, for example, we encounter a
different version of the problem described
above so that:

> A and B are to choose "heads" or "tails" without com-
> municating. If both choose "heads," A gets $3 and B
> gets $2; if both choose "tails," A gets $2 and B gets
> $3. If they choose differently, neither gets any-
> thing. You are A (or B); which do you choose? (Note
> that if both choose at random, there is only a 50-50
> chance of successful coincidence and an expected
> value of $1.25 apiece, less than either $3 or $2.)

Schelling reports that sixteen out of twenty-
two A's and fifteen out of twenty-two B's chose
heads. Given what the A's did, heads was the
best answer for B; given what the B's did, heads
was the best answer for A. Together they did
substantially better than they would have by

choosing randomly, or by trying to win $3 (which would have netted them zero).

An equally interesting aspect of implicit rules is their power to influence negotiation and bargaining even when open communication is possible. This power may be observed in the attractiveness of round numbers in monetary settlements, of the popularity of "majority rules" decision schemes in voting, of the wide use of precedents in strike negotiations, and even of the reliance on natural boundaries in military and political decision making. Mediators, fact finding committees, and research commissions may sometimes make their greatest contribution by suggesting or emphasizing the implicit rule or agreement that will seem most correct or "natural" to the parties in conflict (e.g., "Let's try to even things up here"). Depending upon the problem, they may end up not with the most desirable solution to the conflict, but with a solution that will be agreed upon.

Because tacit rules arise of themselves out of problems, it becomes clear that leaders, negotiators, and others can help groups resolve conflict by formulating and presenting issues to them in such a way as to enhance the salience of tacit rules. The strategy may be as simple as proposing to a conflicting group of four a monetary settlement that is divisible by four or to a group in conflict over hiring one of two men, a compromise candidate. Or the strategy may be relatively complex, such as forming an "umbrella" committee when two committees cannot agree, changing the words used to describe a problem (as from "compensation" to "fringe benefit" or from "dues" to "contribution") or putting together on an agenda two separate issues that will suggest a package deal.

STRATEGY 2: TALKING IT OUT. Most people believe that if parties with competing interests can discuss their differences, conflict can be

resolved. At the least, talking may stall off
outright fighting. But people in conflict are
caught in a dilemma. It often is to their advantage to gain as much information as possible, but to communicate as little as possible. Concealing one's rock-bottom alternative,
for example, may considerably increase one's
bargaining power.

If a mutually advantageous solution to a
conflict exists, (cautious) communication will
sometimes help individuals find it. For example, Scodel (1963) reports that if subjects
playing a prisoner's dilemma game can discuss
how to play the game, cooperation increases.
Deutsch (e.g., 1960) allowed subjects to write
notes to each other before playing a single
game and also found an increase in cooperation. What seems to happen here is that (1) the
advantages of cooperating are made salient
and (2) either implicitly, or explicitly, each
party promises to cooperate. With regard to
the latter, it has been found that stating a
pacific intention significantly increases cooperation (Loomis, 1959), whereas stating an
aggressive intent has the opposite effect.
Asking to be trusted, however, does not always
work. If cooperative promises are not followed
by cooperative behavior, the opponent responds
by competing (Gahagan and Tedeschi, 1968).

Obviously as important as whether people
communicate is what they communicate. As was
noted in Chapter 3, for example, communicating
to clarify the issues, rather than to bargain,
may simply intensify conflict by making salient the degree to which the interests of the
parties are opposed. In bargaining studies
where subjects are instructed to give only
truthful information about their profit structures, no advantage to the quality of the bargaining solution accrues (e.g., Pruitt and
Lewis, 1975). A significant disadvantage seems
to result from having a third party point out
the issues or instruct highly conflicting
parties to discuss what the issues dividing
them are. Erickson et al. (1974) tried out such

a procedure in a study that simulated pretrial negotiations between opposing attorneys. In half the conferences, the judge began the conference by leading the participants through an analysis of the issues. The results showed a 50 percent decrease in settlements when conflict was high, and only a slight increase in settlements when conflict was low.

The third party communication that did benefit participants in the Erickson et al. study was one in which the judge urged the attorneys to discuss the case as a whole and work out a package resolution. The reason why this procedure is effective is apparently that it encourages participants to orient themselves toward mutually beneficial outcomes, rather than to outcomes that benefit only themselves. When conflicting parties search for the former, they are likely to settle on positions that maximize total outcomes.

The content of communications about one's negotiating position (as separate from one's perception of the issues) is an important factor influencing whether or not the conflicting parties settle on mutually beneficial outcomes. It has been found that threats, trying to talk the other into making concessions, early commitments, firm offers on single issues, and conceding or compromising early in negotiations (as in the case beginning this chapter) are all ineffective bargaining methods. Instead, taking one's time and making systematic concessions maximize integrative solutions (Kelley, 1966).

STRATEGY 3: THREATS AND COERCION. Making threats (promises to attack, compete, or increase the other's costs) is not an effective way to negotiate conflict. What happens is that threat is met by threat (Shomer, Davis, and Kelley, 1966), especially when it is perceived as unjust and purposely belligerent. Threat paired with an attack provokes even higher retaliation (Vincent and Tindell, 1969). The result is spiraling aggression, which

usually ends in dissolution of the relationship or annihilation of the parties but, in
some cases, an eventual seeking of detente.

These generalities should not be taken to
imply that threats or coercive acts are never
useful in settling conflict; for example,
making known that one has considerable relative
power to attack may be a significant advantage
to a higher power party. That is, the side that
has at its disposal high coercive power is the
side that can force compliance and deter attacks from the weaker side. The deterrence
argument rests upon the assumption that one
side can retaliate against attacks and can
retaliate on a massive scale; deterrence thus
depends upon high relative power. With equal
power (or, more accurately, equal perceived
power), escalation often results from threat
(Hornstein, 1965). Since groups are likely to
overestimate their own resources (Blake and
Mouton, 1961), the difference in power must be
rather great for the more powerful to use
threat effectively.

A recent experiment by Michener and Cohen
(1973) shows how the relative power to attack
affects dealing with conflict. Pairs of subjects played a game that simulated conflict
between two nations with a history of belliger-
ence. They were to negotiate settlement of a
dispute over ocean facilities and had the
power to threaten and to attack and destroy
their opponent's populations. Within each
pair, one person was randomly given high power
(ability to destroy the other's population);
the other, low power. Twenty-eight combinations
were employed in order to vary the relative
magnitude of coercive power. The results showed
that, as in other studies, threat was met by
threat. But both compliance with demands and
deterrence were affected by differential power.
The lower the low power person's relative
power, the more he complied with the high
power person's demands and the more willing he
was to come to an agreement favorable to the
high power person. In addition, the lower power

person was deterred from attacking; the lower his power, the lower his destructiveness. The higher power person's degree of compliance was affected by neither his own power nor the lower power person's power; his destructiveness, also, was unaffected by his or the other's power. In sum, the capacity to deter attacks and win compliance rested with high power; the degree to which compliance and deterrence were effected depended upon the relative weakness of the low power party.

STRATEGY 4: GAINING RELATIVE POWER. It is obvious that people and groups in conflict will be motivated to increase their relative power, whether it be the power to punish or to reward. Some of the strongest evidence showing attempts to gain power stem from data on coalition formation in groups of three or more. From research and theory (e.g., Gamson, 1961, 1964; Rapoport, 1970) we find that low power people form coalitions when they perceive that banding together will enable them to win a conflict with a person or group having high power. But when forming coalitions, people take into consideration not only whether they can win, but also how much reward they will receive within the coalition. People seek coalitions that will not produce new conflict over the division of resources.

A concern with relative payoffs once the conflict is won induces people to prefer coalitions with those powerful enough to insure successful resolution of the conflict, but not so powerful that their allies will deserve all the rewards of success. The latter is a realistic concern. As Komorita and Chertkoff (1973) argue, those who are weak will seek equality of outcomes, whereas those who are strong will seek parity (division of rewards proportional to resources). People may also be concerned with perceptions and will avoid even winning coalitions in which the ally will be seen as overly superior (e.g., Hoffman, Festinger, and Lawrence, 1954). The data on coalitions provide evidence that, while the cause of conflict may be differences in power, the creation of power differences can also be a strategy for resolving conflict.

SOLUTIONS

Research on strategies for resolving conflict raises the following questions: Which strategies are not simply conflict resolving but also most productive? What kinds of solutions to conflict can we realistically try to attain? Researchers began trying to answer these questions by devising relatively loosely controlled experiments involving cooperation and competition. Later, more highly controlled games of strategy were studied. A classic investigation by Morton Deutsch and Robert Krauss (1962) typifies earlier approaches. Each of two subjects was faced with the problem of sending a truck over a road that at one point narrowed to allow only one truck through. If subjects learned to take turns, they both profited, but if they refused to cooperate in using the roadway, both lost money. Deutsch and Krauss discovered that most pairs of subjects showed a profit, but when they were each given gates to threaten and obstruct the passage of their opponent's trucks, subjects failed to cooperate and suffered large losses.

Since that time, researchers have varied the payoffs involved, the kind and degree of threat, and other factors, such as the possibility of communication between participants. At the same time, interest in the mathematical theory of games increased. Game theory, first discussed formally by Von Neumann and Morganstern in 1944, is a mathematical approach to conflict which concentrates on rational strategies that maximize a player's chances to win and minimize his or her chances for losing. This theoretical approach is used as a model with which the behavior of subjects can be contrasted. It was not long before the prisoner's dilemma game (such as employed in the Engle, Hausen, and Lowe

[1975] study described in Chapter 5), which is readily amenable to mathematical analyses, became the most popular means of investigating conflict.

The situations created by these experimental methods naturally restricted the manner in which conflict could be resolved. For example, if subjects could not leave the experiment, they could not resolve conflict by simply refusing to play. If subjects could not communicate, they could not resolve conflict by agreeing to make payments on the side to a loser. Nemeth (1972) has argued that the context of these studies is too minimal and that they fail to capture the reciprocity of interaction in everyday life. It was not until relatively recently, when other research paradigms (such as bargaining or negotiation simulation games) were used more extensively, that a fuller understanding emerged of the many ways that people solve the problem of conflict.

COOPERATION AND COMPETITION. There are only two solutions to a standard prisoner's dilemma game: cooperation or competition. By definition, the rational solution is to play in order to maximize gains and minimize losses. At best, this means cooperation, but given a zero-sum, prisoner's dilemma situation players should compete, just as the prisoners in the classic situation probably are better off if they confess. Most studies employing the prisoner's dilemma game found that people do compete; fewer than 50 percent cooperative choices are reported in almost every experiment published before 1965 (Steinfatt and Miller, 1974). When the payoff matrix is altered in order to favor cooperative choices, they do increase, although never completely. Subjects apparently "would rather compete than ride the gravy train, even though competition punishes both" (Rapoport, 1966).

STANDOFFS, CAPITULATION, AND ESCALATION. By making the payoffs more nearly approximate pure competition or by creating games in which threats or punishment are possible, researchers have investigated other solutions to conflict. "Chicken" typifies the most dangerous game; a player can win nothing without the other losing. In such games, cooperation really means capitulation (Rapoport, 1971). Subjects in experiments of this type usually bluff each other for a time and end in deadlock. If one party weakens, the solution, of course, is obvious.

When competing individuals are given equal means to threaten or punish each other, deadlocks are common. Thus, deadlock by the seventh trial in a Deutsch and Krauss trucking game is usual. Ackoff and others have developed games in which subjects may attack and thereby increase the costs of an opponent. Many of these games simulate military actions in a war. The solution to these conflicts has sometimes been mutual capitulation, but in one experiment (Ackoff, Conrath, and Howard, 1967), subjects who were not allowed to communicate annihilated each other so frequently that the researchers decided they would have to allow communication in order not to lose the data of so many subjects. Experimenters employing games of strategy that include threat or attack possibilities are especially interested in escalation. Escalation of competitive choices, threats, or attack is easily created in the laboratory, providing some of the more provocative data in this area.

COMPROMISE AND CREATIVE SOLUTIONS. Unless players in most experimental games violate the rules, their alternatives for resolving conflict are extremely limited. But the development of sophisticated games in which subjects role play negotiations has brought to light other ways in which groups can deal with the problem of conflict.

Allowing for negotiations in prisoner's dilemma games involves letting the participants talk, but the structure of the game limits the degree to which different compromises are

reasonably possible. The making of concessions
is discouraged by the nature of the game,
whereas in real conflict situations reciprocal
concession making is common (cf. Nemeth, 1972).
Bargaining games are considerably more open,
and measures can be made of initial negotiating demands, final bargaining demands, bargaining concessions, bargaining endurance, and
coalition formation, as well as various strategies for coming to agreement (e.g., stalling
for time or use of pressure tactics).

The structure of the bargaining game may be
illustrated by describing a task used by
Kelley (1966) and later adapted by Dean Pruitt
and Steven Lewis (1975). Pairs of subjects
take the roles of a buyer and a seller who must
agree on prices for iron, sulfur, and coal.
The buyer can gain his highest profits on iron
and the seller on coal, so that mutually profitable tradeoffs can be negotiated if the
buyer makes heavy concessions on coal and the
seller on iron. They clearly have mixed motives, for to maximize their own outcomes, they
must cooperate to avoid a prolongation or
breakdown of negotiations.

Before they begin negotiations, the buyer
and seller are given a sheet of paper listing
nine prices for each commodity. Table 8.1
shows the profit schedules of each. Next to
each price (designated by a letter) on the
seller's sheet is the profit he will obtain if
he sells the commodity at that price. Next to
each price (also designated by a letter) on
the buyer's sheet is his profit for reselling
the commodity bought at that price.

To understand this bargaining situation,
place yourself for a moment in the position
of the buyer. Now suppose you and the seller
agree, as many pairs of people do, to prices
E for iron, E for sulfur, and E for coal
(E-E-E). At these prices, you will make a
profit of $1,000 on iron, $600 on sulfur, and
$400 on coal, a total of $2,000. The seller
will make profits on those same commodities,
respectively, of $400, $600, and $1,000, also

TABLE 8.1 Buyer and Seller Profit Sheets

Buyer						Seller					
Iron		Sulfur		Coal		Iron		Sulfur		Coal	
Price	Profit	Price	Profit	Price	Profit	Price	Profit	Price	Profit	Price	Profit
A	$2,000	A	$1,200	A	$800	A	$000	A	$000	A	$000
B	$1,750	B	$1,050	B	$700	B	$100	B	$150	B	$250
C	$1,500	C	$900	C	$600	C	$200	C	$300	C	$500
D	$1,250	D	$750	D	$500	D	$300	D	$450	D	$750
E	$1,000	E	$600	E	$400	E	$400	E	$600	E	$1,000
F	$750	F	$450	F	$300	F	$500	F	$750	F	$1,250
G	$500	G	$300	G	$200	G	$600	G	$900	G	$1,500
H	$250	H	$150	H	$100	H	$700	H	$1,050	H	$1,750
I	$000	I	$000	I	$000	I	$800	I	$1,200	I	$2,000

Note: Prices were referred to by letters. The numbers under each commodity represent profits to be made on that commodity at the particular price.

a total of $2,000. Your maximum joint profit is thus $4,000. This joint profit, however, could be much higher. For example, consider the prices B-C-H. The joint yield here is $4,900. Your own profits for B-C-H, however, are $2,750 while the seller's profits are only $2,150. Thus, to increase the joint profit will cause the seller to lose something in relative terms. Or consider the prices A-E-I. This yields the highest joint profit, $5,200. You would individually profit by $2,600 as would your seller. Thus, the highest joint profit, as well as the equitable outcome, goes to the most "diagonal" solution. There are other ways to obtain the highest joint profit (A-B-I, A-F-I, and A-I-I), but these (as in many real-life situations) produce unequal outcomes for individuals.

In these kinds of bargaining situations, two solutions are surprisingly common. Some dyads simply fail to reach agreement within even generous time limits. But most dyads at least begin with the obvious compromise. In the game just described, for example, most participants proposed and agreed upon the same or nearly the same price for all commodities, yielding a joint profit of about $4,000. Relatively few pairs hit on the creative solution— a much lower price for iron than for coal.

How do people in conflict end up with creative or so-called "integrative" solutions— that is, solutions that maximize the greatest gain for all parties. Systematic concession making is one way; it involves beginning with extreme (but not outrageous demands), testing several contracts that are about equally valuable, and making further concessions only when none of these is acceptable. Pruitt and Lewis (1975) found that proposing a general approach and making a number of different proposals were helpful in systematic concession making. They were significantly correlated with joint profits in the bargaining situation we have described. In contrast, giving or asking for information, calling for concessions, and

showing concern for the other were unrelated
to joint profit. Using pressure tactics and
threats was very negatively related to profit.

The advantage to conflicting parties of con-
centrating on maximizing joint outcomes, and
searching for mutually beneficial creative alternatives and package deals has been emphasized by many writers. Deutsch (1960) reported
that subjects instructed to maximize the welfare of both players in the trucking game
profited significantly more than those instructed to look out for themselves or to do
better than the other. Fisher (1964) suggested
the practice of coupling issues in international disputes. Froman and Cohen (1970) have
favorably compared "logrolling" to compromise
in economic disputes. Walton and McKersie
(1965) have noted that "integrative" bargaining
(oriented toward joint outcomes) in labor
negotiations has been far more successful than
"distributive" (individualistic and threatening) bargaining. All of these approaches have
in common a cooperative attitude, but an avoidance of piecemeal bargaining, or an early,
simplistic capitulation such as was illustrated
in the quote that began this chapter.

Summary

This chapter reviews the major lines of research on aggression and conflict. There are
many theories about why aggression exists; some
of them (e.g., instinct theories) have ancient
roots. Most current research suggests that
aggression is learned, especially through
imitation, and that it is aroused by situations in which some hurtful or destructive
intentions and behavior of others is perceived
as unfair, arbitrary, or inappropriate. Once
begun (perhaps in response to an attack),
aggression tends to be escalated; and is usually justified by aggressors as deserved.

Not all aggression derives from emotional

responses to attacks or hostility. There also
exists coercion, or instrumental aggression.
Instrumental aggression is employed as strategy
for gaining certain rewards or reducing costs
(such as for gaining greater relative power),
and the primary motive is not to hurt the opponent. Many political, social and economic
conflicts have resulted in instrumental aggression, war being the chief example.

Conflict among people and groups usually concerns the degree to which they have incompatible interests (but sometimes values or ultimate ends are the source of disagreement). Conflicts of interest may concern how information,
behavior, or outcomes are distributed among
people. Most studies of conflict focus on the
latter type of conflict, and have revealed the
problems people encounter in resolving them.
Thus, for example, people involved in a competition to win money (outcome conflict), may
desire to know their opponent's strategy but
may not be able to find out without making revealing moves themselves. Some of the strategies that work least well are using threats
and attacks and capitulating or compromising
early (see the case beginning this chapter).
Strategies that work better include working
to arrive at mutually beneficial outcomes,
proposing package deals, and making systematic
concessions.

Group Problem Solving

Resolving conflicts about rewards and goals is only part of any group or organization activity. Group members must also define their tasks, their products, and their audiences; develop alternative courses of action; acquire, share, and store information; decide among alternatives; and implement, enforce, or ignore decisions. All of these behaviors constitute the problem solving process. Decision making is part of this process; it is the stage or stages during which one or more alternatives are selected.

The fact that a group or organization is working on a particular task changes its nature. Consider, for example, the following cartoon. The group in the cartoon might face a very simple task; perhaps it is one that any individual could have performed alone. Once a group begins work on it, however, the task changes and is no longer comparable to an

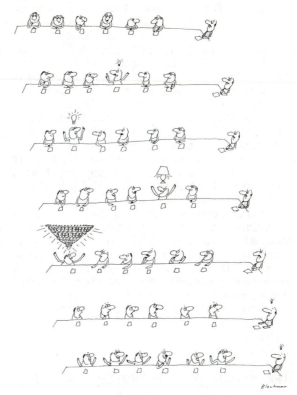

Drawing by R. O. Blechman: 1958 © *Punch* (Rothco).

individual's. Because a group is involved, at least three separate and new problems must be faced: sharing information and ideas, deciding which idea is best (along with deciding how to decide), and gaining acceptance of the best idea. Important aspects of these problems involve organizing so that individual activities can be coordinated, and planning and evaluating the political progress of ideas. These are really social issues.

The social issues of tasks cannot be easily separated from technical issues. For example,

in the cartoon, the issue of how to gain acceptance of an idea is going to be mixed up
with how the chairperson reacts, and that
reaction will affect the definition of what
a "best" idea is. Some experts have argued,
in fact, that the social issues may actually
be the main ones when decisions are made by
a group (cf. Pfeffer, 1978).

This chapter is designed to identify for you
some of the basic dimensions of the problem
solving process in groups. The chapter begins
with a discussion of some different kinds of
tasks that groups work on and how their definitions of those tasks affect the nature of
the problems they actually confront. A later
section reviews the social issues in problem
solving that affect group performance and
decision making. This discussion is meant to
provide a grounding for future study—especially of complex managerial or political
problem solving. The reader is referred to
subsequent books in this series for those
topics. Further detail is provided in Harrison
(1975), Radford (1975), and Janis and Mann
(1977).

THE NATURE OF THE PROBLEM

What a group thinks it must do affects how
a group works together and the outcomes of its
work. The definition of the problem affects
the rest of the problem solving process. It
affects what kinds of information are sought
and considered, who participates in group discussions, what alternatives are considered,
and whose feelings must be satisfied. For example, suppose we are members of a panel of
scientists, chosen from universities across
the country, and asked to review research
grant proposals and to recommend those that
should be funded by the government. Our panel
could take the position that its job was to
make recommendations based only upon scientific
merit, and the discussion would probably turn

to the theoretical and methodological strengths and weakness of the various proposals. The most scientifically prestigious of the panel would probably have greatest influence. If there were too many proposals to consider each carefully, those with the most obvious technical flaws would probably not survive the first cut.

Now let us suppose instead that the definition of the problem is different. Assume that our panel has among its membership scientists who have themselves been working on research applying science to national problems. Suppose these scientists believe that the job of the committee is to recommend funding for research that is socially useful, as well as scientifically worthwhile. This problem definition, assuming it is accepted by at least a significant (or persuasive) minority, will change the work of the panel and its recommendations. For example, the panel must now decide how to weigh usefulness against scientific merit. It now has the problem of defining and choosing among a different set of priorities. The most influential group members may now be those who can find, operationalize, and articulate overlapping objectives such as encouraging excellent scientists to work on applied as well as basic research.

If you consider that this panel is composed of members who belong to various institutions and organizations which may have some competing interests, the difference that the alternative problem definition may make becomes even more apparent. For example, as long as the panel is interested only in science per se, then competition is likely to revolve around the scientific respectability and reputation of applicants in group members' own or preferred areas of research (e.g., claims that one type of research is better than another), but enter a concern with research application, and competition commences over the efficiency and effectiveness of various institutions (e.g., arguments over whether nonprofit institutions are better than universities at conducting "useful" research).

A group's definition of its task—that is, the nature of the problem—is therefore an important issue. It is, however, by no means easy to predict or even specify after the fact how problems develop and how the social issues get worked in with such "objective" aspects of the task as the total amount of information required and whether the information must be widely shared for the task to be completed.

Generally, researchers have examined such objective differences among tasks and not their more subjective social aspects. The groups which researchers have studied have usually been formed just for the laboratory, and they have been given preselected tasks to complete. This approach has not elicited a good representation of what happens in real groups because social issues are not allowed to develop freely or they are minimized as much as possible. Nonetheless, the approach has revealed several differences in the nature of tasks that have large impact on groups, real ones included. One of these, for example, is the difference between a task that requires members to share information with each other vs. a task that does not. This difference results in very different communication patterns (cf. Mackenzie, 1978).

Several investigators have suggested that they might devise a taxonomy of group tasks, particularly a taxonomy that could specify what group behaviors *had* to be enacted in order to achieve at least moderate success.

For instance, Roby and Lanzetta (1958) argued (p. 95):

> We may expect that the most fruitful method of classifying group tasks will be with reference to those aspects of group behavior or procedures which these tasks bring to the foreground. In other words, we would expect that the distinctive features of particular tasks will be the degree to which they require certain group behaviors for adequate performance.

This suggestion was never carried out successfully. So far, formal taxonomy has had little predictive utility (Davis, 1969) and there is no reason, in theory, why such a taxonomy should be either necessary or sufficient to describe a group's work. The objective dimensions of tasks that are known to influence behavior must still be considered as only one of many sources of influence.

The early research on problem solving did not result in a viable taxonomy. It did not fully describe the problem solving process, and certainly did not capture the richness of problem solving in real organizations and groups. But, as we have noted, it did result in the identification of some different types of tasks that differently affect problem solving behavior. There is some value, then, in reviewing and critically examining research on the objective nature of group tasks.

SIMPLE TASKS

Many groups face problems that seem relatively simple because (1) they require few steps to reach a solution and (2) the solution once proposed, is obvious or easily verifiable. Such problems range from very easy tasks (e.g., learning a few code words) to those requiring moderate intellectual skill (e.g., riddles). Indeed, they may involve several activities, including information acquisition, information exchange, and decision making.

Tasks that appeared simple were popular with early researchers because dimensions of some of these problems could be manipulated in the laboratory and because correct answers could be specified. Researchers could easily compare individual against group performance with reference to the time to reach a solution and/ or the number of solutions reached. Comparing individuals to groups was considered an interesting issue although many researchers realized

that group processes change what the task is
and what is considered to be correct or good
performance. A couple of examples will suffice
to illustrate what was done.

1. Perlmutter and de Montmollin (1952) had
   three-person groups learn two-syllable nonsense words. One list was learned by individuals alone (but in the presence of the
   other two); another list was learned co-
   operatively by the group. Half the groups
   worked first as individuals and half worked
   first in the group. The data showed that
   group performance, whether first or second,
   was superior.
2. Shaw (1932) asked isolated individuals and
   four-person groups to solve difficult problems known as the "eureka puzzles." Again,
   groups were superior to individuals. One
   of the problems in which groups excelled
   was this:

   Three Missionaries and three Cannibals are on the
   A-side of the river. Get them across to the B-side by
   means of a boat which holds only two at a time. All
   the Missionaries and one Cannibal can row. Never
   under any circumstances or at any time may the Missionaries be outnumbered by the Cannibals.

Taking together the large number of studies
using such "simple" problems, one may summarize their results as follows: Groups were
superior to individuals in coming up with correct or accurate answers, making fewer errors,
arriving earlier at a learning criterion, and
taking less time per problem. But groups were
inferior when their *relative* efficiency was
calculated: That is, the performance of individuals was superior in terms of the number
of hours required per person. This last generalization has been stated quite succinctly
(p. 74): groups are slow but sure (Kelley and
Thibaut, 1969).

While investigators tried to discover what it
was about group interaction that made group

performance superior, there were scattered reports in the literature, dating back to the
1920s, that even statistical groups were
superior to individuals. For example, Gordon
(1923) asked subjects to rank a set of weights
and correlated their rankings with the true
order of the weights. The average correlation
was .41. Then he created statistical or "nominal" groups by randomly selecting five, ten,
twenty, and fifty subjects and calculating
the average of their individual rankings. For
statistical groups of five, the average correlation with the true order of the weights
was .68, and for statistical groups of fifty,
it was .94. What he had demonstrated was a
statistical principle: the reliability of
measurement is increased by adding items or
independent raters as long as errors are uncorrelated and each item or rater has a fair
chance of predicting the true judgment (Zajonc,
1966).

The observation that, when simple judgments
are required, groups have a statistical advantage over individuals was later found to be
applicable as well to groups which have more
difficult problems, such as the eureka puzzles.
If we can assume that errors are uncorrelated
and that the group knows when it is correct
and if we can calculate the probability that
each member will solve the problem, a statistical model predicting group superiority may
be constructed. Taylor (1954) and Lorge and
Solomon (1955) independently proposed one
model, which the latter called Model A:

$$P_G = 1 - (1 - P_I)^r$$

In this model, P_G is the probability that a
group will solve the problem, P_I is the probability that an individual will solve it, and
r is the size of the group. Lorge and Solomon
reanalyzed three eureka problems used by Shaw
(1932) and found that Model A accounted for
group superiority in two of the problems. A
second statistical model, Model B (which is

similar except it assumes Model A occurs at
each stage of a problem), accounted for group
performance on the third problem.

These statistical models provided a new
baseline for evaluating group problem solving.
They predict that group performance will be
at the level of the most proficient group member and, therefore, that groups will have a
theoretical advantage over nearly all individuals. Comparisons could thus be drawn between
actual group performance and that expected by
statistical calculation.

Studies were performed or reanalyzed with the
new models as a comparison base. What was
found was that actual group performance did
indeed often equal the performance of the
most competent individual group member, but
that there were tasks on which group performance was overpredicted by the models (that
is, the model predicted more success than
actually occurred). Task performances whose
quality was overestimated by Model A were
those in which (1) a number of steps or divisions were required, (2) the correct solution
was not obvious or easily verifiable, and (3)
interpersonal concerns dominated the group.
These exceptions are the very conditions that
characterize most real groups.

For the group to equal the performance of
the most proficient member at least two things
must happen. The group must allow the most
proficient member to solve the problem—that
is, not disrupt performance—and the group
must agree that the solution proposed by the
most proficient member is the correct one. In
real groups these requirements are often not
met. One reason is that the self-defined nature
of the problem makes it practically impossible.
If, for example, an organization must decide
which of two policies to follow with respect
to admitting new members—to admit everyone
or to admit only those who meet certain requirements—there is no easily defined "correct" policy. One of them maximizes "democracy"
at the expense of "exclusiveness" while the

other maximizes "merit" at the expense of "randomness." The real problem, then, might be reaching agreement on a marginally better policy, not discovering the correct answer (Braybrook and Lindblom, 1970).

Even if there is one correct answer and even if the group is ad hoc and has relatively few political concerns, it is by no means certain that the group will allow the most competent member to find the solution or will agree to adopt it. Two factors have been shown to influence whether or not they will permit compliance to take precedence over other concerns. One is the verifiability of the solution itself; the other is their attitudes toward the most competent member. Both factors influence the confidence of members in the most competent person, the confidence of that person, the probability of consensus on the solution, and the rejection of erroneous answers (Kelley and Thibaut, 1969).

In real organizations and groups the effect of considerations other than competence may overwhelm the problem solving process. This occurs even when competence is measurable, facts are available, and success is officially equated with truth. Considerations having this kind of impact include the organization's (or group's) authority to make decisions; its power to implement them; the legality of procedures or decisions; incentives and risks of alternative actions(including their impact on the security of the organization itself); and beliefs about whether a better solution to the current state of affairs exists or is needed.

An article by Sam Adams, who worked as a CIA intelligence analyst during the Vietnam War, provides a good example of how competent people in an organization may come up with verifiably correct answers to a relatively simple question but not have their answers accepted in the organization because of political and social considerations such as those listed above. Adams' job was to estimate Vietcong military strength. After examining military documents carefully and comparing field reports with official ones, he realized that the strength of the Vietcong had been seriously underestimated (600,000 vs. the official count of 270,000). Excitedly, he wrote a report to that effect and told everyone in his office. Nothing happened. No one responded. His numbers, he was finally told, were not acceptable to the military, and it was their responsibility to release official figures. When Adams wrote more memoranda, documenting his estimates with data and demanding a response, the secret CIA estimate was finally revised, but still the military insisted that the official (public) estimate had to remain under 300,000. Low estimates provided support for public statements by the White House that there was light at the end of the tunnel. The CIA organization thus complied with military demands and did not communicate its own estimates to the administration. It was not until many months later, after a devastating offensive by the Vietcong, that the official estimates of its strength were revised.

When Adams tried to expose the previous (and continuing) tampering with data by the military, he was derogated by his own employers and told (p. 68), "Mr. Adams, the real problem is you. You ought to look into yourself." His travel was limited, and he eventually received an unfavorable fitness report. In contrast, some of the military and CIA bureaucrats who abetted the counterfeiting of military intelligence were promoted to more responsible positions. This suggests why an obvious mistake can occur again and again in organizations. A proper analysis of the steps leading to the incorrect solution is avoided. Instead, a single individual or small coalition is blamed. And to blame the one who first pointed out the mistake (who "shook the team") is an easy way to avoid changing procedures and to rid oneself of a group deviant.

MULTIPLE PART TASKS

Now let us return to a consideration of ad
hoc laboratory groups, but consider the effect
of a slightly more complex task—that is, one
which requires members to share information.
Give such a group a task that can be completed
by working out a division of labor by combining
information not uniformly held by all members—
that is, a task with multiple parts—and the
result will sometimes be that the group performs *better* than its most proficient member.
For example, Faust (1959) compared groups and
individuals in their performance on spatial
puzzles and anagram problems. The former are
simple, one-step problems, but the latter are
multiple part problems. (Scrambled words form
a sentence, and people can divide up work on
each word.) He found that groups working on
the spatial puzzles did about as well as the
best individual in nominal groups, but that
groups working on anagrams did better than the
best individual.

The explanation of the group's superiority
on anagrams is again statistical, and predictable from models that take into account
the multiple nature of some problems (e.g.,
Model B in Lorge and Solomon, 1955). That is,
if the errors of individuals can be assumed to
be uncorrelated (randomly distributed), then
statistical averaging results in a pooling of
partial skills or information and a canceling
out of errors. The result is performance higher than that of the most proficient member.
Intuitively, the idea applies to problems of
the anagram sort. The most proficient member
may not think of all the words, but others
can work on those and, moreover, more than one
person can help to store information or hints.
Meanwhile, any redundancy helps to cancel out
errors.

The evidence is very spotty for any advantage to groups on multiple part problems *except*
the statistical one that derives from pooling

answers and canceling errors. In a few laboratory experiments, group members have exceeded
statistical expectations, but more often they
have failed to reach even the levels expected
from statistical models.

MULTIPLE STAGE TASKS

Multiple stage tasks are those which require
working through a sequence of ideas or enacting a sequence of coordinated skills. In contrast to multiple part tasks, multiple stage
intellectual tasks (or decisions) are not
susceptible to a one-time division of labor,
because they require people to place in proper
relation a number of ideas and pieces of information before they can see the answer
(Kelley and Thibaut, 1969). Mackenzie (1978)
discusses multiple stage group problem solving
as a series of stages or "milestones." He shows
that groups develop special structures and
divisions of labor to reach each milestone.

Many researchers have reported that in
laboratory experiments using these kinds of
tasks, ad hoc groups perform significantly
worse than their most proficient member. For
example, Davis and Restle (1963) found that
four-person groups fell short of the level
predicted by Model A on two problems that required a long working through of ideas before
arriving at the best answer. Faucheux and
Moscovici (1958) found that groups working on
Euler's figures performed no better than the
average individual and short of nominal group
scores. (These are problems requiring that
group members follow a common strategy. If
they are not well organized and do not follow
the strategy, members create confusion for
each other.)

Even studies of groups in such games as tug-
of war where physical effort must be coordinated (Dashiell, 1935) indicate that power per
person decreases as group size increases. (In
one study, an eight-man group pulled 249 kilos,

but eight times the average man's pull would
have equalled 504 kilos.)

Almost all of the tasks that real ongoing
groups and organizations have involve multiple
stages. For example, a committee may have the
task of gathering information about an organization's need for raising prices. The task of
gathering information may be amenable to one
division of labor (and in this sense is a
multiple part task), but the committee must
first get organized and decide who is to do
what, a stage which may require a different
division of labor. Later, the group must decide whose information is to be discounted if
there are conflicting pieces of information.
Then it must decide how to publicly announce
the decision and how to implement it. The task
obviously involves a series of steps. The apparent similarity of such tasks to laboratory
experimental tasks on which groups do relatively poorly should not be construed to mean
that real groups would do better if they dis-
banded. We do not really know whether the
tasks are similar (or whether any failure of
the group on the task in question is offset
by successes it has in satisfying other objectives). Yet, given a group working on multiple
stage problems, we ought to examine the difficulties that such a group could encounter—
difficulties which in part are reflected in
experimental studies.

An early study by Thorndike (1938) is illustrative of the coordination difficulties
that such a group might face. He found that
groups did especially poorly in the construction of a crossword puzzle, although with
simpler multiple part construction problems
groups did well, especially if there were
several correct and easily verifiable alternatives. Why? With a crossword puzzle, the relationships of all parts must continually be
kept in mind, and people must coordinate
their activities. A key question concerns the
limitations of short-term memory and information

processing capability. The demands of the problem are not unlike those of the problem the pricing committee has. In both cases the nature of the problem changes the group's ability to work efficiently.

Yet it is not just the demand for coordination and information storage that makes multiple stage problems difficult for groups. The lack of an obvious correct answer or of feedback about the correctness of answers at each stage of the task means that groups decide how they will decide when they are finished with each stage of the task. Should they go with the decision of the most competent member? Should they wait for unanimity? Should they decide that the majority rules? Should they listen to the vociferous member who wants to start over? Whether or not their decision rules are explicit or implicit, they will usually take time to implement and may reduce the productivity of the group. In any case many decisions are required.

DECISIONS

Suppose we give a group of four people, as Olson and Davis (1964) did, five separate and self-contained arithmetic problems. Now they should solve these fairly quickly, because information exchange and simple division of labor are possible. In fact, they should do much better than their most proficient member could do alone. But they will not. Olson and Davis report that twenty-five groups did better than individuals (.64 versus .04 solutions) and better than Model A would predict (.15), but less well than the pooling model (Model B) predicts (.86). The reason is that the groups were as interested in making equalitarian decisions as they were in solving the problems. They were less willing to recognize the skills of more competent members and gave less weight to their answers than they would have if they had been less concerned with being democratic. Davis (1969) reports that rarely have he and his colleagues found groups in the laboratory to work at objectively optimum levels on complex tasks requiring decisions. Their equalitarian decision rules are often inconsistent with objective performance criteria and fail to take full advantage of merit.

It is easy to see how a group's objective productivity may be reduced when decision making does not take account of differential abilities and knowledge. If certain decision rules can hurt the performance of groups working on relatively simple arithmetic problems, imagine the effect on a series of complex decisions such as jury decisions, where choices can never be accurately evaluated for their correctness. In such cases, groups may never discover or may discover too late that their decision rules are causing less than optimum performance by technical or logical criteria.

It is, of course, not always true that equalitarian decision rules are detrimental to a group. An optimum decision in the technical or logical sense that is not politically acceptable or that has been reached by ignoring people's values and commitments can be much worse in the long run. Furthermore, if we have a dictatorship supposedly based on merit, but the dictator is not really a competent member of the group, then problem solving will surely suffer.

The theoretical effect of various decision rules on objective group performance can rather easily be illustrated if we suppose that a group's problem is to choose between two alternatives, A or B. We can even assume that, objectively, A is the best or most correct alternative. Refer to Figure 9.1, adapted from an article on juries by James Davis, Robert Bray, and Robert Holt. It shows for groups of twelve members, and for three different decision rules the probability that a group will choose alternative A as a function of individual preferences for A. (In evaluating the significance of the figure, it may

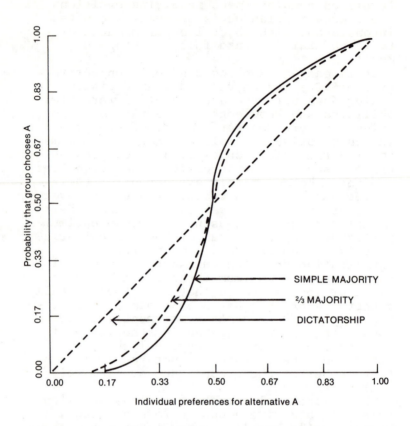

FIGURE 9.1 The Probability that a 12-Person Group, Having Different Decision Rules, Chooses Alternative A Rather Than B As a Function of Individual (and Independent) Choices (Adapted from Davis, Bray and Holt, 1977)

be helpful to imagine that the group is a jury and that "A" is a guilty verdict.) When there is a dictatorship rule, that is, one person decides, the probability of choosing the correct alternative A increases as a direct function of the probability that the dictator prefers A. But a simple-majority decision rule (or a two-thirds majority rule) produces something quite different. When the probability that members prefer A is greater than .5, the group is more likely to choose A than is the dictator. When the probability that members prefer A is less than .5, the group is less likely than the dictator to choose A.

Since majority rule capitalizes on majority sentiments, it is apparent that such a rule will be to a group's advantage if members individually are competent or inclined to be correct. The dictatorship is an advantage when the group members are incompetent or unlikely to prefer the correct decision. The probable effects of other decision schemes can also be calculated, although the figure does not include them. For example, a unanimity rule (all persons must vote for alternative A) or an oligarchy (a fixed subgroup makes the decision) produces a group decision that greatly underestimates individual preferences for A.

Since the nature of a problem (the difficulty of ascertaining correct alternatives, for example) and individual member preferences and competencies affect the efficacy of decision rules, researchers have tried to investigate what decision rules groups actually use in various problem situations. As you would expect, groups have been found to use different decision rules in different situations, and often these rules are by no means optimum from a logical point of view. Davis et al. (1975), for example, found that a two-third majority rule governed simulated jury decisions. Groups failed to reach a decision (a hung jury) whenever a two-thirds majority could not agree. (That is, a two-thirds majority had to prefer one alternative; otherwise, there was a stalemate.)

An interesting finding of the Davis et al. study was that although individual preferences for a guilty verdict added up to a probability of .22, not one jury arrived at a guilty verdict. This seems to indicate that a sizable

minority was "suppressed" by the group during
interaction. Such an effect is an outcome of
majority decision. In groups having any majority decision rule which is followed, group decisions will underestimate minority views and
exaggerate high probability opinions. The
reader is referred to Davis (1973) for a more
complete discussion of this point.

REAL, COMPLEX PROBLEMS

We have been assuming up to this point that
there exists a more or less objectively de-
finable task, an optimum group solution and a
group attempting to reach it. This is often
not the case. Rational solutions, for example,
may not be the issue the group thinks is important. Alternative issues, such as choosing
a politically acceptable procedure for moving
along, may be considered much more important.

The study of decision processes in ongoing
groups and among members of organizations has
revealed many dimensions of complex problems
(cf. Connolly, 1977; Janis and Mann, 1977).
Several of these follow:

1. A real, complex problem is actually a
series of decisions, each of which may have
multiple objectives with varying priorities.
This implies that we must understand how decisions and objectives affect each other and
interact. For instance, if an organization
doesn't have improving its personnel as an
objective, will employment decisions be more
or less subject to the idiosyncratic attitudes
of individuals?

2. Objectives of problem solving are not
always specifiable. For instance, a business
organization may not be able to anticipate
whether it will have much competition or who
its competition will be. Therefore, it will be
unable to identify whether or not it should
plan along those lines. Some organizations try
to deal with this "problem about problems" by
using an analysis of options technique, which

involves planning for alternative situations (Radford, 1975).

3. Available alternatives for solving a problem may not be amenable to quantitative analysis. There may be no objective criteria for weighing them (e.g., a strike versus a year's unsatisfactory wages). The best many groups can do is rank their preferences. Often, groups simply rely upon precedent or traditional standard operating procedures (cf. Tuggle, 1978).

4. Problems are solved by many people; no one can handle all of a complex group issue. Authority, responsibility, and power rarely reside in one and the same person. For example, the theoretical dictator discussed earlier rarely exists in fact. In ongoing groups even the most autocratic leader does not act without being affected by others. If such a leader does make a unilateral decision, others are usually needed to support the decisions and implement them. Sometimes a seeming dictator only acts as a clearinghouse for ideas.

These considerations should make clear why problem solving in groups is so difficult to understand. No current theory is so neat as to discuss a group's success or failure in the singular. Success and failure, of course, depend (among other things) on *which* kind of success the group desires and which kind of failure can be avoided. We turn now to a more systematic consideration of the interpersonal processes affecting what a group wants to do and believes it can do, as well as its attempts to deal with its problems.

INTERPERSONAL PROCESSES IN GROUP PROBLEM SOLVING

CONFORMITY

In earlier chapters, the various processes leading to compliance in groups were described.

One might summarize a major point of that discussion in a single sentence. Groups will move toward unanimity of opinion and compliance with norms because group members want to be accepted and want to be correct. This generalization is no less true in groups working on a specific problem than in freely interacting groups. Thomas and Fink (1961), for example, found that most groups made unanimous decisions about complex problems, even when they were incorrect, and, further, that the members of unanimous groups were more satisfied with their decisions than the members of split groups, whether or not the unanimous decision was correct or incorrect.

The pressure to give a uniform judgment or make a unanimous decision (after, perhaps, a majority vote or consensus develops) is not much of a problem when the task is viewed as simple. In fact, when time is short and alternatives are about equal, the group experiencing high social pressure to agree is at an advantage. But when a free exchange of ideas is necessary, when minority views have value, and when the problem, in general, is complex, as it most usually is, the tendency for group members to promote consensus may be detri-mental to their desired performance (Hoffman, 1965).

Conformity pressures have been demonstrated to have strong effects in two interesting group situations, one in which groups can make risky decisions and another in which groups are supposed to produce creative ideas. The study of risky decisions was begun by Stoner (see Brown, 1965) and Kogan, and Wallach (e.g., Kogan and Wallach, 1964). They gave to individuals, and then to groups of these individuals, a series of problems that required a choice among risky alternatives. On problems of the type illustrated below, group decisions were significantly more risky than individual decisions (Brown, 1965, p. 657):

1. Mr. A, an electrical engineer who is married and has one child, has been working for a large electronics corporation since graduating from college five years ago. He is assured of a lifetime job with a modest, though adequate, salary, and liberal pension benefits upon retirement. On the other hand, it is very unlikely that his salary will increase much before he retires. While attending a convention, Mr. A is offered a job with a small, newly founded company with a highly uncertain future. The new job would pay more to start and would offer the possibility of a share in the ownership if the company survived the competition of the larger firms.

Imagine that you are advising Mr. A. Listed below are several probabilities or odds of the new company's proving financially sound. Please check the *lowest* probability that you consider acceptable to make it worthwhile for Mr. A to take the new job.

☐ The chances are 1 in 10 that the company will prove financially sound.

☐ The chances are 3 in 10 that the company will prove financially sound.

☐ The chances are 5 in 10 that the company will prove financially sound.

☐ The chances are 7 in 10 that the company will prove financially sound.

☐ The chances are 9 in 10 that the company will prove financially sound.

☐ Place a check here if you think Mr. A should *not* take the new job, no matter what the probabilities.

Once the discovery was made that group judgments shifted toward the risky end of the continuum, a number of possible explanations were studied, some of which were subsequently rejected. The risky shift, for example, does not seem to depend upon group members being "entrepreneur" types, because the risky shift appears in groups made up of liberal arts male and female undergraduates as well as of graduate students in industrial management (Wallach, Kogan, and Bem, 1962). Neither does the shift depend upon the experimental situation in which no real losses are involved, for it occurs when risk entails actual monetary costs (Wallach, Kogan, and Bem, 1964) or participation in painful physiological experiments (Bem, Wallach, and Kogan, 1965).

What does seem to be involved in the risky shift is something that happens during the group discussion. But precisely what happens is unclear. Several hypotheses have been advanced, among the most plausible being that (1) taking risks is a behavior valued by group members, who feel pressure to conform by adopting risky positions in public (to be conservative is to be "stuffy" or "afraid"); (2) people in groups feel less personally responsible for mistakes (the "diffusion of responsibility" hypothesis); and (3) people who argue for risk in groups are more persuasive than people who argue for conservative choices because risky positions are inherently more persuasive. Unfortunately, the evidence for each of these hypotheses has been mixed. Further, it has been discovered that consistent *conservative* shifts occur in groups as well (e.g., Burns, 1967; Stoner, 1968).

Because cautious as well as risky shifts are produced by group discussion and because these shifts seem similar to systematic revisions in attitudes commonly found in groups (e.g., in Moscovici and Zavalloni, 1969), some researchers have proposed that the risky (or cautious) shift is part of a very general phenomenon described in the classical problem solving literature (cf. Vinokur and Burnstein, 1974). That is, group members form a consensus around judgments that have the most persuasive weight (or number) in group discussion.

Shifts occur particularly when all the persuasive arguments (or the information on which they are based) are not fully known to each individual initially and when each hears new, more persuasive arguments or information during discussion. During decision making, superior arguments in favor of risk (or caution) cause the risky (or conservative) shift.

"classical" problem solving, the superiority of arguments favoring the correct decision causes a shift in that direction. During decision making, superior arguments in favor of risk (or caution) cause the risky (or conservative) shift.

In this view, the risky shift is based upon the difference between pre-discussion knowledge of pro-risk arguments and the preponderance of pro-risk arguments during discussion, rather than a risk norm per se. This hypothesis is similar to hypothesis (3) above, but does not assume that risk arguments will always be the most persuasive. When individuals' initial information or arguments are only partially shared and when pro-caution arguments are most persuasive or numerous during the information or argument sharing discussion, we would expect a cautious shift.

Many studies appear to fit the hypothesis that risky (or other kinds of) group shifts depend upon the sharing of information in the group and upon social influence processes insuring that group members will change in the direction of the majority or most persuasive view. For example, Lamm (1967) showed that group shifts occur when group members simply hear a discussion of their problem and, in doing so, are exposed to some information they did not have prior to discussion. The direction of such group shifts on decision tasks is highly correlated with the proportion of risky to conservative arguments (Ebbesen .and Bowers, 1974).

The issue is not yet settled, for it is still not clear whether group shifts toward risk or conservatism depend most upon the degree of members' initial lack of information, the degree of credibility of risky (or cautious) arguments themselves, or the confidence and prestige or risky (or cautious) group members. The method of studying the risky shift by using hypothetical problems will not answer these questions. What is fairly certain is that group decisions reflect social influence that is, conformity to persuasive or informed others in the direction of group expectations. Eventually, there is greater uniformity of opinion, and a vote or consensus that may significantly differ from the average of individual judgments.

The study of groups engaged in producing creative ideas has also revealed significant effects of social influence. It has been discovered that groups instructed to come up with new solutions for a problem or creative ideas often do just the reverse: that is, group members tend to pursue rigid lines of thought and criticize those who propose unusual ideas. Moreover, a tendency to evaluate ideas as they come up, instead of waiting until all suggestions have been made and then making choices among the best, has often caused groups to discard or forget relatively good ideas (Hoffman and Maier, 1964).

Osborn (1957) introduced the technique of brainstorming as a way of overcoming pressures toward the conventional and familiar. He gave advertising teams explicit instructions to offer as many ideas as they could during group discussion, however silly, and to meanwhile forego criticism and evaluation. Osborn reported great success with this technique, but experimental tests of the brainstorming technique have shown it to be no panacea. Unless they are well trained in withholding evaluations, brainstorming groups often fail to overcome conformity pressures (e.g., Taylor, Berry, and Block, 1958; Cohen, Whitmyre, and Funk, 1960). Moreover, even when brainstorming groups come up with more unique ideas than individuals, those ideas are not necessarily superior (Weisskopf-Joelson and Eliseo, 1961). A critical problem is that brainstorming groups tend to give up far too early in the discussion, whereas they should instead wait out silences and give people a chance to reflect.

Maximizing the conditions under which groups freely exchange ideas is not the only thing that needs doing to increase their level of performance, for social pressure also makes it likely that group members will in the end reject unique, creative ideas and choose solutions to problems that more closely reflect what is perceived to be normal.

Since conformity with others' opinions and behavior depends upon desires for acceptance and for the reduction of uncertainty, one would expect that the rejection of new or creative solutions to problems is a function of the degree to which group members need approval or are uncertain. This seems to be the case. For example, group members who are less certain of their abilities are more likely than are confident group members to be influenced by others (e.g., Gurnee, 1937), and, in turn, people conform to those who are perceived to be most able, who act confidently, or who have a history of success (e.g., Mausner, 1954).

The tendency to rely upon the judgment of others when one is uncertain applies to the uncertainty of whole groups. When groups are uncertain they turn outward. In contrast, groups that have a history of success are more likely than groups that have a history of failure to conform to average judgments of insiders. Whether or not this tendency helps the group is, of course, a function of the similarity between past and present problems. Hoffman (1965, p. 104) has noted that:

> The omniscient and omnipotent powers . . . given to the [successful] . . . group remind one of those questionable personnel selection decisions which assume that success in one situation predicts success in another: great generals make great executives; the best graduate students make the best professors.

Successful individuals in successful groups can really be myopic when they are faced with new problems, especially when they are under time pressures and decisions must be made to alleviate a crisis (or, alternatively, when there is no time pressure and advice rather than a decision is to be made). The members of such groups may be convinced that they know the most about nearly everything, that there is no time (or need) to ask people outside the group for opinions, and that people outside the group would agree with them anyway, if they knew as much. These groups engage in "groupthink" (Janis, 1972), or, the avoidance of minority and outside opinions and the adoption of a very high degree of in-group social influence.

The result of groupthink is bad decision-making, characterized by the tendency to avoid controversial issues, to fail to question weak arguments, or to call a halt to soft-headed thinking. Here, extracted from Janis and Mann (1977) are eight symptoms of groupthink, each of which may be considered an extreme form of the conformity which normally exists in cohesive groups (pp. 130-131):

1. an illusion of invulnerability
2. collective efforts to rationalize and the discounting of warnings
3. an unquestioned belief in the group's inherent morality
4. stereotyped views of rivals and enemies as evil
5. direct pressure on any member who expresses minority arguments
6. self-censorship of deviations from the group's consensus
7. a shared illusion of unanimity
8. the emergence of self-appointed "mind-guards" against adverse information

COMMITMENT TO THE GROUP AND TO GROUP GOALS

Processes leading to personal commitment in groups will have impact on how group members define their problems and work together. For example, we would expect private feelings of commitment to the group will maximize the perceived importance of loyalty, which, in turn, will cause members to regard with dismay decisions that might reflect badly upon the group.

More subtle effects of commitment are at work, too. For example, personal commitment to the group can reverse the usual effect of organizational rewards which, in turn, affect participation in the organization. An experiment by Barry Staw (1974) illustrates. Staw's study took advantage of the fact that during the Vietnam engagement many male college students had joined the Army Reserve Officer's Training Corps (ROTC) to avoid being drafted. These same men, in late 1969 and early 1970, received a draft lottery number which affected the value of being in ROTC. That is, if they received a low number, the value of ROTC was increased, for they would have been drafted had they not joined ROTC. If they received a high number, the value of ROTC was lowered, because a high number meant they would probably not have been drafted anyway.

Staw assumed that those who signed a contract binding them to ROTC prior to receiving a draft lottery number (but after they had expected to receive one) were highly committed. Those who joined ROTC after receiving a number were presumably less committed. (Support for these assumptions was provided by private attitude measures and by data on joining as a function of lottery number). The major dependent variables of interest to Staw were satisfaction with the ROTC organization, ROTC turnover, and performance ratings. Data were provided for 550 students from universities in the Chicago area.

Table 9.1 shows the effect of high commitment (that is, low external rewards for being in ROTC) on two of the measures, satisfaction and performance. The higher the lottery number (that is, the lower the value of ROTC for avoiding the draft), the higher the indicators of satisfaction and performance in ROTC.

TABLE 9.1 Satisfaction and Performance of Committed ROTC
Students after Receiving Draft Lottery Numbers
(Data from Staw, 1974)

Indicator	Draft Lottery Numbers		
	1–122	123–244	245–366
[a]Satisfaction	2.85	3.11	3.47
[b]Performance	-.25	-.10	.36

[a]The higher the score, the greater was average satisfaction expressed in answer to eight questions.

[b]The higher the score, the higher were average ROTC
grades and percentiles during the semester after the
lottery numbers were distributed. (These are normalized
means.)

The implications of this result are several.
First, satisfaction with a group increases
with commitment. Second, problem solving or
performance consistent with the group's norms
and objectives increases with commitment. Third,
large rewards may reduce commitment, satisfaction, and performance. Perhaps large rewards
cause people to view their motivation as ex-
ternally created or controlled and reduces
their internal motivations. Clearly, commitment to the group must be a consideration in
devising incentives for problem solving. If
they are too low, people will not get involved
enough to become committed in the first place;
if they are too high, the commitment that
exists may be diluted.

ATTRACTION

The tendency for people to like others who
have socially desirable characteristics,
especially high physical attraction, status,

and power, significantly affect problem solving
in groups. People who have those characteristics are judged more talented and competent,
and their opinions are given greater weight.
That their positive features may have little
to do with their actual competence is obvious,
but, ironically, the relative bias is greatest
when their competence is poor. Landy and
Sigall (1974) recently reported that judgments
of an essay were least affected by the physical attractiveness of a (female) writer when
the essay was actually good. When it was bad,
it was evaluated almost as well as a good essay if the writer was physically attractive.

People who talk a great deal also have an
advantage. Riecken (1958) demonstrated that
elegant solutions were rarely adopted when
their proponents were not talkative, but were
almost always adopted when they were very
talkative. Slater (1955) and several others
have reported that persons who talk the most
are most likely to be selected as leaders by
other group members. Mackenzie and Barron
(1970) have shown with a business game
that attempts by a confederate trained with
the optimal solution procedures often fail
because the confederate "fails to try hard. The
best predictor of the rate of adoption of
the optimal technique is not quality but the
quantity of effort by the confederate relative
to the quantity of efforts by others who support conventional wisdom or less optional techniques. The squeaky wheel, then, does get attention.

If talk were highly correlated with performance, the latter phenomenon would benefit
groups, but we know that is not always the
case. People who talk a great deal tend to
be task motivated (Crockett, 1955), active,
and socially extroverted (Mann, 1959). (The
initial letters of the test scales used to
measure these characteristics of talkative
people are "GAS." According to Hoffman [1965],
the acronym is apt in view of the amount of
hot air that emerges.) The three traits,

however, are not correlated with general cognitive ability (Guilford, 1952) and are often
not related to effective group performance
(Fouriezos, Hutt, and Guetzkow, 1950).

In any particular group, interpersonal
attraction and respect may, in fact, be based
upon demonstrable competence, and the person
who talks may actually be the most expert.
Nevertheless, talking and attractiveness are
sometimes signs of too much dominance. Group
leaders who do not dominate but instead encourage the expression of minority views may
act to facilitate problem solving (Maier and
Solem, 1952).

THE EASY WAY OUT

A theme that consistently rings out in the
literature on group interaction is that people
take the easy way out when faced with problems. When they have the choice of facing up
to conflict or avoiding it, planning ahead or
working on routine tasks, discussing which
problem to work on or choosing the most salient, putting ideas on paper or just tossing
them around, group members can be expected to
choose the latter alternatives. It is not
known precisely why this happens, but it is
known that the easy way out can create more
difficult problems for the group in the future.
For example, avoiding written work reduces the
degree to which alternative objectives and
priorities are discussed. Then, when a written
product is tried, the group is caught unpre-
pared for the time it will need to discuss
competing ideas.

Ideational conflict can be conducive to
creative problem solving (cf. Hoffman, 1961).
Experimentally, this has been demonstrated by
Hoffman, Harburg, and Maier (1962), who instructed low status group members to oppose
the suggestions of a high status member and
subsequently found that the resulting conflict produced more creative solutions. For
conflict to be productive, Hoffman maintains,

it should be based upon substantive issues,
not likes and dislikes among group members.
Guetzkow and Gyr (1954) demonstrated this
when they showed that successful management
conferences were punctuated by substantive
conflict, whereas the unsuccessful ones were
characterized by interpersonal, emotional conflict. It is not easy, however, to stick to
substance in a conflict, for when people disagree, they tend to dislike each other (see
Chapter 7). That may be why so often they take
the easy way and avoid all kinds of confrontation.

Planning in advance, especially scheduling
time and writing down things to be done, may
help groups avoid unexpected contingencies.
Small groups can overcome some information and
response distribution difficulties by spending
time getting organized. Many of the problems
large groups and organizations have could be
at least partially surmounted by short and
medium range planning. For instance, it has
been pointed out by Cyert, March and others
that top management often must rely on second,
third, fourth, fifth, or sixth-hand information in making a decision. This information
is both biased and condensed. As a result,
management does not really make the decision;
instead, there seems to be a progressive commitment along the line toward a particular
course of action (March, 1959). Planning and
organization to reduce information bias and
oversimplification can force decision makers
to attend to many relevant facts and ideas.
Planning can also benefit the group by focusing
attention on the requirements of the problem
and perhaps identifying which problem of many
should be worked on.

The need for planning is not usually the
most salient feature of situation, whereas
immediate problems and work are (Cohen, March,
and Olsen, 1972). Moreover, to plan ahead is
to deal with uncertain utilities and contingencies. It is easier to simply go directly to
problem solving or decision making, especially

if it is routine. At Carnegie-Mellon, March, Simon, and their colleagues had subjects handle relatively simple administrative jobs. These jobs involved sending routine communications to clerks about warehouse inventories, assigning clerks to warehouses, and suggesting any other changes in procedure that might be effective in the future. Although the jobs were described as equally important, the subjects spent considerably more than one-third of their time on routine matters. And as their work load increased, less and less time was spent on planning.

Similar difficulties in allocating time to planning are characteristic of observed behavior in actual large-scale organizations. It is psychologically easier to work on problems as they present themselves than to systematically search for the most profitable use of one's time. Managers in modern organizations are sometimes trained in the use of options analysis and cost-benefit analysis in order to force their attention to planning. This does not necessarily render their planning useful, however, since *what* is planned may have little to do with what the organization finds useful later. Planning exercises may, for example, be used to provide seemingly objective rationalizations for self-interested objectives and procedures.

In conclusion, groups lean toward the easy way out, which is not to their advantage if they can plan and confront conflict sensibly. If, on the other hand, confronting conflict means acting out emotions and if planning means rationalizing, then the easy way out is probably the better way out.

SITUATIONAL FACTORS

Whenever researchers leave the laboratory and test their hypotheses in the field (or design programs based upon laboratory research), the impact of uncontrolled situational factors becomes of special concern. Small but psychologically significant differences between laboratory conditions and field situations can make it difficult to demonstrate the generalizability of a hypothesis. Yet there is a heuristic advantage in field studies because it is just those differences, if one can identify them, that provide new insights and theoretical changes which can be tested later in the laboratory. One difference that repeatedly presents itself is that in real settings there are other groups around which may exert influence on the "experimental" group as well as environmental conditions which may make certain behaviors that people enact in the laboratory much less probable. Among these conditions are acts of nature (e.g., drought) and acts of other nations (e.g., missile installations [Allison, 1971]).

The effect of the larger social environment has been noted both in discussions of the problem solving literature and in many other areas of social psychology. We may point, for example, to the research on altruism. In the laboratory, a sizable group of subjects have in experiment after experiment failed to help people in trouble. Partly, this is because the situation is ambiguous (Latané and Darley, 1970). That is, subjects do not really know whether the emergency is real and whether their help is needed. The presence of other subjects also reduces helping because people depend on them to take whatever risks are involved in altruistic acts (Latané and Darley, 1963).

In contrast, researchers field testing the effect of bystanders, the need for help, and other variables have found that the degree of altruism is sometimes quite high. For instance, in a high percentage of cases (62 of 65), passengers on a subway helped a person in distress (Piliavin, Rodin, and Piliavin, 1969). That led Staub and Baer (1974) to guess that the difficulty of escape was an important factor in altruism. Subjects in the laboratory expected to

leave soon and were frequently placed in a room
different from the victim in need of help, whereas passengers on a moving subway train could
neither leave nor ignore the victim. In a
subsequent study, Staub and Baer showed that
the difficulty of escape was indeed important.
Pedestrians who encountered a heart attack
victim in their path were more likely to offer
aid than were pedestrians on the opposite side
of the street.

In the area of problem solving, the extreme
complexity of most real group problems and
the presence of outside pressure groups has
reduced the generalizability of some hypotheses
discovered in the laboratory. Charles Lindblom
(1959) has discussed this in a paper on policy
decisions in government. He notes that laboratory studies of problem solving (as well as
the more complicated studies involving systems
analysis and operations research) focus upon
the importance of clear objectives, explicit-
ness of evaluation, a high degree of information exchange and review, and quantification
of values. But, he argues, public administrators cannot follow these lines easily.

How does one specify the utility of all possible objectives when (1) possible objectives
are practically endless, (2) different groups
weigh values quite differently, (3) objectives
cannot actually be divorced from the policies
that would lead to them, and (4) long-term
objectives cannot be completely reached without sacrificing other important goals? Actually, administrators must choose among a few
possible alternatives, which are not too different from the old policy and which combine
actions or programs in ways attractive to different groups. For example, in formulating
an urban renewal policy, they must choose
among policies that can satisfy objectives
such as the following: emptying old buildings
quickly, finding suitable accommodations for
current tenants, and avoiding friction with

people in areas to which the current tenants are sent. Such practical difficulties led Lindblom to propose that policy making in real groups is often accomplished by the method of successive limited comparisons (e.g., comparing two similar alternatives for taking a first step, and waiting until later to consider the next step). Researchers have studied some factors that influence such comparisons.

One factor is the presence of other groups with conflicting objectives (cf. Pfeffer, 1978). If these other groups are powerful, it is essential that one choose a policy that will be acceptable to them, and, in fact, agreement among groups may become the only practical test of a policy's correctness. It is therefore quite logical that a group's problem solving approach may involve a search for solutions agreeable to other groups but with avoidance of specifying objectives too clearly. If such solutions can be found, it might indeed be quite disruptive to examine whether there is also agreement on objectives among groups or even to reexamine the policy in light of the group's own objectives. Lindblom argues that the proliferation of different groups in our society has increased the chance that various objectives will eventually have a chance of being reached, so that perhaps it is not bad to ignore discussion of objectives among groups.

The variety of recent laboratory studies in which expectations of future interaction were manipulated may be viewed as an attempt to investigate, under controlled conditions, the influence of conflicting group pressures on problem solving. Traditionally, problem solving groups in the laboratory meet with strangers who will never see each other again, and the group product does not have to be reconciled with the opinions of people in other groups. By having some groups of subjects expect to interact with each other again, researchers can examine how concern about the future

implication of an individual's or group's
behavior affects present behavior.

Some interesting effects have emerged. Shapiro
(1975), for example, found that divisions of
reward among people who had made unequal work
contributions were changed when people expected to interact with them again. Instead of
equitably distributing rewards (i.e., rewarding people in accordance with their work),
people divided rewards equally. This sort of
behavior is probably analogous to public
policy decisions that are based upon the acceptability of outcomes, the avoidance of
future conflict, or the decision to invest in
certain constituencies.

THE VALUE OF PROBLEM SOLVING IN GROUPS

Whether or not groups perform at optimum
levels defined by some criterion of absolute
correctness is no longer a meaningful question, for what is optimum depends upon the
group. Even so, it is clear that many groups
do not perform as well as they would like.
Members of government committees, for example,
may be heard to complain that (1) their meetings are a waste of time; (2) decisions could
have been predicted beforehand (i.e., were
a foregone conclusion); and/or (3) the chairperson (or other designated individual) could
have done the job better if he or she had
worked alone.

Are too many problems and decisions made in
groups? Is participation overrated? Consider
what would happen if problems were solved and
decisions made by competent individuals, armed
only with computers and masses of quantitative
data. Their solution to any problem might indeed surpass that of a group, but the likelihood of others understanding, accepting, and
acting upon the solution would be considerably
reduced. Since group maintenance, member
satisfaction, member motivation, and individual performance are dramatically effected by
the degree to which members participate in

organizing themselves and in problem solving
(e.g., Bass and Leavitt, 1963; Liem, 1975),
group problem solving in the long run may be
more superior and more economical than problem
solving that is done by expert individuals
(Thibaut and Kelley, 1961).

Further, whatever one's arguments for individual problem solving, group problem solving
is here to stay anyway. Kelley and Thibaut
(1969) argue the case effectively (p. 89):

> Group decision making is an inevitable and omni-
> present phenomenon whether effective or not. So long
> as group members are interdependent in attaining
> their goals, they will wish to be involved in deci-
> sions regarding the priority to be given these goals
> and the means to be chosen for their attainment.
> . . . Faced with widespread desire for group deci-
> sions—indeed, faced with group decision making as an
> essential ingredient of interdependent life—we must
> understand and manage these processes as well as pos-
> sible.

IMPROVING THE PRODUCTIVITY OF GROUPS

The chances are rather high that the reader
of this book will find himself or herself at
some time the leader of a work or decision-
making group. Given that you know some of the
problems that groups face, something about
what happens in groups, and some understanding
of why groups sometimes falter or do a poor
job, what could you do about it? The following
objectives illustrate how some experienced and
successful group leaders have improved the
productivity of their own groups.

ESTABLISHING A ROLE AS LEADER

Most effective leaders view themselves as
responsible for the work of their group and
will try to maintain or establish the respect
of group members so that this responsibility

can be carried out. It is equally important
to induce group members to see themselves, also, as responsible for the group's work. If
they do not, the leader will wind up with all
the work and with lack of consensus on the end
product besides. It is necessary, then, to
establish one's credentials as a viable leader
without reducing the commitment of group members to the task (the latter phenomenon arises
when group members view responsibility for a
final product or solution as the leader's and
their job as simply to provide opinions).

It has been said that a poor leader is one
who is blamed for everything that goes wrong,
that a good leader is one who receives admiration and credit, and that a great leader is
someone surrounded by people who think they
themselves have done a great job. Being a merely
adequate leader may require that one overwhelm the group with one's "inputs" or credentials; being a really top-notch leader requires demonstrating to group members that one
can support what group members want to do.

Accomplishing this last objective usually
demands a great deal more effort than the
usual attempt to gain respect and attention,
for it means becoming a useful follower
as well as a leader in the classical sense.
In many situations the effort will have to be
limited, but any leader can at least consider
it an objective that is worth doing something
about. How is it done?(cf. Kiesler, 1976).

1. The leader must help the group define the
   situation and the task in a way that not
   only gets the job done well, but also fits
   with his or her own strengths. In this way,
   the leader's skills and expertise can be
   made useful to the group. Some leaders, for
   example, have very good social skills and,
   in trying to help the group reach a consensus, will want to emphasize interpersonal interaction and group meetings. In the
   same situation, leaders who are perhaps
   more introverted but highly sensitive to

the views of others may prefer written or
informal communications with individuals.
If overlapping goals are identified and if
the best of several views are synthesized
(perhaps through written documents), such a
leader can de-emphasize group meetings.
Meetings of the formal sort can proceed
relatively quickly and be used not to reach
but to review the consensus that the leader
has already discovered and articulated to
individuals.

2. The leader must be well prepared for group
   meetings so that time is not wasted on
   last-minute searches for information, on
   rehashing information that was not made
   easily available, on personal ego problems
   that were left unattended, or on conflict
   that cannot be handled effectively because
   it was not anticipated. To be prepared
   means knowing not only the hard data,
   but knowing the views of group members as
   individuals and planning for discussions in
   which individual perceptions and concerns
   about the task can be raised.

3. The leader must try to "sit in the skin" of
   group members as people and be helpful to
   them in reaching their own objectives.
   Group members will want to know what's going on and to be reassured that their perspectives are receiving some attention.

4. It is important to accept self-interested
   remarks, "ego trips," failures to work, and
   emotional outbursts as human expressions of
   personal interests and commitments. Interests and commitments should be viewed as
   something to work with, not against. Almost
   anyone's commitments will feed into goals
   that are important to the group, and one
   can discover sources of strength for the
   group even in egotistical people. It is
   equally desirable for a group leader to
   view his or her own interests and emotions
   with as much objectivity and openness as
   possible so that they do not interfere with
   the task. Group members are very sensitive

to biases, whether actual or perceived, on
the part of group leaders. The facts are
much less important than perceptions in
this regard. If group members perceive that
the leader's biases are interfering with
the group process or with their own, then
the leader should reconsider his or her own
behavior, not seek out ways to prove the
"truth."

DEFINING A SOLVABLE PROBLEM

In the foregoing chapters we have seen that
group members work together best on a problem
(1) that is of their own choosing, (2) that is
reasonably clear, (3) that is framed in a way
which fits with the members' definition of the
situation, and (4) that is perceived as solvable. Yet many groups whose problem meets
these criteria become stymied or even compound
their problem. Watzlawick, Weakland, and Fisch
(1974) have written a book called *Change* that
is filled with illustrations of this phenomenon along with a theoretical approach to it.
Basically, the real problem of the group is
that it has not defined a solvable problem.
Consider the following:

1. A few years ago, New York State attempted
   to crack down on illegal drug traffic by
   enacting tough new laws for the quick,
   severe punishment of drug suppliers,
   dealers, and users. Nevertheless, drug
   traffic remained as high as in states
   without such laws, court delays increased,
   and millions of dollars were diverted from
   other public services. This case illustrates
   the defining of a long-run, difficult social problem as one that is short-run and
   traceable to a relatively few individuals.
   In doing so, the group insures that the
   problem will be unsolvable. Problems such
   as earthquakes, crime, smuggling, drug
   abuse, prejudice, cruelty, and war are
   centuries old. There is no known quick "cure"

for these problems, and they cannot be defined as though there were.

2. A large industry in this country advertises and sells means for the attainment of the "ideal" or nearly ideal marriage. Doubtless, this endeavor has caused many couples to become dissatisfied with their own relationship, since quite normal disagreements and changes in relationships are seen as needing therapeutic attention. When all the advice promoted in encounter weekends, manuals, magazines, and books inevitably fails to help the couples attain their ideal state, it is taken as a sign that the marriage is hopeless (rather than hopelessly normal).

   As in this latter case, many groups seek solutions to problems that are not problems or search for problems to match solutions (or group rationale) they already have. The change thus attempted may then create difficulties that did not exist before. This phenomenon is not farfetched or unusual. Examples are legion in groups which try to attain ultimate happiness or other utopian states for their members or others, to "clearly communicate their goals" to other groups, or to change the private attitudes and feelings of people whose behavior is actually quite reasonable.

3. About four years ago, a legal aid clinic for the poor was established in a small city in the southern United States. When the clinic lawyers turned their attention from individual problems such as divorces and wills to certain predatory businesses in the city, a group of business executives representing the shadier, marginal side of the business community decided to get even. They began courting elected officials to narrow the clinic's range of acceptable litigation, created through various fronts apparent "agitation" by organizations representing the poor, and through various other techniques aroused ire against the clinic for diverting funds from "more pressing" issues.

The clinic fought back as best it could but lost more public support and resources. Soon it seemed that legal aid for the poor in the city would have to be abandoned. At this stage, the director of the clinic commenced a major suit against the businesses employing fraudulent selling and credit techniques and asked the local court for an injunction to stop all illegal debt collection practices. With this message of strength, the clinic captured the support of the legitimate business community and created disarray among its enemies, who abandoned their attack.

This case illustrates that groups must often do more than redefine their problem. In formulating a problem that is solvable, many groups may find that they redefine the situation itself. It would have helped the clinic very little to seek the "real" causes of the attacks against it or to attempt further to defend or justify its actions. To survive, the clinic had to leave the "You shove, I push, you shove, I push" situation and create a "We act, you support, we act" situation. Many conflicts can be resolved satisfactorily only in this manner because the "I push, you shove" or the "You attack, I defend" syndrome is a circular one that feeds upon itself.

Watzlawick, Weakland, and Fisch (1974) give us some thoughtful advice that can be adapted by leaders to help their groups through such difficulties:

1. Begin by defining the problem of the group in objective behavioral terms, such as "We have lower sales in area II than in other areas" (rather than "We have an image problem in area II") or "The trustees are reallocating our funds after we have already decided how to spend them" (rather than "Our morale is low because the trustees are interfering with us"). In doing so, the

leader identifies what the objective problem
is and is able to help the group discard
problems that either do not exist, are
framed in ways that can never be solved, or
simply must be accepted as facts of life.
2. Identify the solutions that have been tried
so far, and investigate whether these solutions have created more problems than they
solved, cost more than their benefits, or
are directed at the wrong problem.
3. Identify the changes that are desired in objective behavioral terms, as "to increase
sales 5 percent per year in area II" (not
"to improve our image") or "to reduce by 50
percent the number of patients who do not
pay their bills" (not "to tighten up billing
practices"). Groups should distinguish vague
goals from actual objectives, separate problems from solutions (or real problems from
problems merely implied by their solutions),
and be able to recognize when objectives or
motives behind objectives, are what is perceived as the problem.
4. In making a plan to bring about the change
desired, consider whether definitions of
the situations must be reframed. For example, can an impending confrontation be
reframed as a situation in which the parties
have a common aim? Can conflict be reframed
as a situation in which the groups involved
are perceived as acting independently? To
illustrate, take this example cited by
Watzlawick, Weakland, and Fisch (p. 107):
In 1943, the Nazis ordered all Jews in
Denmark to wear a yellow Star of David arm-
band. The king of Denmark successfully reframed the situation by announcing that,
since there were no differences among Danes,
the Nazis' order applied to all Danes and
that he would be the first to wear the Star
of David.
    The handling of the Cuban missile crisis
by President Kennedy in 1962 is another
example. The crisis was begun when it was
confirmed that the Russians had installed

missiles in Cuba. The Americans responded
with a blockade. On Friday, October 26 the
President received a private message from
the USSR that the Soviets would be willing
to withdraw the offensive missiles if the
United States pledged not to invade Cuba.
Yet, on the following day, the Russians
publicly announced that they would withdraw
their missiles only if the United States also dismantled its rocket bases in Turkey.
The solution was discovered by Robert
Kennedy: to act as though the Saturday message had never existed and to publicly accept the message received on Friday. This
"Trollope Ploy" (named after the scene in
one of Anthony Trollope's stories in which
a young woman interprets a young man's
squeezing her hand as a proposal of marriage) successfully created a new face saving definition of the situation that was
acceptable to both şides and permitted each
to withdraw threats without seeming to lose
(Hilsman, 1967).

MAKING PROGRESS

Groups and leaders of groups often delude
themselves about their own progress because
they get bogged down in administrative goals
(e.g., quarterly progress reports) or operating
procedures (e.g., meetings) as a means of
evaluating progress. Group members who are coming to understand each other's expertise may
feel they are making a great deal of progress
when actually getting to know people is only a
means for making progress. The leader, then,
must help the group define and separate its
ends from its means and must continually reas-
sess his or her own progress towards ends.
The meaning of "progress" should depend on
the ends desired. For example, in groups that
have a decision to make, but where almost any
decision will do, the leader must keep an eye
on progress toward consensus. In contrast,
where the quality of the decision is important,

progress toward a decision that has been pre-
ceded by careful searches for information and
consideration of minority views is essential.
Progress will usually be much slower, and care
must be taken not to so alter the end desired
that no decision is really made at all. This
happens in groups that have very hard decisions
to make. That is, the end product is redefined
in such a way that progress seems more rapid
but no great progress is really made. For example, a group that has to decide whether to
forego salary increases for employees or to
give up some investments might so prolong the
discussions that conflict resolution itself
becomes the major goal. By then, a number of
incidents may have occurred (such as direct
confrontations with employees) that have in
effect closed off the options of the group and
forced a resolution of the problem by default.
The leader, then, must continually reevaluate
the progress of the group towards its objectives, not allowing the legitimate concern for
full deliberation or side issues to *inappropri-
ately* interfere with the group's movement. That
takes delicate balancing.

HELPING A GROUP DEAL WITH CONFLICT

It is essential for a leader to be helpful
to a group in its beginning stages. When conflict arises, as in most groups it should, the
leader can then command enough respect to
arbitrate and mediate different perspectives.
Mediating conflict, however, does not necessarily mean that the leader induces group members to compromise. As we have seen in an
earlier section of this book, compromise can
be a poor second to a creative, unique solution.

Helping a group deal with conflict requires
coping with tendencies toward groupthink, a
concept described earlier. Groupthink leads to
defensive avoidance of conflict (Janis and
Mann, 1977). In defensive avoidance, the group
reacts to uncertainty and to stress by closing

off its search for information and debate.
Minority views are not heard or are rejected.
The outcome of this may be a group that (1) decides not to decide—letting things stand as
they are without considering the advantages of
making a change; (2) decides to let some other
group or person make the decision; or (3) decides on a solution that is not supported by
the data—whether these data be the opinions
of outsiders or objective information. In each
case the group may bolster its decision by convincing itself that its beliefs are superior to
those of others, that its information is more
unique or exclusive, and that its members are
more qualified to make the decision (have higher inputs) than others.

The group leader must take responsibility
for preventing defensive avoidance, leading the
group members to feel that listening to minority views and considering all relevant information are neither threatening nor boring:

1. Group members cannot consider all relevant
information if the information is given to them
as it comes in. Our memory and perceptual processes are limited, and too much information
simply overwhelms us. In fact, decision makers
often fail to make good decisions because they
are trying to consider too many bits and pieces
of information. A group leader, then, must
condense, reformulate, and analyze information
so that it is presented to group members in
useful, easily understood form. All relevant
information is then available, but not in an
undistilled state. A side benefit of condensing
information (in spite of the work involved) is
that it prevents group members from walking
away from important jobs just because they
have already read or considered great quanti-
ties of material.

2. Group members need to be informed about
the views of others, particularly minority
views or views not represented in the group.
Leaders can present minority opinions themselves or call for such opinions to be expressed.

3. There will be pressures for equity in any group. A leader should satisfy the need for equity by making sure that people are treated equitably. Doing so is *not* the same as treating every opinion, bit of information, or position as though it were equally correct or important. There is a tendency in groups governed by democratic decision rules to equate equal treatment of people with equality of ideas, as long as they gain majority support. A leader can make sure everyone's opinions are considered, without permitting the group to count all popular solutions to problems as if they were of equal merit.

4. Careful consideration of interpersonal needs and concerns does not mean that group leaders must be personally close to group members. Closeness, in fact, is not correlated with group success (that is, it works in some kinds of groups and not others). Far more important is that the group leader is seen as someone who is fair, open, and careful to check the reality of his or her perceptions of people.

These few guidelines do not by any means cover all the territory that one might desire; they certainly do not capture the specific skills and knowledge necessary to lead groups, nor do they address the problems of large groups or organizations. The objectives should give a flavor of what is possible to attempt, however.

SUMMARY

This chapter describes some ways that groups formulate and deal with problems. Every task a group has to perform may be viewed as a set of problems. These problems range from the relatively technical (e.g., information distribution among members) to the relatively social (e.g., decisions about recognition or credit). The subjective perceptions of all such problems are just as important to consider as any technical analysis of them.

The performance of groups in addressing their problems depends in part on the structural properties of their tasks. For example, where tasks demand relatively little coordination of effort and correct answers can be recognized when they are suggested, groups have a statistical advantage over individuals and, theoretically, should perform as well as their most proficient member. Groups often do not do as well as they might, however, because social and political problems interfere. In reaching a decision, for example, a group might ignore correct minority opinions because the majority is convinced it is the more expert.

The social and political problems of groups arise from interpersonal processes. Those which affect group performance include conformity, commitment to the group, and interpersonal attraction. For example, groups which are successful, (or are comprised of successful people) are often cohesive (i.e., there is high mutual attraction), and cohesiveness encourages conformity. If conformity pressures are too great, the group may engage in "groupthink," avoid conflict over substance, and make poor decisions.

Because groups often perform poorly does not imply individuals could do better. If one considers social issues and individual motives, such as the need to participate in decisions affecting oneself, group problem solving may be superior. Experienced leaders capitalize on interpersonal processes to maximize the performance of their groups. Among the objectives they try to attain are (1) to establish their role as a supportive, useful person, (2) to define solvable problems for the group, (3) to make progress toward important ends, and (4) to help the group deal with conflict.

References

Abelson, R. P., Aronson, E., McGuire, W. J. Newcomb, T. M., Rosenberg, M. J., and Tannenbaum, P. (Eds.). *Theories of cognitive consistency: A sourcebook.* Chicago: Rand McNally, 1968.

Ackoff, R. L., Conrath, D. W., and Howard, N. *A model study of the escalation and de-escalation of conflict.* Vol. 1. Philadelphia: Management Science Center, University of Pennsylvania, 1967.

Adams, J. S. Toward an understanding of inequity. *Journal of Abnormal and Social Psychology*, 1963, *67*, 422-436.

Adams, J. S., and Rosenbaum, W. E. The relationship of worker productivity to cognitive dissonance about wage inequity. *Journal of Applied Psychology*, 1962, *46*, 161-164.

Adams, S. Vietnam cover-up; Playing war with numbers. *Harper's*, 1975, *250* (May), pp. 41-44, 62-73.

Ajzen, I., and Fishbein, M. Attitudes and normative

beliefs as factors influencing behavioral intentions. *Journal of Personality and Social Psychology*, 1972, *21*, 1-9.

Allison, G. T. *Essence of decision: Explaining the Cuban missile crisis,* Boston: Little, Brown, 1971.

Allport, F. H. *Social psychology.* Boston: Houghton Mifflin, 1924.

Allport, G. W. *The nature of prejudice.* Reading, Mass.: Addison-Wesley, 1954.

Allport, G. W. Six decades of social psychology. In S. Lundstedt (Ed.), *Higher education in social psychology.* Cleveland, Ohio: The Press of Case Western Reserve University, 1968, pp. 9-19.

Altman, I., and Haythorn, W. W. Interpersonal exchange in isolation. *Sociometry*, 1965, *28*, 411-426.

Altman, I., and Taylor, D. A. *Social penetration: The development of interpersonal relationships.* New York: Holt, Rinehart, and Winston, 1973.

Altman, I., Taylor, D. A., and Wheeler, L. Ecological aspects of group behavior in social isolation. *Journal of Applied Social Psychology*, 1971, *1*, 76-100.

Amoroso, D. M., and Walters, R. H. Efforts of anxiety and socially mediated anxiety on reduction of paired-associated learning. *Journal of Personality and Social Psychology*, 1969, *11*, 308-396.

Anderson, A. B. Combined effects of interpersonal attraction and goal-path clarity on the cohesiveness of task oriented groups. *Journal of Personality and Social Psychology*, 1975, *31*, 68-75.

Anderson, M. P. A model of group discussion. In R. S. Cathcart and L. A. Samovar (Eds.), *Small group communication: A reader*. Dubuque, Iowa: William C. Brown, 1971, pp. 103-115.

Apfelbaum, E. On conflicts and bargaining. In L. Berkowitz (Ed.), *Advances in experimental social psychology*. Vol. 7. New York: Academic Press, 1974.

Argyris, C. *Some causes of organizational ineffectiveness within the Department of State*. Washington, D. C.: Department of State Occasional Paper, No. 2, 1967.

Ariès, P. *Centuries of childhood* (translated by R. Baldick), New York: Knopf, 1962.

Aristotle. *The poetics.* In S. H. Butcher (Trans.), *Aristotle's theory of poetry and fine art.* (4th ed.). New York: Dover Press, 1951.

Aronson, E., and Linder, D. Gain and loss of esteem as determinants of interpersonal attractiveness. *Journal of Experimental Social Psychology*, 1965, *1*, 156-171.

Aronson, E., and Mills, J. Effect of severity of initiation on liking for a group. *Journal of Abnormal and Social Psychology*, 1959, *59*, 177-181.

Aronson, E., Turner, J. A., and Carlsmith, J. M. Communicator credibility and communication discrepancy as determinants of opinion change. *Journal of Abnormal and Social Psychology*, 1963, *67*, 31-36.

Asch, S. E. Studies of independence and conformity. A minority of one against a unanimous majority. *Psychological Monographs*, 1956, *70*, No. 9, (Whole No. 416).

Austin, W., and Walster, E. H. Participants' reaction to "equity with the world." *Journal of Experimental Social Psychology*, 1974, *10*, 528-548.

Azrin, N. H., Hutchinson, R. R., and Hake, D. F. Pain-induced fighting in the squirrel monkey. *Journal of Experimental Animal Behavior*, 1963, *6*, 620-621.

Bales, R. F. *Personality and interpersonal behavior.* New York: Holt, Rinehart and Winston, 1970.

Bandura, A. Vicarious processes: A case of no-trial learning. In L. Berkowitz (Ed.), *Advances in experimental social psychology.* Vol. 2. New York: Academic Press, 1965, pp. 3-57.

Bandura, A., Ross, D., and Ross, S. Transmission of aggression through imitation of aggressive models. *Journal of Abnormal and Social Psychology*, 1961, *63*, 575-582.

Bandura, A., and Walters, R. H. *Adolescent aggression.* New York: Ronald Press, 1959.

Barton, A. H. Consensus and conflict among American

leaders. *Public Opinion Quarterly*, 1974-75 (Winter), 507-530.

Bass, B. M., and Leavitt, H. J. Some experiments in planning and operating. *Management Science*, 1963, *9*, 574-585.

Batson, C. D. Attribution as a mediator of bias in helping. *Journal of Personality and Social Psychology*, 1975, *32*, 455-466.

Bavelas, A. Morale and training of leaders. In G. Watson (Ed.) *Civilian morale*. Boston: Houghton Mifflin, 1942.

Becker, H. S. Becoming a marijuana user. *American Journal of Sociology*, 1953, *59*, 235-242.

Becker, H. S. *Outsiders: Studies in the sociology of deviance*. New York: The Free Press, 1963.

Bell, D. *The coming of post-industrial society. A venture in social forecasting*. New York: Basic Books, 1973.

Bem, D. J., Wallach, M. A., and Kogan, N. Group decision making under risk of aversive consequences. *Journal of Personality and Social Psychology*, 1965, *1*, 453-460.

Bennis, W. G., Berkowitz, N., Affinito, H., and Malone, M. Authority, power, and the ability to influence. *Human Relations*, 1958, *11*, 143-155.

Bennis, W. G., and Shepard, H. A. A theory of group development. *Human Relations*, 1965, *9*, 415-457.

Berkowitz, L. *Aggression: A social psychological analysis*. New York: McGraw-Hill, 1962.

Berkowitz, L., and Green, J. A. The stimulus qualities of the scapegoat. *Journal of Abnormal and Social Psychology*, 1962, *64*, 293-301.

Berkowitz, L., Lepenski, J. P., and Angulo, E. J. Awareness of own anger level and subsequent aggression. *Journal of Personality and Social Psychology*, 1969, *11*, 293-300.

Berscheid, E., Boye, D., and Walster, E. H. Retaliation as a means of restoring equity. *Journal of Personality and Social Psychology*, 1968, *10*, 370-376.

Berscheid, E., and Walster, E. H. When does a harm-doer compensate a victim? *Journal of Personality and Social Psychology*, 1967, *6*, 435-441.

Berscheid, E., and Walster, E. H. *Interpersonal attraction*. Reading, Mass.: Addison-Wesley, 1978.

Bickman, L. Environmental attitudes and actions. *Journal of Social Psychology*, 1972, *87*, 323-324.

Billig, M., and Tajfel, H. Social categorization and similarity in intergroup behavior. *European Journal of Social Psychology*, 1973, *3*, 27-51.

Biondo, J., and MacDonald, A. P., Jr. Internal-external locus of control and response to influence attempts. *Journal of Personality*, 1971, *39*, 407-419.

Bixenstine, V. E., and Gaebelein, J. W. Strategies of "real" opponents in eliciting cooperative choice in a prisoner's dilemma game. *Journal of Conflict Resolution*, 1971, *15*, 157-166.

Blake, R. R., and Mouton, J. S. Comprehension of one's own and of outgroup positions under intergroup competition. *Journal of Conflict Resolution*, 1961, *5*, 304-310.

Blau, P. M. Patterns of interaction among a group of officials in a government agency. *Human Relations*, 1954, *7*, 337-348.

Blau, P. M. *Exchange and power in social life*. New York: John Wiley and Sons, 1964.

Bordon, R. C. *Public speaking—as listeners like it*. New York: Harper and Row, 1935.

Bowers, J. W. Communication strategies in conflicts between institutions and their clients. In G. R. Miller and H. W. Simons (Eds.), *Perspectives on communication in social conflict*. Englewood Cliffs, N.J.: Prentice-Hall, 1974, pp. 125-152.

Bramel, D. Interpersonal attraction, hostility, and perception. In J. Mills (Ed.), *Experimental social psychology*. New York: Macmillan, 1969.

Braybrook, D., and Lindblom, C. E. *A strategy of decision: Policy evaluation as a social process*. New York: The Free Press, 1970.

Brehm, J. W. *A theory of psychological reactance*. New York: Academic Press, 1966.

Brehm, J. W., and Cohen, A. R. *Explorations in cognitive dissonance*. New York: John Wiley and Sons, 1962.

Brehm, J. W., Gatz, M., Goethals, G., McCrimmon, J., and Ward, L. Psychological arousal and interpersonal attraction. (Mimeo.) Lawrence: University of Kansas, 1970.

Brehm, J. W., and Rozen, E. Attractiveness of old alternatives when a new attractive alternative is introduced. *Journal of Personality and Social Psychology*, 1971, *20*, 261-266.

Brock, T. C. Communicator-recipient similarity and decision change. *Journal of Personality and Social Psychology*, 1965, *1*, 650-654.

Brown, B. R., and Garland, H. The effects of incompetency, audience acquaintanceship, and anticipated evaluative feedback on face-saving behavior. *Journal of Experimental Social Psychology*, 1971, *7*, 490-502.

Brown, R. W. *Social psychology*. New York: The Free Press, 1965.

Buchanan, J. M., and Tullock, G. *The calculus of consent*. Ann Arbor: University of Michigan Press, 1962.

Burns, J. F. An extremity-variance analysis of group decisions involving risk. Unpublished doctoral dissertation, Massachusetts Institute of Technology, 1967.

Burns, T. The reference of conduct in small groups: Cliques and cabals in occupational milieux. *Human Relations*, 1955, *8*, 467-486.

Burnstein, E., Stotland, E., and Zander, A. Similarity to a model and self-evaluation. *Journal of Abnormal and Social Psychology*, 1961, *62*, 257-264.

Buss, A. H. Instrumentality of aggression, feedback, and frustration as determinants of physical aggression. *Journal of Personality and Social Psychology*, 1966, *3*, 153-162.

Buss, A. H., Booker, A., and Buss, E. Firing a weapon and aggression. *Journal of Personality and Social Psychology*, 1972, *22*, 296-302.

Byrne, D. *The attraction paradigm*. New York: Academic Press, 1971.

Caplan, N., Morrison, A., and Stambaugh, R. J. The use of social science knowledge in policy decisions at the national level: A report to respondents. Ann Arbor: Institute for Social Research, University of Michigan, 1975.

Cartwright, D., and Zander, A. (Eds.) *Group dynamics: Research and theory* (3rd ed.). New York: Harper and Row, 1968.

Centers, R. *The psychology of social classes.* Princeton, N.J.: Princeton University Press, 1949.

Cialdini, R. B., Brover, S. L., and Lewis, S. K. Attributional bias and the easily persuaded other. *Journal of Personality and Social Psychology*, 1974, *30*, 631-637.

Cialdini, R. B., Vincent, J. E., Lewis, S. K., Catalan, J., Wheeler, D., and Darby, B. L. Reciprocal concessions procedure for inducing compliance: The door-in-the-face technique. *Journal of Personality and Social Psychology*, 1975, *31*, 206-215.

Clausewitz, C. *On war.* Washington, D.C.: Infantry Journal Press, 1950.

Clore, G. L., Hirschberg (Wiggins), N., and Itkin, J. Gain and loss in attraction: Attributions from non-verbal behavior. *Journal of Personality and Social Psychology*, 1975, *31*, 706-712.

Cloward, R. A., and Ohlin, L. E. *Delinquency and opportunity: A theory of delinquent gangs.* New York: The Free Press of Glencoe, 1960.

Coch, L., and French, J. R., Jr. Overcoming resistance to change. *Human Relations*, 1948, *1*, 512-532.

Cohen, D., Whitmyre, J. W., and Funk, W. H. Effect of group cohesiveness and training upon creative thinking. *Journal of Applied Psychology*, 1960, *44*, 319-322.

Cohen, M. D., and March, J. G. *Leadership and ambiguity: The American college president.* New York: McGraw-Hill, 1974.

Cohen, M. D., March, J. G., and Olsen, J. P. A garbage can model of organizational choice. *Administrative Science Quarterly*, 1972, *17*(1), 1-25.

Collins, B. E., and Hoyt, M. F. Personal responsibility-for-consequences: An integration and extension of the forced compliance literature. *Journal of Experimental Social Psychology*, 1972, *8*, 558–593.

Collins, B. E., and Raven, B. H. Group structure: Attraction, coalitions, communication, and power. In G. Lindzey and E. Aronson (Eds.), *The handbook of social psychology*. Vol. 4. Reading, Mass.: Addison-Wesley, 1969. Pp. 102–204.

Connolly, T. Information processing and decision making in organizations. In B. M. Staw and G. R. Salancik (Eds.), *New directions in organizational behavior*. Chicago: St. Clair Press, 1977. Pp. 205–234.

Cooper, J. Personal responsibility and dissonance: The role of foreseen consequences. *Journal of Personality and Social Psychology*, 1971, *18*, 354–363.

Cooper, J., and Worchel, S. Role of undesired consequences in arousing cognitive dissonance. *Journal of Personality and Social Psychology*, 1970, *16*, 199–206.

Cottrell, N. B. Performance in the presence of other human beings: Mere presence, audience and affiliation effects. In E. C. Simmel, R. A. Hoppe, and G. A. Milton (Eds.), *Social facilitation and imitative behavior*. Boston: Allyn and Bacon, 1968.

Cottrell, N. B., Wack, D. L., Sekerak, G. J., and Rittle, R. H. Social facilitation of dominant responses by the presence of an audience and the mere presence of others. *Journal of Personality and Social Psychology*, 1968, *9*, 245–250.

Crawford, J. L. Task uncertainty, decision importance, and group reinforcement as determinants of communication processes in groups. *Journal of Personality and Social Psychology*, 1974, *29*, 619–627.

Crockett, W. H. Emergent leadership in small decision-making groups. *Journal of Abnormal and Social Psychology*, 1955, *51*, 378–383.

Cronbach, L. J. *Essentials of psychological testing*. New York: Harper and Row, 1970.

Crozier, M. *The bureaucratic phenomenon*. Chicago: University of Chicago Press, 1964.

Crutchfield, R. S. Conformity and character. *American Psychologist*, 1955, *10*, 191-198.

Cyert, R. M., and March, J. G. *A behavioral theory of the firm*. Englewood Cliffs, N.J.: Prentice-Hall, 1963.

Daniels, L. R., and Berkowitz, L. Liking and response to dependency relationships. *Human Relations*, 1963, *16*, 141-148.

Darley, J. M. Fear and social comparison as determinants of conformity behavior. *Journal of Personality and Social Psychology*, 1966, *4*, 73-78.

Darley, J. M., and Latané, B. Norms and normative behavior: Field studies of social interdependence. In J. Macaulay and L. Berkowitz (Eds.), *Altruism and helping behavior*. New York: Academic Press, 1970. Pp. 83-101.

Darley, S. A., and Cooper, J. Cognitive consequences of forced noncompliance. *Journal of Personality and Social Psychology*, 1972, *24*, 321-326.

Dashiell, J. F. Experimental studies of the influence of social situations in the behavior of individual human adults. In C. Murchison (Ed.), *Handbook of social psychology*. Worcester, Mass.: Clark University Press, 1935. Pp. 1097-1158.

Davis, J. H. Group decision and social interaction: A theory of social decision schemes. *Psychological Review*, 1973, *80*, 97-125.

Davis, J. H. *Group performance*. Reading, Mass.: Addison-Wesley, 1969.

Davis, J. H., Bray, R. M., and Holt, R. W. The empirical study of decision processes in juries: A critical review. In J. Tapp and F. Levine (Eds.). *Law, justice and the individual in society: Psychological and legal perspectives*. New York: Holt, Rinehart and Winston, 1977. Pp. 326-361.

Davis, J. H., Kerr, N. L. Atkin, R. S., Holt, R., and Meek, D. The decision processes of 6- and 12-person mock juries assigned unanimous and two-third's majority rules. *Journal of Personality and Social Psychology*, 1975, *32*, 1-14.

Davis, J. H., Kerr, N. L., Sussmann, M., and Rissman, A. K. Social decision schemes under risk. *Journal of Personality and Social Psychology*, 1974, *30*, 248-271.

Davis, J. H., and Restle, F. The analysis of problems and prediction of group problem solving. *Journal of Abnormal and Social Psychology*, 1963, *66*, 103-116.

Davis, K. E., and Jones, E. E. Changes in interpersonal perception as a means of reducing cognitive dissonance. *Journal of Abnormal and Social Psychology*, 1960, *61*, 402-410.

DeCharms, R., and Wilkins, E. S. Some effects of verbal expression of hostility. *Journal of Abnormal and Social Psychology*, 1963, *66*, 462-470.

Deutsch, M. The effects of cooperation and competition upon group process. *Human Relations*, 1949, *2*, 129-152 and 199-231.

Deutsch, M. The effect of motivational orientation upon trust and suspicion. *Human Relations*, 1960, *13*, 123-139.

Deutsch, M., and Collins, M. E. *Interracial housing: A psychological evaluation of a social experiment.* Minnapolis: University of Minnesota Press, 1951.

Deutsch, M., and Gerard, H. A study of normative and informational social influences upon individual judgment. *Journal of Abnormal and Social Psychology*, 1955, *51*, 629-636.

Deutsch, M., and Krauss, R. M. Studies of interpersonal bargaining. *Journal of Conflict Resolution*, 1962, *6*, 52-76.

Dion, K. K., and Berscheid, E. Physical attractiveness and sociometric choice in nursery school children. (Mimeo.) Minneapolis: University of Minnesota, 1972.

Dion, K. K., and Dion, K. L. Self-esteem and romantic love. *Journal of Personality*, 1975, *43*, 39-57.

Dollard, J., Doob, L., Miller, N., Mowrer, O., and Sears, R. *Frustration and aggression.* New Haven: Yale University Press, 1939.

Doob, A. N., Carlsmith, J. M., Freedman, J. L., Landauer, T. K., and Tom, S., Jr. Effect of initial selling price on subsequent sales. *Journal of Personality and Social Psychology*, 1969, *11*, 345-350.

Doob, A. N., and Wood, L. Catharsis and aggression: The effects of annoyance and retaliation on aggressive behavior. *Journal of Personality and Social Psychology*, 1972, *22*, 156-162.

Douvan, E. Social status and success strivings. *Journal of Abnormal and Social Psychology*, 1956, *52*, 219-223.

Dovidio, J. F., and Morris, W. N. Effects of stress and commonality of fate in helping behavior. *Journal of Personality and Social Psychology*, 1975, *31*, 145-149.

Duval, S., and Wicklund, R. A. *A theory of objective self awareness*. New York: Academic Press, 1972.

Dweck, C. S. The role of expectation and attribution in the alleviation of learned helplessness. *Journal of Personality and Social Psychology*, 1975, *31*, 674-685.

Eagly, A. H. Comprehensibility of persuasive arguments as a determinant of opinion change. *Journal of Personality and Social Psychology*, 1974, *29*, 758-773.

Ebbesen, E. B., and Bowers, R. J. Proportion of risky to conservative arguments in a group discussion and choice shift. *Journal of Personality and Social Psychology*, 1974, *29*, 316-327.

Edelman, M. *The symbolic uses of politics*. Urbana: University of Illinois Press, 1964.

Ellis, R. A., and Keedy, T. C., Jr. Three dimensions of status: A study of academic prestige. *Pacific Sociological Review*, 1960, *3*, 23-28.

Enzle, M. E., Hansen, R. D., and Lowe, C. A. Causal attribution in the mixed-motive game: Effects of facilitory and inhibitory environmental forces. *Journal of Personality and Social Psychology*, 1975, *31*, 50-54.

Epstein, S., and Taylor, S. P. Instigation to aggression as a function of degree of defeat and perceived aggressive intent of the opponent. *Journal of Personality*, 1967, *35*, 265-289.

Erickson, B., Holmes, J. G., Frey, R., Walker, L., and Thibaut, J. Functions of a third party in the resolution of conflict: The role of a judge in pretrial conferences. *Journal of Personality and Social Psychology*, 1974, *30*, 293-306.

Evan, W. M. Conflict and performance in R & D organizations. *Industrial Management Review*, 1965, *7*, 37-45.

Faucheux, C., and Moscovici, S. Études sur la créativité des groupes: I. Tâche, situation individuelle et groupe. *Bulletin de Psychologie*, 1958, *11*, 863-874.

Faust, W. L. Group versus individual problem solving. *Journal of Abnormal and Social Psychology*, 1959, *59*, 68-72.

Fellner, C. H., and Marshall, J. R. Kidney donors. In J. Macaulay and L. Berkowitz (Eds.), *Altruism and helping behavior*. New York: Academic Press, 1970. Pp. 269-281.

Festinger, L. Informal social communication. *Psychological Review*, 1950, *57*, 271-282.

Festinger, L. *A theory of cognitive dissonance.* Evanston, Ill.: Ron Peterson, 1957.

Festinger, L. A theory of social comparison processes. *Human Relations*, 1954, *7*, 117-140.

Festinger, L., and Carlsmith, J. M. Cognitive consequences of forced compliance. *Journal of Abnormal and Social Psychology*, 1959, *58*, 203-210.

Festinger, L., and Kelley, H. *Changing attitudes through social contact.* Ann Arbor: University of Michigan, Research Center for Group Dynamics, 1951.

Festinger, L., Schachter, S., and Back, K. *Social pressures in informal groups: A study of human factors in housing.* Stanford: Stanford University Press, 1950.

Fiedler, F. E. A contingency model of leadership effectiveness. In L. Berkowitz (Ed.), *Advances in experimental social psychology*. Vol. 1. New York: Academic Press, 1964. Pp. 150-191.

Fisher, R. Fractionating conflict. In R. Fisher (Ed.), *International conflict and behavioral science*. New York: Basic Books, 1964.

Fouriezos, N. T., Hutt, M. L., and Guetzkow, H. Measurement of self-oriented needs in discussion groups.

Journal of Abnormal and Social Psychology, 1950, *45*, 682-690.

Freedman, J. L. Confidence, utility and selective exposure: A partial replication. *Journal of Personality and Social Psychology*, 1965, *2*, 778-780.

Freedman, J. L., and Doob, A. N. *Deviancy: The psychology of being different.* New York: Academic Press, 1968.

Freedman, J. L., and Fraser, S. C. Compliance without pressure: The foot-in-the-door technique. *Journal of Personality and Social Psychology*, 1966, *4*, 195-202.

French, J. R. P., Jr. Organized and unorganized groups under fear and frustration. *University of Iowa Studies in Child Welfare*, 1944, *20*, 231-308.

French, J. R. P., Jr., and Raven, B. H. The bases of social power. In D. Cartwright (Ed.), *Studies in social power.* Ann Arbor: University of Michigan Press, 1959. Pp. 150-167.

Freud, S. *Introductory lectures on psychoanalysis (1916-1917): A general introduction to psychoanalysis.* Garden City, New York: Garden City Publishing Co., 1943.

Freud, S. *Beyond the pleasure principle (1920).* New York: Macmillan, 1953.

Frey, D., and Irle, M. Some conditions to produce a dissonance and an incentive effect in a 'forced compliance' situation. *European Journal of Social Psychology*, 1972, *2*, 45-54.

Froman, L. A., Jr., and Cohen, M. D. Compromise and logroll: Comparing the efficiency of two bargaining processes. *Behavioral Science*, 1970, *15*, 180-183.

Gahagan, J. P., and Tedeschi, J. T. Strategy and the credibility of promises in the prisoner's dilemma game. *Journal of Conflict Resolution*, 1968, *12*, 224-234.

Gallo, P. S. *The effects of different motivational orientations in a mixed-motive game.* Unpublished doctoral dissertation, University of California, Los Angeles, 1963.

Gallo, P. S., and McClintock, C. G. Cooperative and competitive behavior in mixed-motive games. *Journal of Conflict Resolution*, 1965, *9*, 68–78.

Gamson, W. A. A theory of coalition formation. *American Sociological Review*, 1961, *26*, 231–244.

Gamson, W. A. Experimental studies of coalition formation. In L. Berkowitz (Ed.), *Advances in experimental social psychology*. Vol. 1. New York: Academic Press, 1964. Pp. 82–110.

Gamson, W. A. *Power and discontent*. Homewood, Ill.: Dorsey Press, 1968.

Garrett, J., and Libby, W. L., Jr. Role of intentionality in mediating responses to inequity in the dyad. *Journal of Personality and Social Psychology*, 1973, *28*, 21–27.

Geen, R. G., Stonner, D., and Shope, G. L. The facilitation of aggression by aggression: Evidence against the catharsis hypothesis. *Journal of Personality and Social Psychology*, 1975, *31*, 721–726.

Geller, D. M., Goodstein, L., Silver, M., and Steinberg, W. On being ignored: The effects of the violation of implicit rules of social interaction. *Sociometry*, 1974, *37*, 541–556.

Gerard, H. B., and Mathewson, G. C. The effects of severity of interaction on liking for a group: A replication. *Journal of Experimental Social Psychology*, 1966, *2*, 278–287.

Gergen, K. J. The effects of interaction goals and personalistic feedback on the presentation of self. *Journal of Personality and Social Psychology*, 1965, *1*, 413–424.

Gergen, K. J. *Altruism from the recipient's viewpoint: Individual and international perspectives*. Swarthmore College, 1968. (Mimeo.)

Gergen, K. J. *The psychology of behavior exchange*. Reading, Mass.: Addison-Wesley, 1969.

Gergen, K. J., Ellsworth, P., Maslach, C., and Seipel, M. Obligation, donor resources, and reactions to aid in three cultures. *Journal of Personality and Social Psychology*, 1975, *31*, 390–400.

Gergen, K. J., Gergen, M. M., and Barton, W. H. Deviance in the dark. *Psychology Today*, 1973, *7* (Oct.), 129–130.

Gergen, K. J., and Wishnor, B. Others' self-evaluation and interaction anticipation as determinants of self-presentation. *Journal of Personality and Social Psychology*, 1965, *2*, 348–358.

Goethals, G. R., and Cooper, J. Role of intention and post-behavioral consequence in the arousal of cognitive dissonance. *Journal of Personality and Social Psychology*, 1972, *23*, 298–301.

Goffman, E. *The presentation of self in everyday life.* Garden City, New York: Doubleday, 1959.

Goffman, E. On cooling the mark out: Some aspects of adaptation to failure. *Psychiatry*, 1952, *15*, 451–463.

Goffman, E. *Stigma: Notes on the management of spoiled identity.* Englewood Cliffs, N.J.: Prentice-Hall, 1963.

Goffman, E. *Behavior in public places: Notes on the organization of gatherings.* New York: The Free Press, 1966.

Goldstein, J. H., Davis, R. W., and Herman, D. Escalation of aggression: Experimental studies. *Journal of Personality and Social Psychology*, 1975, *31*, 162–170.

Gordon, K. A study of esthetic judgments. *Journal of Experimental Psychology*, 1923, *6*, 36–43.

Gouldner, A. W. The norm of reciprocity: A preliminary statement. *American Sociological Review*, 1960, *25*, 161–178.

Grabitz-Gneich, G. Some restrictive conditions for the occurrence of psychological reactance. *Journal of Personality and Social Psychology*, 1971, *19*, 188–196.

Grant, J. *Black protest: History, documents, and analyses: 1619 to the present.* New York: Fawcett World Library, 1968.

Greenberg, M. S., and Frisch, D. M. Effect of intentionality on willingness to reciprocate a favor. *Journal of Experimental Social Psychology*, 1972, *8*, 99–111.

Gross, N., Mason, W., and McEachern, A. *Explorations*

in role analysis. New York: John Wiley and Sons, 1958.

Guetzkow, H. Differentiation of roles in task-oriented groups. In D. Cartwright and A. Zander (Eds.), *Group dynamics: Research and theory.* (2nd ed.). Evanston, Ill.: Row, Peterson, 1960. Pp. 683-704.

Guetzkow, H., and Gyr, J. An analysis of conflict in decision-making groups. *Human Relations,* 1954, *7,* 367-382.

Guetzkow, H., and Simon, H. A. The impact of certain communication nets upon organization and performance in task-oriented groups. *Management Science,* 1955, *1,* 233-250.

Guilford, J. S. Temperament traits of executives and supervisors measured by the Guilford personality inventories. *Journal of Applied Psychology,* 1952, *36,* 228-233.

Gurnee, H. A comparison of collective and individual judgments of facts. *Journal of Experimental Psychology,* 1937, *21,* 106-112.

Haire, M. Group dynamics in the industrial situation. In A. Kornhauser, R. Dubin, and A. M. Ross (Eds.), *Industrial conflict.* New York: McGraw-Hill, 1954. Pp. 373-385.

Hamblin, R. L. Leadership and crises. *Sociometry,* 1958, *21,* 322-335.

Harris, M. B. Mediators between frustration and aggression in a fixed experiment. *Journal of Experimental Social Psychology,* 1974, *10,* 561-571.

Harris, V. A., and Jellison, J. M. Fear arousing communications, false physiological feedback, and the acceptance of recommendation. *Journal of Experimental Social Psychology,* 1971, *7,* 269-279.

Harrison, E. F. *The managerial decision-making process.* Boston: Houghton Mifflin, 1975.

Harvey, J. H., Ickes, W. J., and Kidd, R. F. (Eds.), *New directions in attribution research.* Vol. 1. Hillsdale, N.J.: Lawrence Erlbaum Associates, 1976.

Hastorf, A. H., Schneider, D. J., and Polefka, J. *Person perception.* Reading, Mass.: Addison-Wesley, 1970.

Hazen, M. D., and Kiesler, S. B. Communication strategies affected by audience opposition, feedback and persuasibility. *Speech Monographs*, 1975, *42*, 56-68.

Heider, F. *The psychology of interpersonal relations*. New York: John Wiley and Sons, 1958.

Helmreich, R., and Collins, B. E. Studies in forced compliance: Commitment and magnitude of inducement to comply as determinants of opinion change. *Journal of Personality and Social Psychology*, 1968, *10*, 75-81.

Hendrick, C., and Seyfried, B. A. Assessing the validity of laboratory-produced attitude change. *Journal of Personality and Social Psychology*, 1974, *29*, 865-870.

Hendricks, M., and Brickman, P. Effects of status and knowledgeability of audience on self-presentation. *Sociometry*, 1974, *37*, 440-449.

Hilsman, R. *To move a nation*. Garden City, N.Y.: Doubleday, 1967.

Hoffman, L. R. Conditions for creative problem solving. *Journal of Psychology*, 1961, *52*, 429-444.

Hobbes, T. *Leviathan*. New York: E. P. Dutton and Company, 1950.

Hoffman, L. R. Group problem solving. In L. Berkowitz (Ed.), *Advances in experimental social psychology*. Vol. 2. New York: Academic Press, 1965. Pp. 99-132.

Hoffman, L. R., Harburg, E., and Maier, N. R. F. Differences and disagreement as factors in creative problem solving. *Journal of Abnormal and Social Psychology*, 1962, *64*, 206-214.

Hoffman, L. R., and Maier, N. R. F. Valence in the adoption of solutions by problem-solving groups: Concept, method, and results. *Journal of Abnormal and Social Psychology*, 1964, *69*, 264-271.

Hoffman, P. J., Festinger, L., and Lawrence, D. Tendencies toward group comparability in competitive bargaining. *Human Relations*, 1954, *7*, 141-159.

Hollander, E. P. Conformity, status, and idiosyncrasy credit. *Psychological Review*, 1958, *65*, 117-127.

Holmes, D. S. Aggression, displacement and guilt. *Journal of Personality and Social Psychology*, 1972, *21*, 296-301.

Holmes, D. S., and Jackson, T. H. Influence of locus of control on interpersonal attraction and affective reactions in situations involving reward and punishment. *Journal of Personality and Social Psychology*, 1975, *31*, 132–136.

Homans, G. C. *The human group*. New York: Harcourt, Brace, 1950.

Homans, G. C. *Social behavior: Its elementary forms*. New York: Harcourt, Brace & World, 1961.

Hornstein, H. A. The effects of different magnitudes of threat upon interpersonal bargaining. *Journal of Experimental Social Psychology*, 1965, *1*, 282–293.

Horowitz, M. The recall of interrupted group tasks: An experimental study of individual motivation in relation to group goals. *Human Relations*, 1954, *7*, 3–38.

Hoyt, M. F., and Janis, I. L. Increasing adherence to a stressful decision via a motivational balance-sheet procedure: A field experiment. *Journal of Personality and Social Psychology*, 1975, *31*, 833–839.

Hurwitz, J. I., Zander, A. F., and Hymovitch, B. Some effects of power on the relations among group members. In D. Cartwright and A. Zander (Eds.), *Group dynamics: Research and theory*. New York: Harper and Row, 1968. Pp. 291–300.

Israel, J., and Tajfel, H. (Eds.) *The context of social psychology: A critical assessment*. New York: Academic Press, 1972.

Jabes, J. *Individual processes in groups and organizations*. Arlington Heights, Ill.: AHM Publishing Corp., 1978.

Jacobs, R., and Campbell, D. The perpetuation of an arbitrary tradition through several generations of a laboratory microculture. *Journal of Abnormal and Social Psychology*, 1961, *62*, 649–659.

Janis, I. L. *Psychological stress*. New York: John Wiley and Sons, 1958.

Janis, I. L. *Victims of groupthink*. Boston: Houghton Mifflin, 1972.

Janis, I. L., and Mann, L. *Decision making: A psychological analysis of conflict, choice and commitment.* New York: The Free Press, 1977.

Joad, C. E. M. *Why war?* Harmondsworth, England: Penguin Special, 1939.

Johnson, J. E., and Levanthal, H. Effects of accurate expectations and behavioral instructions on reactions during a noxious medical examination. *Journal of Personality and Social Psychology*, 1974, *29*, 710-718.

Johnson, R. E., Conlee, M. C., and Tesser, A. Effects of similarity of fate on bad news transmission: A re-examination. *Journal of Personality and Social Psychology*, 1974, *29*, 644-648.

Johnson, W. The fateful process of Mr. A. talking to Mr. B. *Harvard Business Review*, 1969, *31*, 49-56.

Jones, C., and Aronson, E. Attribution of fault to a rape victim as a function of respectability of the victim. *Journal of Personality and Social Psychology*, 1973, *26*, 415-419.

Jones, E. E. *Ingratiation.* Appleton-Century, 1964.

Jones, E. E., Gergen, K. J., Gumpert, P., and Thibaut, J. W. Some conditions affecting the use of ingratiation to influence performance evaluation. *Journal of Personality and Social Psychology*, 1965, *1*, 613-625.

Jones, E. E., Gergen, K. J., and Jones, R. G. Tactics of ingratiation among leaders and subordinates in a status hierarchy. *Psychological Monographs*, 1963, *77*.

Jones, E. E., Kanouse, D. E., Kelley, H. H., Nisbett, R. E., Valins, S., and Weiner, B. *Attribution: Perceiving the causes of behavior.* Morristown, N.J.: General Learning Press, 1972.

Jones, E. E., and Nisbett, R. E. The actor and the observer: Divergent perceptions of the causes of behavior. In E. E. Jones, D. E. Kanouse, H. H. Kelley, R. E. Nisbett, S. Valins, and B. Weiner (Eds.), *Attribution: Perceiving the causes of behavior.* Morristown, N.J.: General Learning Press, 1972. Pp. 79-94.

Jones, E. E., and Wortman, C. *Ingratiation: An attri-*

butional approach. Morristown, N.J.: General Learning Press, 1973.

Jourard, S. M. *The transparent self.* Princeton, N.J.: D. Van Nostrand, 1964.

Julian, J. W., Bishop, D. W., and Fiedler, F. E. Quasi-therapeutic effects of intergroup competition. *Journal of Personality and Social Psychology,* 1966, *3*, 321-327.

Kahn, M. The physiology of catharsis. *Journal of Personality and Social Psychology,* 1966, *3*, 278-286.

Kanfer, F. H., Cox, L. E., Greiner, J. M., and Karoly, P. Contracts, demand characteristics, and self-control. *Journal of Personality and Social Psychology,* 1974, *30*, 605-619.

Kanter, R. M. *Commitment and community: Communes and utopias in sociological perspective.* Cambridge, Mass.: Harvard University Press, 1972.

Kaplan, N. Reference groups and interest group theories of voting. In H. H. Hyman and E. Singer (Eds.), *Readings in reference group theory and research.* New York: The Free Press, 1968. Pp. 461-472.

Kaplan, K. J., Firestone, I. J., Degnore, R., and Moore, M. Gradients of attraction as a function of disclosure probe intimacy and setting formality: On distinguishing attitude oscillation from attitude change-study one. *Journal of Personality and Psychology,* 1974, *30*, 638-646.

Katz, D. Psychological barriers to communication. *The Annals of the Academy of Political and Social Science,* 1947, *250*, 17-25.

Katz, D. The two-step flow of communication: An up-to-date report on an hypothesis. *Public Opinion Quarterly,* 1957, *21*,. 61-78.

Kelley, H. H. Communication in experimentally created hierarchies. *Human Relations,* 1951, *4*, 39-56.

Kelley, H. H. Two functions of reference groups. In G. E. Swanson, T. M. Newcomb, and E. L. Hartley (Eds.), *Readings in social psychology.* New York: Holt, Rinehart and Winston, 1952. Pp. 410-414.

Kelley, H. H. A classroom study of the dilemma in interpersonal negotiations. In K. Archibald (Ed.), *Strategic interaction and conflict.* Berkeley: Institute of International Studies, University of California, 1966.

Kelley, H. H., and Thibaut, J. W. Group problem solving. In Lindzey, G., and Aronson, E. (Eds.), *The handbook of social psychology.* (2nd ed.) Vol. 4. Reading, Mass.: Addison-Wesley, 1969. Pp. 1-101.

Kelley, H. H., Thibaut, J. W., Radloff, R., and Mundy, D. The development of cooperation in the "minimal social situation." *Psychological Monographs*, 1962, *76*, No. 19 (Whole No. 538).

Kiesler, C. A. *The psychology of commitment: Experiments linking behavior to belief.* New York: Academic Press, 1971.

Kiesler, C. A. A theory of stimulus incongruity. (Mimeo.) Lawrence, Kansas: University of Kansas, 1975.

Kiesler, C. A. Personal communication, 1976.

Kiesler, C. A., Collins, B. E., and Miller, N. *Attitude change: A critical analysis of theoretical approaches.* New York: John Wiley and Sons, 1969.

Kiesler, C. A., and DeSalvo, J. The group as an influencing agent in a forced compliance paradigm. *Journal of Experimental Social Psychology*, 1967, *3*, 160-171.

Kiesler, C. A., and Kiesler, S. B. Role of forewarning in persuasive communication. *Journal of Abnormal and Social Psychology*, 1964, *68*, 547-549.

Kiesler, C. A., and Kiesler, S. B. *Conformity.* Reading, Mass.: Addison-Wesley, 1969.

Kiesler, C. A., Roth, T. S., and Pallak, M. S. Avoidance and reinterpretation of commitment and its implications. *Journal of Personality and Social Psychology*, 1974, *30*, 705-715.

Kiesler, C. A., and Sakumura, J. A test of a model for commitment. *Journal of Personality and Social Psychology*, 1966, *3*, 349-353.

Kiesler, S. B. Stress, affiliation and performance.

Journal of Experimental Research in Personality, 1966, *1*, 227-235.

Kiesler, S. B. Actuarial prejudice toward women and its implications. *Journal of Applied Psychology*, 1975, *5*, 201-216.

Kiesler, S. B. The preference for predictability or un-predictability as a mediator of reactions to norm violations. *Journal of Personality and Social Psychology*, 1973, *27*, 354-359.

Kiesler, S. B., and Baral, R. L. The search for a romantic partner: The effects of self-esteem and physical attractiveness on romantic behavior. In K. Gergen and D. Marlowe (Eds.), *Personality and social behavior*. Reading, Mass.: Addison-Wesley, 1970. Pp. 155-165.

Kiesler, S. B., and Coffman, B. *Emotions in experiential groups: Effects of arousal and trainer cues*. (Mimeo.) Lawrence, Kansas: University of Kansas, 1975.

Kinsey, A. C., Pomeroy, W. B., and Martin, C. E. *Sexual behavior in the human male*. Philadelphia: Saunders, 1948.

Kleck, R. E. Physical stigma and nonverbal cues emitted in face-to-face interaction. *Human Relations*, 1968, *21*, 19-28.

Kleck, R. E., Ono, H., and Hastorf, A. H. The effects of physical deviance upon face-to-face interaction. *Human Relations*, 1966, *19*, 424-436.

Kleck, R. E., and Rubenstein, C. Physical attractive-ness, perceived attitude similarity, and interpersonal attraction in an opposite-sex encounter. *Journal of Personality and Social Psychology*, 1975, *31*, 107-114.

Kleinke, C. L., Staneski, R. A., and Weaver, P. Evalua-tion of a person who uses another's name in ingrati-ating and noningratiating situations. *Journal of Experimental Social Psychology*, 1972, *8*, 457-466.

Kogan, N., and Wallach, M. A. *Risk taking: A study in cognition and personality*. New York: Holt, 1964.

Komorita, S. S., and Chertkoff, J. M. A bargaining the-ory of coalition formation. *Psychological Review*, 1973, *80*, 149-162.

Kursh, C. O. The benefits of poor communication. *Psycho-analytic Review*, 1971, *58*, 189-208.

Kutak, R. I. Sociology of crisis: The Louisville Flood of 1937. *Social Forces*, 1938, *17*, 66-72.

Lamm, H. Will an observer advise higher risk taking after hearing a discussion of the decision problem? *Journal of Personality and Social Psychology*, 1967, *6*, 467-471.

Landy, D., and Sigall, H. Beauty is talent: Task evaluation as a function of the performer's physical attractiveness. *Journal of Personality and Social Psychology*, 1974, *29*, 299-304.

Lanzetta, J. T. Group behavior under stress. *Human Relations*, 1955, *8*, 29-52.

Lanzetta, J. T. *Uncertainty as a motivating variable.* Paper read at Conference on Experimental Social Psychology, Vienna, Austria, April, 1967.

Lanzetta, J. T., and Driscoll, J. M. The effects of uncertainty and importance on information search in decision making. *Journal of Personality and Social Psychology*, 1968, *10*, 479-486.

Lasswell, H. D. The study of political elites. In H. D. Lasswell and D. Lerner (Eds.), *World revolutionary elites*. Cambridge, Mass.: M.I.T. Press, 1965.

Latané, B., and Darley, J. M. Group inhibition of bystander intervention in emergencies. *Journal of Personality and Social Psychology*, 1968, *10*, 215-221.

Latané, B., and Darley, J. M. *The unresponsive bystander: Why doesn't he help?* New York: Appleton-Century-Crofts, 1970.

Lawler, E. E. *Pay and organizational effectiveness: A psychological view*. New York: McGraw-Hill, 1971.

LeCarre, J. *A murder of quality*. New York: Pocket Books, 1970.

Lee, I. *How to talk with people*. New York: Harper and Brothers, 1952.

Lee, T. J. Why discussions go astray. In R. S. Cathcart and L. A. Samovar (Eds.), *Small group communication:*

A reader. Dubuque, Iowa: Wm. C. Brown, 1970. Pp. 289-299.

Leighton, A. *The governing of men.* Princeton, N.J.: Princeton University Press, 1945.

Lerner, D. The coercive ideologists in perspective. In H. D. Lasswell and D. Lerner (Eds.), *World revolutionary elites: Studies in coercive ideological movements.* Cambridge, Mass.: M.I.T. Press, 1966.

Leventhal, H., Singer, R., and Jones, S. Effects of fear and specificity of recommendations upon attitudes and behavior. *Journal of Personality and Social Psychology*, 1965, *2*, 20-29.

Lewin, K. Forces behind food habits and methods of change. *Bulletin of the National Research Council*, 1943, *108*, 35-65.

Lewin, K. *Resolving social conflicts.* New York: Harper, 1948.

Lewin, K. *Field theory in social science.* New York: Harper, 1951.

Liem, G. R. Performance and satisfaction as affected by personal control over salient decisions. *Journal of Personality and Social Psychology*, 1975, *31*, 232-240.

Lin, N. The McIntire March: A study of recruitment and commitment. *Public Opinion Quarterly*, 1974-1975 (Winter), *38*, 562-573.

Lindblom, C. E. The science of "meddling through." *Public Administration Review*, 1959, *19*, 78-88.

Linder, D. E., Cooper, J., and Jones, E. E. Decision freedom as a determinant of the role of incentive magnitude in attitude change. *Journal of Personality and Social Psychology*, 1967, *6*, 245-254.

Loftis, J., and Ross, L. Effects of misattribution of arousal upon the acquisition and extinction of a conditioned emotional response. *Journal of Personality and Social Psychology*, 1974, *30*, 673-682.

Loomis, J. L. Communication, the development of trust, and cooperative behavior. *Human Relations*, 1959, *12*, 305, 315.

Lorenz, K. *On aggression.* New York: Harcourt, Brace & World, 1966.

Lorge, I., and Solomon, H. Two models of group behavior in the solution of eureka-type problems. *Psychometrika,* 1955, *20,* 139-148.

Lowe, C. A., and Goldstein, J. W. Reciprocal liking and attribution of ability: Mediating effects of perceived intent and personal involvement. *Journal of Personality and Social Psychology,* 1970, *16,* 291-298.

McGregor, D. M. *The human side of enterprise.* New York: McGraw-Hill, 1960.

McGuire, W. J. Discussion of William N. Schoenfeld's paper. In O. Klineberg and R. Christie (Eds.), *Perspectives in social psychology.* New York: Holt, Rinehart, & Winston, 1965. Pp. 135-140.

McGuire, W. J. The nature of attitudes and attitude change. In G. Lindzey and E. Aronson (Eds.), *The handbook of social psychology.* (2nd ed.) Vol. 3. Reading, Mass.: Addison-Wesley, 1969. Pp. 136-314.

Machiavelli, N. *The prince.* New York: E. P. Dutton and Company, 1948.

Mackenzie, K. D. The effects of status on group risk taking. *Organizational behavior and human performance,* 1970, *5,* 517-541.

Mackenzie, K. D. Analysis of risky shift experiments. *Organizational behavior and human performance,* 1971, *6,* 283-303.

Mackenzie, K. D. *Organizational structures.* Arlington Heights, Ill.: AHM Publishing Corp., 1978.

Mackenzie, K. D., and Barron, F. H. Analysis of a decision-making investigation. *Management Science,* 1970, *17,* 226-241.

McNamara, J. D. *The impact of bureaucratic dysfunctions on attempts to prevent police corruption.* Paper read at American Psychological Association, New Orleans, 1974.

Maier, N. R. F., and Solem, A. R. The contribution of a discussion leader to the quality of group thinking: The effective use of minority opinions. *Human Rela-*

tions, 1952, *5*, 277-288.

Manis, M., Cornell, S. D., and Moore, J. C. Transmission of attitude-relevant information through a communication chain. *Journal of Personality and Social Psychology*, 1974, *30*, 81-94.

Mann, R. D. *The relation between personality characteristics and individual performance in small groups.* Unpublished doctoral dissertation, University of Michigan, 1959.

Manning, S. A., and Taylor, D. A. Effects of viewed violence and aggression: Stimulation and catharsis. *Journal of Personality and Social Psychology*, 1975, *31*, 180-188.

March, J. G. Business decision making. *Industrial Research*, 1959 (Spring).

March, J. G., and Simon, H. A. *Organizations.* New York: John Wiley and Sons, 1958.

Marchetti, V., and Marks, J. D. *The CIA and the cult of intelligence.* New York: Dell, 1975.

Marx, K. *Capital.* Vol. 1. New York: E. P. Dutton, & Co., 1951.

Maslow, A. H. *Motivation and personality.* Harper & Brothers, 1954.

Mausner, B. The effect of one's partner's success in a relevant task on the interaction of observer pairs. *Journal of Abnormal and Social Psychology*, 1954, *49*, 557-560.

Mayo, E. *The human problems of an industrial civilization.* New York: Macmillan, 1933.

Mazis, M. B. Antipollution measures and psychological reactance theory: A field experiment. *Journal of Personality and Social Psychology*, 1975, *31*, 654-660.

Mechanic, D. Sources of power of lower participants in complex organizations. *Administrative Science Quarterly*, 1962, *7*, 349-364.

Medow, H., and Zander, A. Aspirations for the group chosen by central and peripheral members. *Journal of Personality and Social Psychology*, 1965, *1*, 224-228.

Mehrabian, A. Inference of attitudes from the posture, orientation, and distance of a communicator. *Journal of Consulting and Clinical Psychology*, 1968, *32*, 296-308.

Merton, R. K. The self-fulfilling prophecy. *Antioch Review*, 1948, *8*, 193-210.

Merton, R. K. *Social theory and social structure.* Glencoe, Ill.: Free Press, 1957.

Mettee, D. R. The true discerner as potent source of positive affect. *Journal of Experimental and Social Psychology*, 1971, *7*, 292-303.

Meyers, A. E. Team competition, success, and adjustment of group members. *Journal of Abnormal and Social Psychology*, 1962, *65*, 325-332.

Michener, H. A., and Cohen, E. D. Effects of punishment magnitude in the bilateral threat situation. *Journal of Personality and Social Psychology*, 1973, *26*, 427-438.

Milgram, S. Some conditions of obedience and disobedience to authority. *Human Relations*, 1965, *18*, 57-76.

Milgram, S., and Toch, H. Collective behavior: Crowds and social movements. In G. Lindzey and E. Aronson (Eds.), *The handbook of social psychology.* (2nd ed.) Vol. 4. Reading, Mass.: Addison-Wesley, 1969. Pp. 507-610.

Miller, N. Involvement and dogmatism as inhibitions of attitude change. *Journal of Experimental Social Psychology*, 1965, *1*, 121-132.

Miller, R. L., Brickman, P., and Bolen, D. Attribution versus persuasion as a means for modifying behavior. *Journal of Personality and Social Psychology*, 1975, *31*, 430-441.

Mills, J., and Aronson, E. Opinion change as a function of the communicator's attractiveness and desire to influence. *Journal of Personality and Social Psychology*, 1965, *1*, 173-177.

Minard, R. D. Race relationships in the Pocahontas coal field. *Journal of Social Issues*, 1952, *8*, 29-44.

Mischel, W. *Personality and assessment.* New York: John Wiley and Sons, 1968.

Mogy, R. B., and Pruitt, D. G. Effects of a threatener's enforcement costs on threat credibility and compliance. *Journal of Personality and Social Psychology*, 1974, *29*, 173-180.

Montagu, M. F. A. *Man and aggression*. New York: Oxford University Press, 1968.

Morgan, S. W., and Mausner, B. Behavioral and fantasied indicators of avoidance of success in men and women. *Journal of Personality*, 1973, *41*, 456-470.

Morse, S., and Gergen, K. J. Social comparison, self consistency and the concept of self. *Journal of Personality and Social Psychology*, 1970, *16*, 148-156.

Moscovici, S. Society and theory in social psychology. In J. Israel and H. Tajfel (Eds.), *The context of social psychology: A critical assessment*. New York: Academic Press, 1972. Pp. 17-68.

Moscovici, S., and Zavalloni, M. The group as a polarizer of attitudes. *Journal of Personality and Social Psychology*, 1969, *12*, 125-135.

Moyer, K. E. The physiology of aggression and the implications for aggression control. In J. L. Singer (Ed.), *The control of aggression and violence*. New York: Academic Press, 1971.

Mulder, M. Group structure and group performance. *Acta Psychologica*, 1959, *16*, 356-402.

Mulder, M. The power variable in communication experiments. *Human Relations*, 1960, *13*, 241-257.

Mulder, M. Unpublished remarks from a conference held at Carleton University, Ottawa, Canada. July, 1974.

Mulder, M., and Stemerding, A. Threat, attraction to group, and need for strong leadership: A laboratory experiment in a natural setting. *Human Relations*, 1963, *16*, 317-334.

Nance, J. *The gentle Tasaday*. New York: Harcourt Brace Jovanovich, 1975.

Neath-Gelvin, J. *A review of social comparison theory*. (Mimeo.) Lawrence, Kansas: University of Kansas, 1975.

Nemeth, C. A critical analysis of research utilizing

the prisoner's dilemma paradigm for the study of bargaining. In L. Berkowitz (Ed.), *Advance in experimental social psychology*. Vol. 6. New York: Academic Press, 1972. Pp. 203-234.

Nemeth, C., and Wachtler, J. Creating the perceptions of consistency and confidence: A necessary condition for minority influence. *Sociometry*, 1974, *37*, 529-540.

Newcomb, T. M. Attitude development as a function of reference groups: The Bennington study. In G. E. Swanson, T. M. Newcomb, and E. L. Hartley (Eds.), *Readings in social psychology*. New York: Holt, Rinehart and Winston, 1952.

Okun, M. A., and DiVesta, F. J. Cooperation and competition in coacting groups. *Journal of Personality and Social Psychology*, 1975, *31*, 615-620.

Olson, P., and Davis, J. H. Divisible tasks and pooling performance in groups. *Psychological Reports*, 1964, *15*, 511-517.

Orne, M. T., and Evans, F. J. Social control in the psychological experiment. *Journal of Personality and Social Psychology*, 1965, *1*, 189-200.

Orvis, B. R., Kelley, H. H., and Butler, D. Attributional conflict in young couples. In J. H. Harvey, W. J. Ickes, and R. F. Kidd (Eds.), *New directions in attribution research*. Vol. 1. Hillsdale, N.J.: Lawrence Erlbaum Associates, 1976. Pp. 353-386.

Osborn, A. F. *Applied imagination*. 3rd ed. New York: Scribner's, 1963.

Pallak, M. S., and Heller, J. F. Interactive effects of commitment to future interaction and threat to attitudinal freedom. *Journal of Personality and Social Psychology*, 1971, *14*, 39-45.

Pallak, M. S., Sogin, S. R., and Van Zante, A. Bad decisions: Effect of volition, locus of causality, and negative consequences on attitude change. *Journal of Personality and Social Psychology*, 1974, *30*, 217-227.

Pepitone, A. Toward a normative and biocultural social psychology. *Journal of Personality and Social Psychology*, 1976, *34*, 641-653.

Pepitone, A., and Kleiner, R. The effects of threat and

frustration on group cohesiveness. *Journal of Abnormal and Social Psychology*, 1957, *54*, 192–199.

Pepitone, A., and Reichling, G. Group cohesiveness and the expression of hostility. *Human Relations*, 1955, *8*, 327–337.

Perlmutter, J. V., and de Montmollin, G. Group learning of nonsense syllables. *Journal of Abnormal and Social Psychology*, 1952, *47*, 762–769.

Pfeffer, Jeffrey. *Organizational Design*. Arlington Heights, Ill.: AHM Publishing Corp., 1978.

Piliavin, I. M., Rodin, J., and Piliavin, J. A. Good samaritanism: An underground phenomenon. *Journal of Personality and Social Psychology*, 1969, *13*, 289–299.

Plato. *The republic*. F. M. Cornford (Trans.). New York: Oxford University Press, 1964.

Porter, L. W., and Lawler, E. E. *Managerial attitudes and performance*. Homewood, Ill.: Dorsey Press, 1968.

Pounds, W. The process of problem finding. *Industrial Management Review*, 1969 (Fall), 1–19.

Prince, S. H. *Catastrophe and social change*. New York: Columbia University Press, 1920.

Pruitt, D. G. Reciprocity and credit building in a laboratory dyad. *Journal of Personality and Social Psychology*, 1968, *8*, 143–147.

Pruitt, D. G., and Lewis, S. A. Development of integrative solutions in bilateral negotiation. *Journal of Personality and Social Psychology*, 1975, *31*, 621–633.

Rabinowitz, L., Kelley, H. H., and Rosenblatt, R. M. Effects of different types of interdependence and response conditions in the minimal social situation. *Journal of Experimental Social Psychology*, 1966, *2*, 169–197.

Radford, K. J. *Managerial decision making*. Reston, Va.: Reston Publishing Co., 1975.

Raine, A. Group training. In J. A. Gibson (Ed.), *Strive! An athlete's handbook*. Waterloo, Ontario: Mutual Life of Canada, 1974.

Radloff, R. Opinion evaluation and affiliation. *Journal of Abnormal and Social Psychology*, 1961, *62*, 578-585.

Rapoport, A. Editorial comment on gaming. *Journal of Conflict Resolution*, 1966, *10*, 209.

Rapoport, A. Conflict resolution in the light of game theory and beyond. In P. Swingle (Ed.), *The structure of conflict*. New York: Academic Press, 1970. Pp. 1-44.

Rapoport, A. Editorial comment on gaming. *Journal of Conflict Resolution*, 1971, *15*, 487-488.

Raven, B. H. Social influence and power. In I. D. Steiner and M. Fishbein (Eds.), *Current studies in social psychology*. New York: Holt, Rinehart and Winston, 1965.

Raven, B. H., and French, J. R. P., Jr. Legitimate power, coercive power, and observability in social influence. *Sociometry*, 1958, *21*, 83-97.

Raven, B. H., and Rietsma, J. The effects of varied clarity of group goals and group path upon the individual and his relation to his group. *Human Relations*, 1957, *10*, 29-44.

Report of the National Advisory Commission on Civil Disorders. New York: Bantam Books, 1968.

Riecken, H. W. Some problems of consensus development. *Rural Sociology*, 1952, *17*, 245-252.

Riecken, H. W. The effect of talkativeness on ability to influence group solutions of problems. *Sociometry*, 1958, *21*, 309-321.

Rieff, P. *Freud: The mind of the moralist*. New York: Viking Press, 1959.

Roby, T. B., and Lanzetta, J. T. Considerations in the analysis of group tasks. *Psychological Bulletin*, 1958, *55*, 88-101.

Rogers, C. R. Process of the basic encounter group. In J. F. T. Bugental (Ed.), *Challenges of humanistic psychology*. New York: McGraw-Hill, 1967.

Rokeach, M., and Kliejunas, P. Behavior as a function of attitude-toward-object and attitude-toward-situation. *Journal of Personality and Social Psychology*, 1972, *22*, 194-201.

Rosen, S., and Tesser, A. On reluctance to communicate undesirable information: The MUM effect. *Sociometry*, 1970, *33*, 253-263.

Rosenfeld, H. M. Approval-seeking and approval-inducing functions of verbal and nonverbal responses in the dyad. *Journal of Personality and Social Psychology*, 1966, *4*, 597-605.

Rosenfeld, H. M. Nonverbal reciprocation of approval: An experimental analysis. *Journal of Experimental Social Psychology*, 1967, *3*, 102-111.

Rosenthal, R. Teacher expectations. In G. S. Lesser (Ed.), *Psychology and the educational process*. Glenview, Ill.: Scott, Foresman, 1971.

Rosenthal, R., and Jacobson, L. *Pygmalion in the classroom: Teacher expectation and pupils' intellectual development*. New York: Holt, Rinehart and Winston, 1968.

Rousseau, J. J. *The social contract and discourses*. New York: E. P. Dutton and Company, 1950.

Rubin, Z. Disclosing oneself to a stranger: Reciprocity and its limits. *Journal of Experimental Social Psychology*, 1975, *11*, 233-260.

Saegert, S., Swap, W., and Zajonc, R. B. Exposure, context, and interpersonal attraction. *Journal of Personality and Social Psychology*, 1973, *25*, 234-242.

Sakuri, M. M. Small group cohesiveness and detrimental conformity. *Sociometry*, 1975, *38*, 340-357.

Salancik, G. R., and Pfeffer, J. The bases and use of power in organizational decision making: The case of a university. *Administrative Science Quarterly*, 1974, *19*, 453-473.

Sampson, E. E., and Brandon, A. C. The effects of role and opinion deviation on small group behavior. *Sociometry*, 1964, *27*, 261-281.

Schachter, S. Deviation, rejection, and communication. *Journal of Abnormal and Social Psychology*, 1951, *46*, 190-207.

Schachter, S. *The psychology of affiliation*. Stanford, Ca.: Stanford University Press, 1959.

Schachter, S. The interaction of cognitive and physiological determinants of emotional state. In L. Berkowitz (Ed.), *Advances in experimental social psychology*. Vol. 1. New York: Academic Press, 1964. Pp. 49–81.

Schachter, S., Ellertson, N., McBride, D., and Gregory, D. An experimental study of cohesiveness and productivity. *Human Relations*, 1951, *4*, 229–238.

Schachter, S., and Singer, J. E. Cognitive, social and physiological determinants of emotional state. *Psychological Review*, 1962, *69*, 379–399.

Scheff, T. J. Control over policy by attendants in a mental hospital. *Journal of Health and Human Behavior*, 1961, *2*, 93–105.

Schein, E. H. The Hawthorne group studies revisited: A defense of Theory Y. In E. L. Cass and F. G. Zimmer (Eds.), *Man and work in society*. New York: Van Nostrand Reinhold, 1975. Pp. 78–94.

Schelling, T. C. Bargaining, communication, and limited war. *The Journal of Conflict Resolution*, 1957, *1*, 19–36.

Schelling, T. C. *The strategy of conflict*. Cambridge, Mass.: Harvard University Press, 1960.

Schneider, D. J., and Eustis, A. C. Effects of ingratiation motivation, target positiveness, and revealingness on self-presentation. *Journal of Personality and Social Psychology*, 1972, *22*, 149–155.

Schneider, D. J., and Turbot, D. Self-presentation following success or failure: Defensive self-esteem. *Journal of Personality*, 1975, *43*, 127–135.

Schopler, J., and Bateson, N. The power of dependence. *Journal of Personality and Social Psychology*, 1965, *2*, 247–254.

Schur, E. M. *Labeling deviant behavior*. New York: Harper & Row, 1971.

Scodel, A. Effects of group discussion on cooperation in a prisoner's dilemma game. Paper read at California Psychological Association, December, 1963.

Seashore, S. *Group cohesiveness in the industrial work*

group. Ann Arbor, Mich.: Institute for Social Research, 1954.

Secord, P. F., and Backman, C. W. *Social psychology*. New York: McGraw-Hill, 1974.

Segal, M. W. Alphabet and attraction: An unobtrusive measure of the effect of propinquity in a field setting. *Journal of Personality and Social Psychology*, 1974, *30*, 654-657.

Shapiro, E. G. Effect of expectations of future interaction on reward allocations in dyads: Equity or equality. *Journal of Personality and Social Psychology*, 1975, *31*, 873-880.

Shaw, M. E. Comparison of individuals and small groups in the rational solution of complex problems. *American Journal of Psychology*, 1932, *44*, 491-504.

Shaw, M. E. Communication networks. In L. Berkowitz (Ed.), *Advances in experimental social psychology*. Vol. 1. New York: Academic Press, 1964. Pp. 111-149.

Sherif, C. W., Kelley, M., Rodgers, H. L., Jr., Sarup, G., and Tittler, B. T. Personal involvement, social judgment, and action. *Journal of Personality and Social Psychology*, 1973, *27*, 311-327.

Sherif, M. *The psychology of social norms*. New York: Harper, 1936.

Sherif, M., Harvey, O. J., White, B. J., Hood, W. R., and Sherif, C. W. *Intergroup conflict and cooperation: The robbers' cave experiment*. Norman, Okla.: University Book Exchange, 1961.

Shomer, R. W., Davis, A. H., and Kelley, H. H. Threats and the development of coordination: Further studies of the Deutsch and Krauss trucking game. *Journal of Personality and Social Psychology*, 1966, *4*, 119-126.

Siegel, A. E., and Siegel, S. Reference groups, membership groups, and attitude change. *Journal of Abnormal and Social Psychology*, 1957, *55*, 360-364.

Silka, L., and Kiesler, S. Couples who choose to remain childless. *Family Planning Perspectives*, 1977, *9*, 16-25.

Simmons, Richard E. *Managing Behavioral Processes: Applications of Theory and Research.* Arlington Heights, Ill.: AHM Publishing Corp., 1978.

Simon, H. A. Testimony to the House Subcommittee on Science, Research and Technology. February 19, 1976. (Mimeo.) Pittsburg: Carnegie Mellon University, 1976.

Simon, H. A. *Administrative behavior: A study of decision-making processes in administrative organization.* 3rd Ed., New York: Free Press, 1976.

Simon, R. J. *The jury and the defense of insanity.* Boston: Little, Brown, 1967.

Simons, H. W. The carrot and the stick as handmaidens of persuasion in conflict situations. In G. R. Miller and H. W. Simons, *Perspectives on communication in social conflict.* Englewood Cliffs, N.J.: Prentice-Hall, 1974. Pp. 172-205.

Slater, P. E. Role differentiation in small groups. *American Sociological Review*, 1955, *20*, 300-310.

Smith, C. S. *Self definition change as a function of interpersonal similarity: A test of a psychological spacing model.* Unpublished master's thesis, University of Kansas, 1975.

Snyder, M., and Cunningham, M. R. To comply or not comply: Testing the self-perception explanation of the "foot-in-the-door" phenomenon. *Journal of Personality and Social Psychology*, 1975, *31*, 64-67.

Solomon, L. The influence of some types of power relationships and game strategies upon the development of interpersonal trust. *Journal of Abnormal and Social Psychology*, 1960, *61*, 223-230.

Staub, E., and Baer, R. S., Jr. Stimulus characteristics of a sufferer and difficulty of escape as determinants of helping. *Journal of Personality and Social Psychology*, 1974, *30*, 279-284.

Staw, B. M. Attitudinal and behavioral consequences of changing a major organizational reward: A natural field experiment. *Journal of Personality and Social Psychology*, 1974, *29*, 742-751.

Stedry, A. C., and Kay, E. The effects of goal difficulty on performance: A field experiment. *Behavioral
Science*, 1966, *11*, 459-470.

Steinfatt, T. M., and Miller, G. R. Communication in
game theoretic models of conflict. In G. R. Miller
and H. W. Simons (Eds.), *Perspectives on communication in social conflict.* Englewood Cliffs, N.J.:
Prentice-Hall, 1974. Pp. 14-75.

Stockford, L., and Bissell, H. W. Factors involved in
establishing a merit rating scale. *Personnel*, 1949,
26, 94-116.

Stoner, J. A. F. Risky and cautious shifts in group
decisions: The influence of widely held values.
Journal of Experimental Social Psychology, 1968, *4*,
442-459.

Storms, M. D. Videotape and the attribution process:
Revising actors' and observers' points of view.
Journal of Personality and Social Psychology, 1973,
27, 165-175.

Storms, M. D., and McCaul, K. D. Attribution processes
and the emotional exacerbation of dysfunctional behavior. In J. H. Harvey, W. J. Ickes, and R. F. Kidd
(Eds.), *New directions in attribution research.*
Vol. 1. Hillsdale, N.J.: Lawrence Erlbaum Associates,
1976. Pp. 143-164.

Stouffer, S. A., Lumsdaine, A. A., Lumsdaine, M. H.,
Williams, R. H., Jr., Smith, M. B., Janis, I. L.,
Star, S. A., and Cottrell, L. S., Jr. *The American
soldier: Combat and its aftermath.* Vol. 2. Princeton,
N.J.: Princeton University Press, 1949.

Strodtbeck, F. L., and Hook, L. H. The social dimensions of a twelve man jury table. *Sociometry*, 1961,
24, 397-415.

Strodtbeck, F. L., James, R. M., and Hawkins, D.
Social status in jury deliberations. *American
Sociological Review*, 1957, *22*, 713-719.

Strodtbeck, F. L., and Mann, R. D. Sex role differentiation in jury deliberations. *Sociometry*, 1956, *19*,
3-11.

Sullivan, J. J., and Pallak, M. S. The effect of commitment and reactance on action taking. *Personality and Social Psychology Bulletin*, 1976, *2*, 179–182.

Tannenbaum, F. *Crime and community*. Boston: Ginn, 1938.

Tajfel, A. Experiments in intergroup discrimination. *Scientific American*, 1970, *2*, 96–102.

Taylor, D. A., Wheeler, L., and Altman, I. Self-disclosure in isolated groups. *Journal of Personality and Social Psychology*, 1973, *26*, 39–47.

Taylor, D. W. Problem solving by groups. *Proceedings of the Fourteenth International Congress of Psychology*. Montreal, June, 1954.

Taylor, D. W., Berry, P. C., and Block, C. H. Does group participation when using brainstorming facilitate or inhibit creative thinking? *Administrative Science Quarterly*, 1958, *3*, 23–47.

Taylor, S. E. On inferring one's attitudes from one's behavior: Some delimiting conditions. *Journal of Personality and Social Psychology*, 1975, *31*, 126–131.

Tedeschi, J. T. Threats and promises. In P. Swingle (Ed.), *The structure of conflict*. New York: Academic Press, 1970.

Tedeschi, J. T., Smith, R. B., III, and Brown, R. C., Jr. A reinterpretation of research on aggression. *Psychological Bulletin*, 1974, *81*, 540–562.

Terkel, S. *Working*. New York: Avon Books, 1975.

Tesser, A., Rosen, S., and Conlee, M. C. News valence and available recipient as determinants of news transmission. *Sociometry*, 1972, *35*, 619–628.

Thibaut, J. W., Friedland, N., and Walker, L. Compliance with rules: Some social determinants. *Journal of Personality and Social Psychology*, 1974, *30*, 792–801.

Thibaut, J. W., and Kelley, H. H. *The social psychology of groups*. New York: John Wiley and Sons, 1961.

Thomas, E. J., and Fink, C. F. Models of group problem solving. *Journal of Abnormal and Social Psychology*, 1961, *68*, 53–63.

Thompson, J. D. *Organizations in action*. New York: McGraw-Hill, 1967.

Thompson, V. A. *Modern organizations*. New York: A. A. Knopf, 1961.

Thorndike, R. L. On what type of task will a group do well? *Journal of Abnormal and Social Psychology*, 1938, *33*, 409–413.

Toch, H. H. *Violent men: An inquiry into the psychology of violence*. Chicago: Aldine, 1969.

Triplett, N. The dynamogenic factors in pacemaking and competition. *American Journal of Psychology*, 1897, *9*, 507–533.

Tubbs, S. L., and Moss, S. *Human communication: An interpersonal perspective*. New York: Random House, 1974.

Tuggle, Francis D. *Organizational Processes*. Arlington Heights, Ill.: AHM Publishing Corp., 1978.

Varela, J. A. *Psychological solutions to social problems: An introduction to social technology*. New York: Academic Press, 1971.

Vernon, T. A., and Bigelow, D. A. Effect of information about a potentially stressful situation on responses to stress impact. *Journal of Personality and Social Psychology*, 1974, *29*, 50–59.

Vincent, J. E., and Tindell, J. O. Alternative cooperative strategies in a bargaining game. *Journal of Conflict Resolution*, 1969, *13*, 494–510.

Vinokur, A., and Burnstein, E. The effects of partially shared persuasive arguments on group-induced shifts: A group-problem-solving approach. *Journal of Personality and Social Psychology*, 1974, *29*, 305–315.

Von Neumann, J., and Morganstern, O. *The theory of games and economic behavior*. Princeton, N.J.: Princeton University Press, 1944.

Wallach, M. A., Kogan, N., and Bem, D. J. Group influence on individual risk taking. *Journal of Abnormal and Social Psychology*, 1962, *65*, 75–86.

Wallach, M. A., Kogan, N., and Bem, D. J. Diffusion of

responsibility and level of risk taking in groups. *Journal of Abnormal and Social Psychology*, 1964, *68*, 263-274

Walster, E. The effect of self-esteem on romantic liking. *Journal of Experimental and Social Psychology*, 1965, *1*, 184-197.

Walster, E., Aronson, E., and Abrahams, D. On increasing the persuasiveness of a low prestige communicator. *Journal of Experimental and Social Psychology*, 1966, *2*, 325-342.

Walster, E., Aronson, V., Abrahams, D., and Rottman, L. Importance of physical attention in dating behavior. *Journal of Personality and Social Psychology*, 1966, *5*, 508-516.

Walster, E., Berscheid, E., and Walster, G. W. New directions in equity research. *Journal of Personality and Social Psychology*, 1973, *25*, 151-176.

Walster, E., and Prestholdt, P. The effect of misjudging another: Overcompensation or dissonance reduction? *Journal of Experimental Social Psychology*, 1966, *2*, 85-97.

Walster, E., Walster, G. W., and Berscheid, E. *Equity: Theory and research*. Boston: Allyn and Bacon, 1978.

Walton, R. E. From Hawthorne to Topeka and Kolmar. In E. L. Cass and F. G. Zimmer (Eds.), *Man and work in society*. New York: Van Nostrand Reinhold, 1975. Pp. 116-134.

Walton, R. E., and McKersie, R. B. *A behavioral theory of labor negotiations: An analysis of a social interaction system*. New York: McGraw-Hill, 1965.

Watzlawick, P., Beavin, J. H., and Jackson, D. D. *Pragmatics of human communication: A study of interactional patterns, pathologies, and paradoxes*. New York: W. W. Norton, 1967.

Watzlawick, P., Weakland, J. H., and Fisch, R. *Change: Principles of problem formation and problem resolution*. New York: W. W. Norton, 1974.

Weber, M. *The theory of social and economic organization*. Oxford: Oxford University Press, 1947.

Weick, K. E. *The social psychology of organizing.* Reading, Mass.: Addison-Wesley, 1969.

Weiner, B. New conceptions in the study of achievement motivation. In B. Maher (Ed.), *Progress in experimental personality research.* Vol. 5. New York: Academic Press, 1970. Pp. 67–109.

Weiss, R. F., and Miller, F. G. The drive theory of social facilitation. *Psychological Review*, 1971, *78*, 44–57.

Weisskopf-Joelson, E., and Eliseo, T. An experimental study of the effectiveness of brainstorming. *Journal of Applied Psychology*, 1961, *45*, 45–49.

Whorf, B. L. Science and linguistics. In J. B. Carroll (Ed.), *Language, thought and reality. Selected writings of Benjamin Lee Whorf.* New York: John Wiley and Sons, 1956. Pp. 207–219.

Whyte, W. F. *Street corner society: The social structure of an Italian slum.* Chicago: The University of Chicago Press, 1943.

Whyte, W. F. *Men at work.* Homewood, Ill.: Irwin-Dorsey Press, 1967.

Wicklund, R. A. *Freedom and reactance.* Potomac, Md.: Lawrence Erlbaum AssocIztes, 1974.

Wicklund, R. A., and Brehm, J. W. Attitude change as a function of felt competence and threat to attitudinal freedom. *Journal of Experimental Social Psychology*, 1968, *4*, 64–75.

Wildavsky, A. Political complications of budgetary reform. *Public Administration Review*, 1961, *21*, 183–190.

Wilensky, H. L. *Intellectuals in labor unions.* Glencoe, Ill.: The Free Press, 1956.

Wilmot, W. W. *Dyadic communication: A transactional perspective.* Reading, Mass.: Addison-Wesley, 1975.

Worchel, S., and Arnold, S. E. The effect of combined arousal states on attitude change. *Journal of Experimental and Social Psychology*, 1974, *10*, 549–560.

Worchel, S., and Cooper, J. *Understanding social psychology.* Homewood, Ill.: Dorsey, 1976.

Worchel, S., and Brehm, J. W. Direct and social restoration of freedom. *Journal of Personality and
Social Psychology*, 1971, *18*, 294-304.

Word, C. O., Zanna, M. P., and Cooper, J. The nonverbal
mediation of self-fulfilling prophecies in interracial
interaction. *Journal of Experimental and Social
Psychology*, 1974, *10*, 109-120.

Wrightsman, L. The effects of waiting with others on
changes in level of felt anxiety. *Journal of Abnormal
and Social Psychology*, 1960, *61*, 216-222.

Zajonc, R. B. Social facilitation. *Science*, 1965, *149*,
269-274.

Zajonc, R. B. *Social psychology: An experimental approach*. Belmont, Ca.: Brooks/Cole, 1966.

Zajonc, R. B. Attitudinal effects of mere exposure.
Journal of Personality and Social Psychology, 1968,
9, 2-27.

Zajonc, R. B. Attitudinal effects of mere exposure.
In S. Himmelfarb and A. H. Eagly. *Readings in
attitude change*. New York: John Wiley and Sons,
1974. Pp. 52-80.

Zajonc, R. B., and Sales, S. M. Social facilitation
of dominant and subordinate responses. *Journal of
Experimental and Social Psychology*, 1966, *2*, 160-168.

Zander, A. Group aspirations. In D. Cartwright and
A. Zander (Eds.), *Group dynamics*. New York: Harper
& Row, 1968. Pp. 418-429.

Zander, A., Cohen, A. R., and Stotland, E. *Role relations in the mental health professions*. Ann Arbor:
University of Michigan, Institute for Social Research, 1957.

Zander, A., and Curtis, T. Effects of social power on
aspiration setting and striving. *Journal of Abnormal
and Social Psychology*, 1962, *64*, 63-74.

Zander, A., and Medow, H. Individual and group levels of
aspiration. *Human Relations*, 1963, *16*, 89-105.

Zander, A., Medow, H., and Dustin, D. Social influences
on group aspirations. In A. Zander and H. Medow (Eds.),
Group aspirations and group coping behavior. Ann

Arbor, Mich.: Institute for Social Research, 1964.

Zander, A., and Newcomb, T. Group levels of aspiration in United Fund campaigns. *Journal of Personality and Social Psychology*, 1967, *6*, 157-162.

Zanna, M. P., Goethals, G. R., and Hill, J. F. Evaluating a sex-related ability: Social comparison with similar others and standard setters. *Journal of Experimental Social Psychology*, 1975, *11*, 86-93.

Ziller, R. C., Hagey, J., Smith, M. D. C., and Long, B. H. Self-esteem: A self-social construct. *Journal of Consulting and Clinical Psychology*, 1969, *33*, 84-95.

Zimbardo, P. G., and Ebbesen, E. G. Experimental modification of the relationship between effort, attitude and behavior. *Journal of Personality and Social Psychology*, 1970, *16*, 207-213.

Author Index

Subject Index